Copy - p. 114
p. 98
p. 50.

All About House Plants

THEIR SELECTION, CULTURE AND PROPAGATION, AND HOW BEST TO USE THEM FOR DECORATIVE EFFECT

by Montague Free

STAFF HORTICULTURIST OF *THE HOME GARDEN*
(FORMERLY HORTICULTURIST, BROOKLYN BOTANIC GARDEN)

FULLY ILLUSTRATED WITH COLOR
PHOTOGRAPHS AND HALFTONES
AND WITH DRAWINGS BY EVA
MELADY, JOHN BRIMER, GEORGE
HOLLROCK & MAUD H. PURDY

The American Garden Guild, Inc., &
Doubleday & Company, Inc., **1948**

Printed at The Country Life Press, Garden City, N. Y.

TO MY WIFE

Contents

Part Three—Types of House Plants

*(Cultural Requirements of the Different Groups, and
Recommended Varieties)*

Part Four—Lists of Plants

Illustrations

COLOR PLATES

HALF TONES

All About House Plants

CHAPTER I

What House Plants Bring to the Home

MY EARLY recollections of house plants go back to the Gay Nineties when I, a snub-nosed lad, admired a magnificent Fuchsia and a "French" Lavender which were my mother's pride and joy. My father used to knock out the ashes from his pipe into their pots (doubtless the ashes provided desirable potash!) and extinguish his matches by pushing them headfirst into the soil. These practices at times resulted in minor domestic storms. I used to suck the rather negligible amount of nectar from the fallen Fuchsia flowers and enjoy the fragrance of the crushed leaves of the Lavender. Fuchsias are still available in an ever-increasing number of varieties, but I doubt whether French Lavender (which, in case you are interested, is *Lavandula dentata*) could be acquired without a long and arduous search of catalogues.

But the cultivation of plants in homes goes back far beyond the Gay Nineties—just how far it is difficult to say with any certainty. The early Greeks and the Romans grew plants in pots, and perhaps it is safe to assume that at times these were brought into their homes. Sir Hugh Platt in the *Garden of Eden,* printed in 1660, refers to the possibilities of growing plants in homes and says: "I have known Mr. Jacobs of the Glassehouse to have carnations all the winter by benefit of a room that was near his glassehouse fire." Apparently various Citrus fruits were grown in England in the early 1600s and were accommodated during the winter in "orangeries"—which might be long rooms with many windows. The former orangery in the Royal Botanic Gardens at Kew (now used as a museum) is an example.

About a hundred years ago books began to appear on the cultivation of house plants in England and in France. In 1824 there was published *The Greenhouse Companion—also the Proper Treatment of Flowers in Rooms,* by John Claudius Loudon; and in 1842 Nathaniel Ward published his book *On the Growth of Plants in Closely Glazed Cases*—the beginning of terrarium culture. In this country *The Parlor Gardener,* translated from the French and adapted to American use by C. J. Randolph, was published in Boston in 1861. Since that time books on house plants have appeared in increasing numbers, indicating great interest in this phase of gardening.

The lists of plants recommended for house culture have not changed greatly in the last seventy-five years or so. I have just been poring through a book called *Window Gardening,* edited by Henry T. Williams, which was in its sixth edition in 1873. As it was poorly printed and in small type most trying to these aging eyes, I had great difficulty in getting a comprehensive picture of the plant material recommended because there is no index. The plants are scattered hither and yon throughout the book, and the lists are, for the most part, not alphabetically arranged. However, it was possible to discern that some which are in the front rank of house plants today were equally favored in 1873—Begonia, Cacti in variety, Camellia, English Ivy, Fuchsia, hardy bulbs, and Pelargonium all receiving considerable attention. Some of these plants recommended we do not rate very highly today, because they are unfitted for culture in homes with central heating, because fashions have changed, or because they are practically unobtainable. Plants falling in one or other of these categories are: Calceolaria, Carnation, Cineraria, Erica, Epacris, and Mahernia. The Musk Plant (*Mimulus moschatus*), which is among those recommended, in its fragrant form has been lost to cultivation. In my young days almost every cottage window had its pot of Musk, but with the loss of fragrance the chief incentive for growing it has disappeared, so that it is seldom seen nowadays.

I was interested to notice that numerous winter-hardy plants were recommended for house culture. While a few of these, mostly early spring-flowering plants, are suggested in this book in Chapter XVII, it would seem that Arborvitae, Barberries, Dianthus, Honeysuckle, Lychnis, Mahonia, and Peony, as recommended in 1873, are scarcely appropriate. A list of sixty or more so-called "alpine" plants is given—these to be kept outdoors or in a cold cellar during winter and brought into the house in March. Alpine-plant enthusiasts may see some merit in a suggestion such as this, especially if the plants are restricted largely to those very early species whose flowers, when produced outdoors, are likely to be marred by the weather sometimes experienced in late winter and early spring. Many alpines are diminutive plants whose charms can be fully appreciated only when they are inspected closely. Bringing them indoors gives us a chance to see them more nearly at eye level.

Some of the plants that are among the most important for house culture today are missing from these early works. African-violets; the many species belonging in the Pineapple Family; Peperomias; many species of Philodendron and related Aroids; the Picka-back Plant, Snake-plant, and many others, get no mention because they are comparative newcomers to the house-plant scene.

Incidentally, when thumbing over the pages of this old book, I came across an item which rather intrigued me—a Turnip basket. This is made by scooping out the center of a Turnip (presumably a Rutabaga), starting from the root end, and leaving a shell about an inch thick. The hollow is filled with soil, Morning-glory seed planted in it, and kept watered. Then the whole contraption is suspended by cords from a bracket in the window. The Morningglories climb up the cords, leaves grow from what is now the base of the Turnip, providing an allegedly lovely combination. This is reminiscent of the modern practice of planting seeds of a dwarf variety of Sweet Alyssum in eggshells to be used as Easter favors. This involves carefully decapitating the matutinal eggs and saving a sufficient number of shells so that the seeds can be sown nine or ten weeks prior to the desired date of flowering.

Value of house plants. Surely it is unnecessary nowadays to waste much ink in selling the proposition that the culture of house plants is well worth the effort required. The fact that there are so many house-plant addicts even in large cities where growing conditions are at their worst is sufficient evidence of the pleasure and interest they give. Perhaps they are valued even more in the city than they are in the country, for the greenness of their leaves and the brightness of their flowers bring relief from the everlasting bricks, mortar, stone, and asphalt. The superintendent of nurses of the largest medical center in New York once told me that the nurses there, fresh from the country, would go crazy if they were not allowed and encouraged to have living plants in their rooms.

It has often been suggested that the culture of house plants provides a suitable occupation for invalids and others who are housebound. This is true enough; but I submit that it is also an absorbing hobby for the hale and hearty, both men and women, who can expect dividends in beauty and interest if they follow it with knowledge and skill.

Growing plants in the home, especially if one is not content to string along with nothing but the old standbys, presents problems just as great as those one meets when growing them outdoors; and the thrill of accomplishment that is the result of solving them is eminently satisfying.

One gets a little closer to plants grown indoors and therefore gains a better insight into their idiosyncrasies, their beauty, and their adaptations to environment. One has the feeling he is something of a chemist when compounding soils and fertilizers; a budding naturalist when dealing with the bugs that may infest them; very much of a craftsman when he successfully performs the operations of grafting and making cuttings; and a creative artist when he sets up a dish garden or terrarium.

With all these and other amenities it must be recognized that there is a concomitant responsibility to provide regular and intelligent care, and that there are certain limitations. Although there are a few plants which can exist for almost incredible periods in dim corners, most of the plants you will wish to grow (unless you are thinking of Mushrooms) demand a well-lighted situation, and some must have abundant sunshine. The lack of humidity in the air may inhibit the culture of some plants unless they are grown in terrariums, and here spatial limitations enter the picture. Not all plants can adapt themselves to house conditions, though as we shall see later the number of tolerant kinds is large enough to satisfy any reasonable demands. Insufficient interest and lack of knowledge of the requirements of plants are perhaps the most potent limiting factors. Many plants demand cultural skill and meticulous attention to watering, temperature, resting, potting, et cetera, as indicated in the following chapters.

POSSIBILITIES

On the other hand, the possibilities inherent in house-plant culture are tremendous. Although over 300 genera and upward of a thousand species and varieties (this is an estimate—they haven't been counted) are included in this book, even this extensive listing does not represent all the kinds that have been recommended for house culture from time to time in diverse places. And I am sure there are others, as yet untried as house plants, that would succeed if given a fair chance.

Where conditions are reasonably good from a plant standpoint it is possible, by making a suitable selection of varieties, to manage them in such a way that the home is never entirely devoid of flowering plants. They can be incorporated in a definitive decorative scheme, or enjoyed as individuals without making any special attempt to display them effectively. They can be assembled in miniature gardenesque arrangements, grown in terrariums, or, under water, in aquariums. Many groups contain large numbers of species and varieties, which render them of great interest to the collector who wishes to specialize.

Plants which can be grown in homes, for part time at least, run the gamut from Aroids to vegetables, from those which are found in deserts to denizens of the rain forests; and their natural habitats range from the Arctic to the Equator.

CHAPTER II

Give Them a Chance to Live

Most of the failures experienced with house plants are due to attempting to grow them under unsuitable conditions. In other words, the environment is at fault. The chief job, therefore, of the would-be grower of house plants is to provide the right growing conditions, and if the mountain will not come to Mohammed, why, Mohammed must go to the mountain—meaning that if the environment cannot be changed, plants must be selected which will endure the environment.

In certain plant families we find a number of subjects which are well adapted to growth under house conditions. Many of these belong in the Lily Family. These include: dwarf varieties of *Aloe; Asparagus* species grown for ornament such as Emerald Feather, and Asparagus-fern; *Aspidistra,* known as Cast-iron Plant, because of its toughness; *Dracaena,* in several species and varieties; *Gasteria* and *Haworthia,* interesting South African succulents; and *Sansevieria* (Snake-plant) which, according to some, can be killed only by overwatering.

The Jack-in-the-pulpit Family (Aroids) is the one par excellence for providing candidates for home growing, though most of them, with the exception of Calla-lilies and Anthuriums, are regarded chiefly as foliage plants. There are a dozen or more handsome and different kinds of *Philodendron* suitable for house culture. *Dieffenbachia, Aglaonema* (including the well-known Chinese Evergreen), *Homalomena, Monstera, Nephthytis, Pothos, Schismatoglottis,* and *Syngonium* are among other genera in this family containing one or more species that can "take it."

Desert plants, especially Cacti and other succulents, are excellent whenever a sunny window is available and are particularly valuable in rooms where the air is excessively dry. Some of them, such as the Christmas Cactus, Mistletoe Cactus, and Orchid Cactus will endure some shade but need more atmospheric moisture.

Succulents, in addition to those mentioned above, include such well-known genera as *Bryophyllum* (Sprouting-leaf), *Crassula* (Jade Plant), *Kalanchoe,* and *Sedum,* all belonging in the Orpine Family. *Fenestraria* and *Lithops,* Windowed Plants and Living Stones; and *Faucaria,* Tiger's Jaw, are a few of the many succulent members of the Fig-marigold Family, which are grown as house plants by fanciers of this group.

Doubtless plants of this nature are able to survive because the impervious cuticle covering their leaves, which enables them to thrive under the hot desert sun and the lack of moisture, also enables them to get along in the dry air of the living room.

Other plants with tough constitutions are Grape relatives such as *Cissus rhombifolia,* Grape-ivy; *C. antarctica,* Kangaroo Vine; and *C. capensis,* Cape Grape. Many plants in the Pineapple Family (Bromeliads), especially *Neoregelia,* Painted Fingernail; *Billbergia, Cryptanthus,* and *Nidularium,* will grow in dry air and with little light, but are rather scarce and consequently difficult to obtain. *Pandanus, Ficus,* various Citrus fruits, English Ivy (if not kept too hot), and *Howea* (Curly Palm) also are excellent.

In general those plants which have tough leathery leaves like those of the well-known "Brooklyn" Rubber Plant, and those whose leaves are shiny, are best bets for the living room, though there are some excellent house plants with hairy leaves such as African-violets and Gloxinias. These hairs serve much the same purpose as thickened and hardened skin in preventing loss of moisture by transpiration. The drawback to these hairy types from the standpoint of the housewife is that they are too efficient as dust catchers.

It is fortunate for us that these plant "toughies," which can endure almost anything, are available, but if we restrict ourselves to them we are deprived of a large number of attractive plants that can be grown in the home if conditions are reasonably good. Therefore, if you are really interested in growing house plants, every endeavor should be made to change the environment to fit the plants which are likely to thrive under the conditions you are able to supply.

Familiarity with the unfavorable conditions which make house plants miserable is helpful in enabling us to see just what has to be overcome and in devising means for setting things to rights.

TEMPERATURE, HUMIDITY, GAS, AND VENTILATION

Temperature and atmospheric moisture are most important. These two factors are linked because the higher the temperature of the air, the greater its capacity for moisture. High temperatures, with the resultant reduction in humidity, are responsible for many house-plant ills.

Humidify the air as much as possible. If you do this, you will find that you yourself will be comfortable at a lower temperature than is the case when the air is deficient in moisture. (See page 82.)

Gas is harmful: Artificial gas used in cooking and heating is deadly to most plants and it does not have to be present in high concentration—one part in 200,000 parts of air is sufficient to injure Tomato plants, and a concentration of 1 to 400,000 upsets Castor Bean plants. By taking precautions and selecting enduring plants, even this handicap can be overcome to a large extent. (See page 83.)

Ventilation is desirable whenever the weather permits because it admits moist outdoor air and dilutes the concentration of injurious gas if any is present.

Light essential: Insufficient light often limits the variety of plants available for house culture. Some, such as Aspidistra, Fiddle-leaf Fig, and some of the Philodendrons, are able to exist for months in dark corners. Snake-plants set around a pool in the lobby of a neighborhood movie house, where there is practically no natural light and that provided by electricity is on the dim side, look as though they might be able to last through the winter. But, for the most part, plants need to be kept as close as possible to windows, provided this does not involve setting them on top of an active radiator.

It is well known that country dwellers are able to grow to perfection a greater variety of house plants than those whose lot is cast in a big city. They do not have to contend with the dust, fumes from factories, and impure air generally that accompany city life. In most cases the plants are not subject to gas injury because cooking is done on a coal, wood, or electric range. In many of the homes where the best house plants are grown, central heating is lacking. Consequently, the rooms are only moderately warm, and the air, because of this, is comparatively humid. Furthermore, the bubbling kettle and the seething soup pot, almost always in operation on the range, add their quota of water vapor to the air. Often farmers' wives can grow plants of such good quality that professional gardeners, with all the conveniences of a greenhouse, cannot match them.

Acclimatization: The sudden transition from the excessively humid conditions of a greenhouse to the aridity of the living room is sometimes disastrous. To overcome this, plants should be raised at home, or they should be obtained during the spring and summer months or early in the fall before it is necessary to use artificial heat. Plants bought at such times have a chance to adapt themselves to their new environment without the discomfiture attendant upon the dry air which usually accompanies artificial heat. Another reason for purchasing plants during the warm months is that there is no danger of their suffering from chilling during transit from the florist's store to the home.

Do not be too despondent if leaves start to turn yellow and fall off within a few days after the plants are received. Often this is just a passing phase—a sort of homesickness which is overcome after the plants become acclimated.

One way of helping to keep house plants healthy is to maintain them in a state of constant juvenility. This implies propagation by cuttings, air-layering, or seeds in your own home. If you are able to do this, you avoid the necessity of having to condition the plants to a sudden change.

And, lastly, it must not be forgotten that due attention must be given to watering, fertilizing, the use of right soil mixtures, resting, timing, pest fighting, and other factors previously mentioned which are concerned in good culture and may be looked on as part of the environment. These and other elements will be discussed in greater detail in subsequent chapters.

CHAPTER III

Real Gardens Indoors

INDOOR GARDENING, like gardening outdoors, develops two distinct kinds of plant enthusiasts. One is the cultivator who grows plants because of their interest and intrinsic beauty, and who makes no attempt to display them in an artistic ensemble. He sometimes has a touch of collectors' mania, often complicated with something akin to parental instinct which makes him fuss around with sickly plants whose proper niche is the garbage pail. The other is the decorator who cares little for plants as individuals and uses them in much the same way as a painter uses his pigments. He is not interested in *growing* plants and is perfectly content to use transitory material, obtained from the florist, which is discarded without a tear when it begins to look shabby. It is the individual whose attitude toward house plants lies between these two extremes who is likely to get the most out of indoor gardening. He has the fascination of watching the plants develop under his care and the thrill of pride that comes from producing a perfect specimen. Realizing that a jumble of potted plants set down haphazardly is not likely to be very attractive, he gives time and thought to arranging the plants effectively, thus achieving a decorative effect that is pleasurable to others as well as to himself.

Usually the most satisfactory window gardens are those which make use of both permanent and transient material—the first to frame and provide a background to the composition, and the latter to provide color and change of scene.

Vines will be desirable to frame the window. They may be planted in the ends of a window box (more about this later) or grown in pots standing on the sill. They can be trained upward by fastening their shoots with unobtrusive tape and thumbtacks to the casing, or a simple narrow trellis can be provided to which they are tied. Good vines for this purpose are: Cape Grape, English Ivy, Grape-ivy, Morning-glories (these need something around which they can twine), and Nephthytis.

Instead of using vines which grow upward, you may prefer those which hang down; or perhaps a combination of the two. These droopers are grown in pots (provided with saucers to eliminate the nuisance of drips) attached by brackets to the casing toward the top of the window. Good droopers are:

Ceropegia woodi, Hearts Entangled; English Ivy varieties (select suitable specimens from the greenhouse of your local florist—Little Beauty is a good one if you can get it) ; *Nepeta hederacea variegata,* variously known as Ground-ivy, Gill-over-the-ground, Field-balm, et cetera; *Philodendron cordatum; Scindapsus (Pothos) aureus; S. pictus argyraeus; Thunbergia alata,* Black-eyed Susan Vine; *Trades-cantia fluminensis* vars.; and *Zebrina pendula* vars.—both genera known as Wandering Jew.

Having reversed the usual procedure by first constructing the frame, the next step is to make the picture. It may be decided that there is room for one or more hanging plant shelves. These should be of clear glass so that no more sun is shut out of the room than is absolutely necessary. They may be supported by light metal hangers attached to the sash frame, or by brackets fastened to the casing. Browse around in five-and-ten-cent, hardware, and department stores until you find the kind of contraption that will fit your window.

On the shelves, hung near eye level for most convenient observations, small pots of decorative Cacti and succulents may be set. The pots can be left as is, or painted white, or any color to suit, and should stand in drip saucers which ought to be of clear glass so they will not block off light. The rows of small painted pots have a certain decorative quality when seen as a whole, but the plants in them should also be interesting enough to bear close inspection. A selection from the following will provide variety in color, shape, and texture.

Cacti: *Astrophytum myriostigma,* Bishop's Hood Cactus; *Cephalo-cereus senilis,* Old Man Cactus; *Chamaecereus sylvestri,* Peanut Cactus; *Echinocactus grusoni,* Golden Ball Cactus; *Echinopsis eyriesi; Espostoa lanata; Mamillaria bocasana; M. elongata,* Golden Lace Cactus; *M. fragilis; Opuntia microdasys,* Rabbit Ears Cactus, and its variety *albescens.*

Hanging plant shelves. Heavy wire supports, with wire brackets welded in place, support glass shelves under which they pass. These and similar contraptions are available at seed and department stores

Succulents other than Cacti: *Crassula lycopodioides; C. rupestris* (*perfossa*) *; Echeveria secunda; E. leucotricha; Faucaria tigrina,* Tiger's Jaw; *Gasteria verrucosa; Haworthia margaritifera, H. truncata; Kalanchoe lanceolata* (*pilosa*), Panda Plant; and any of the Flowering Stones (*Lithops* spp., et cetera) ; or the allied Windowed Plants—*Fenestraria* spp., et cetera.

Cacti and other succulents are suggested for the shelves partly because they are just what is needed decoratively; and partly because their cultural requirements are met by the light, airy, and dry environment.

Next the sills will need attention. So far the plant material suggested is, we hope, of a permanent nature but not especially colorful. Therefore it might be well to plan to brighten up the composition by using more floriferous plants on the sills, which may involve rather frequent changes of material. This will require the provision of another plant room, preferably a cool one, in which Azaleas, Camellias, hardy bulbs and the like, can be brought along to the bud stage before putting them on display. Lacking such a room, one may make frequent purchases of plants in bud or bloom from the florist. If the state of the pocketbook does not permit extensive splurges in the acquisition of plants, and if it is not possible to provide a room in which to grow or store plants when they are not in bloom, one has to rely on those of long flowering habit such as *Begonia scharffi*, Wax Begonia, Patience Plant, and Shrimp Plant. Brightly colored foliage plants also can play a part—Coleus in winter and fancy-leaved Caladiums in summer and fall.

When the window ledge is equipped with a watertight tray filled with pebbles, the potted plants may be stood on them. The plants should be arranged as effectively as possible. But you may feel that with numerous pots on brackets and shelves there are enough of them on view already and will be inclined to try to hide these additional pots. This can be done by having boxes made to fit the window space. They ought to be 7 inches deep and as much wide—the wider the better, within reason, to allow for flexibility in arranging plants. Drainage holes are desirable, and this requires a water-holding tray beneath them to catch drips. Sufficient room can be partitioned off at each end of the box to contain soil in which the framing climbers are planted. The remainder of the box is filled with moist peatmoss in which the pots of the flowering plants are plunged and thus effectively hidden. Peatmoss is suggested because it is clean to handle and its loose texture makes it easy to remove and insert the pots when changes are made. It also reduces the necessity of frequent watering, and the evaporation of moisture from it helps to keep the air humid, thus prolonging the life of the flowers.

Except when one is restricted to long-blooming flowering plants the content of the window boxes will vary with the seasons. In winter the mainstay will be hardy forcing bulbs—Tulips, Narcissi, et cetera; in spring, Cineraria, Genista, and Hydrangea will supply the color; in summer, Achimenes, Tuberous Begonias, Fuchsias, and Gloxinias; in fall, Chrysanthemums, Wax Begonia, and Lantana.

Plants can be effectively displayed on stands made of wood or metal. These should, of course, be set up in a well-lighted situation. They are particularly valuable for porch decoration during the summer months.

The maker of an indoor garden has to decide whether it is to face the street or the room. Almost invariably the best side of plants is that which is toward the source of light; consequently, when they are required to look well when seen from inside, it is necessary to turn them rather frequently—usually about once a week. Vines and plants too large to be given a weekly turnabout always appear at their best to the observer on the outside looking in and there is nothing much that can be done about it.

There are a few things always to be kept in mind—things small in themselves, but which, if neglected, can detract immensely from any planned decorative effect: the pots in which the plants are growing should be painted a uniform color, scrubbed clean, or hidden; sickly plants should either be discarded or promptly removed to a room set apart to serve as a sanitarium—they have no place in what sets out to be an ornamental display; and yellowing leaves and faded flowers must be picked off daily.

WINDOW BOXES

House plants can be grown or displayed in window boxes to serve a dual purpose: that of room decoration in winter, and outdoors in spring, summer, and fall on the porch rail or window ledge.

The metal "self-watering" window boxes are desirable for this purpose because they eliminate the nuisance of drips through the drainage holes, and are not too heavy to be moved around by a couple of huskies, even when filled with moist soil and plants. The ones I have are 36 × 7 × 7 inches but, as I remember it, they are also available in smaller sizes. If these types do not appeal, boxes of wood or metal can be constructed to fit the window spaces. They should be at least 6 inches wide and of equal depth and not so long that they are too heavy to move easily. There must be provision for the escape of surplus water. This, unless the boxes are constructed with a false bottom along the lines of the "self-watering" kinds, requires the presence of a watertight tray beneath to catch drips.

The box may be filled with soil and the plants set directly in it; or potted plants may be plunged in peatmoss to give the effect of a planted box. If the first method is followed, the variety of suitable plants is limited. Kinds should be chosen which have a presentable appearance throughout the year and which possess tough constitutions. This means that the planting will be confined largely to "foliage" plants such as Boston and Holly Ferns; small Palms; Dracaena;

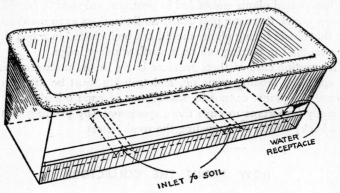

A "self-watering" window box. Water is applied at the base, and soaks *up* through the soil. Several types, constructed on the same principle, are available at seed stores

Emerald Feather Asparagus; Chlorophytum; Philodendron, English Ivy, Tradescantia, and Zebrina (to trail over edge); Snake-plant; Aspidistra; with long-blooming flowering plants such as Patience Plant, Wax Begonia, and House Geraniums.

When the time comes to set the boxes out in spring, it may be that some of the plants will be so woebegone that it will be a kindness to remove them. The vacancies left by their passing can be filled with free-flowering material such as Balcony Petunias and Dwarf Marigolds to provide color throughout the summer. Before planting them as much soil as possible should be removed from the planting spaces without disturbing the roots of the plants remaining in the box. The holes thus made should be filled with rich, new soil.

In the fall the plants should be cleaned of fading flowers, dead leaves, and branches—if this was not done, as it should have been, at weekly intervals throughout the summer. If the annual material is still flowering and in good condition, leave it until it becomes ratty. When this occurs remove it; and consider if the box is in need of complete or partial replanting, and if some of the plants have to be discarded (because they have grown too big, are shabby, or because you feel the need of a change) and replaced with new ones. If replanting is decided upon, remove all the plants from the box, taking care not to injure the roots any more than is absolutely necessary, discard the soil remaining in the box and replace with new.

When potted plants embedded in peatmoss are used to furnish the window boxes, there are practically no limitations as to material, except that shade-loving plants should not be included in a box that is to be exposed to blazing sun on a south window ledge.

The routine care of these window boxes in the matter of watering, spraying, feeding, pruning, and training must be attended to. Because the plants cannot be moved out of each other's way, it is especially important to curb those specimens (by pruning or tying them back) which are crowding the weak sisters.

HOW ABOUT THE COLLECTOR?

The serious cultivator of house plants often discovers that certain groups have a special appeal—either because they thrive exceedingly well, or because they have features which make them especially interesting. When this happens, he is vulnerable to the collecting bug and any day is likely to become the willing victim of an absorbing hobby.

I once had a collector friend whose specialty was small succulents. His addiction to them led him to construct a small "greenhouse" over the cellar window on the south side of the house. The plants were inconveniently tended and admired by standing on a box in the cellar and thrusting head and shoulders through the window. One hopes that such devotion provided compensations other than those afforded by the plants—I have a suspicion that it also gave him a rather uncomfortable retreat where he could smoke his pipe in peace. Plants grown in such a situation add nothing to the amenities of the living room, but it is unnecessary to worm oneself into a frame over a cellar window to enjoy Cacti and succulents, for they are more resistant to dry air and gas than most plants, and they thrive in any sunny window.

Cacti and succulents, however, comprise too many species to permit the formation of a comprehensive collection in a dwelling, so it is wise to limit oneself to a section within the group, or even to a single genus. If the objective is the cultivation of a large number of species and varieties—and a true collector may want to grow all available kinds within his limit—it is better to select a group the

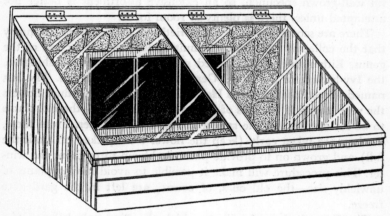

A homemade frame built of window sash and tongued- and grooved boards can be used by the indoor gardener for growing house plants and other purposes, such as propagating, starting seedlings, carrying along bulbs for forcing, and the like. Cellar window admits heat in winter; hinged sash provide for ventilation

members of which never attain any great size; or one in which the individuals can easily be maintained as small specimens by periodic propagation. Plants filling these specifications are found among the Mammillarias, belonging to the Cacti, many of which have the additional merit of flowering while still very small. Living Stones and Windowed Plants, those strange inhabitants of the South African deserts, never get very large; neither do *Haworthia, Faucaria,* and selected species of *Crassula* and *Echeveria.* The tropical and subtropical Sedums can easily be brought down to earth again, when old plants get too large, by making cuttings of their shoots which root with ridiculous ease.

If sunny windows are not available a collection of Ferns could be installed; or one might make a hobby of getting together all the named forms of Fuchsia, or of African-violet, and it will be found that there is a surprisingly large number of these.

A collection of Begonias is almost never without some individuals in bloom—many of them producing their flowers over long periods —and most of them have leaves that are colorful, of interesting form, or otherwise attractive. Some Begonias, however, may grow to considerable size and there is a natural reluctance to discard a beautiful well-grown specimen, so an extensive assortment is better not attempted unless there is plenty of room for it.

There are scores of species and varieties of *Pelargonium*—so many that the collector will probably limit himself to one section of the genus. Either the scented-leaved group, the Martha Washington, the Ivy-leaved, or the Zonal Geraniums could be chosen. The last named, sometimes known as House Geraniums, will produce flowers the year 'round if two lots of plants are maintained—the old plants to be set outdoors in the spring to bloom all summer. From these, cuttings are taken early (keep the flower buds picked off until the fall) and grown on to provide plants to bloom throughout the winter. This procedure will make it possible to avoid having plants of unwieldy size—the old ones, of course, are left in the garden to freeze.

The Bromeliads, a family to which the Pineapple belongs (see page 158), are tremendously varied in leaf form and in habit of growth. Often their leaves are brilliantly colored, and the flowers of many species exhibit combinations of color found nowhere else in the vegetable kingdom. *Billbergia nutans,* for example, has blue-edged green petals, conspicuous golden stamens, and striking red bracts. These plants take kindly to house conditions, and those who are willing to go to the trouble of acquiring a collection (they are not carried by every florist) will be well repaid.

I know a man whose hobby is the cultivation of tropical and sub-tropical fruits as house plants. In many ways this is not an ideal selection, for some—Pomegranate and Fig—are leafless during the winter and, as they are kept outdoors during the summer, are house plants only by virtue of their winter occupancy of the cellar. Avocado is never likely to produce any fruit when grown as a house plant; Papaya and Banana, even the comparatively dwarf Chinese variety, are far too large for the average home. But the Citrus fruits—Kumquat, Lemon, Otaheite Orange, et cetera—the Surinam Cherry, Strawberry Guava, and Pineapple, have definite possibilities.

There may be those with the collecting instinct who desire more variety than is afforded by the cultivation of one group. Even though space is limited, they need not be deterred, for there is the possibility of making use of those plants which have a dormant period at different seasons so that growing space is occupied by one group while the other is resting—analogous to the practice of sleeping men in relays sometimes adopted when transporting troops. Fuchsias actively grow and blossom during spring, summer, and fall, and can be kept dormant in the cellar during the winter, during which time their place in the window garden can be occupied by a collection of winter-flowering bulbous plants such as Lachenalias, Oxalis, et cetera. Or a collection of summer-flowering Achimenes, Tuberous Begonias, or Gloxinias could be alternated with winter-flowering annuals, and so on.

The collector does not, perhaps, have as much opportunity to produce decorative results as those who grow and display a greater variety of plant material, but at least he can, in common with those whose aim is primarily interior decoration, be faithful in attending to those small chores mentioned on page 14.

CHAPTER IV

Terrariums

DRY AIR is one of the greatest obstacles to the successful culture of house plants. Growing them in terrariums enables us to overcome this handicap and permits the cultivation of a variety of plants which would be certain to die quickly if exposed to the air of the average living room. They are especially valuable for the city dweller because they enable him to maintain a moist atmosphere around his plants no matter how assiduously the janitor attempts to reproduce in his apartment the climate of Death Valley.

Personally I do not like the term "terrariums" because I feel that Nathaniel Ward, F.R.S., F.L.S., a London physician who, more than a hundred years ago, discovered that plants could be grown in closed containers, should be commemorated in the name given them. Therefore, I prefer to hear them called "Wardian cases."

Ward greatly desired an old wall covered with a growth of Ferns and Mosses. There was no difficulty whatever about the old wall—that was already there—but the good doctor, residing in the dirt and smoke of London, could not make plants grow in it or on it. He was interested in all natural phenomena, and in the summer of 1829, wishing to see the emergence of an adult sphinx moth, he buried the chrysalis in soil contained in a glass jar which he then covered with a metal lid. Nothing is known about the fate of the chrysalis—Ward was too excited about a Fern and a Grass which appeared in the bottle and continued to thrive there with no attention and without additional water for nearly four years. There is no telling how long these two plants might have flourished if, during Ward's absence from home, the lid had not rusted and let rain into the jar, waterlogging the soil, which caused the plants to rot.

The spontaneous growth of a plant belonging to a group which he had so far failed to grow in spite of all his efforts caused Ward to experiment with a variety of plants in all sorts of containers. He began with one of the most intractable of all plants under cultivation —a Filmy Fern (*Trichomanes radicans*) which grows wild in Killarney in Ireland but is the despair of most gardeners. It grew happily for four years in a wide-mouthed bottle covered with oiled silk, without any added water, and then became too crowded, necessitating its removal to a Fern house. There, covered with a bell jar (thus continuing the principle of a closed container), it developed fronds 15 inches long—larger than those of specimens in its native haunts.

After experimenting with more than a hundred species of Ferns and thoroughly proving the success of the system as far as this group is concerned, Ward constructed a glass case about 8 feet square which he placed outside a window on the north side of his house. In this case, which might easily be called an unheated greenhouse, he grew a great variety of hardy material including Ferns and flowering plants, and also two Palms. These flourished but, says Ward, "the atmosphere was too moist, and there was too little sun for them to ripen seed, with the exception of the *Mimulus,* the *Oxalis,* and the *Cardamine* . . ."

The "Drawing-room case," which contained Palms, Ferns, Club Mosses, Aloes, and Cacti, was very successful, and Ward says of it: "The Palms have now been enclosed for fifteen years . . . they will continue for many years without outgrowing their narrow bounds." The association of moisture-loving Ferns, et cetera, with desert plants is incongruous and presents cultural difficulties, but these were overcome by growing the former in the bottom of the case, and suspending the Cacti and succulents from a bar near the roof where the only water available to them was that contained as vapor in the air.

Wardian cases, or terrariums, whichever you prefer, enable us to control the amount of atmospheric moisture around the plants grown in them. In those which are tightly closed the moisture evaporated from the soil and that transpired by the leaves condenses on the glass, runs down to the soil, and again becomes available for the use of the roots in a sort of perpetual-motion cycle.

The late W. A. Manda, a superb plantsman, once gave me a fishbowl terrarium, tightly covered with a pane of glass, in which a variety of plants were growing. I left it on a southeast window sill with no attention whatever for nearly a year—just to see what would happen. As a result of neglecting to apply those curbs which are a part of routine care, one plant, *Fittonia argyroneura,* had grown so vigorously that all the rest were smothered, but it was perfectly healthy and the terrarium was still presentable except for the depressing remains of the murdered plants.

Although many plants grow well in tightly closed cases, for our purposes a modification of the principle is desirable. When tightly closed, moisture often condenses on the glass, obscures the plants within, and defeats our objective of displaying decorative plants; also some plants object to an atmosphere in which the humidity is constantly kept at 100 per cent. So, except in special instances, it is desirable to provide some means of ventilation which can be increased or decreased according to circumstances.

The plants in terrariums are protected from dust, temperature changes are gradual, and the plants are not exposed to drafts. All these are helpful factors when growing plants under the abnormal conditions of the living room. Ward maintained that the plants in closed cases were not exposed to direct contact with any current of noxious gases and that the law regulating the diffusion of gases prevents their admission in sufficient quantity to affect the plants. I am not enough of a physicist to know whether or not this contention is correct; if it is, those of us who experience difficulties in growing plants in houses in which heating, cooking, et cetera, are done with artificial gas should find terrariums a great boon. I can agree that the plants are protected against direct currents of deleterious gases, but am inclined to question whether the air of the case is very different from that of the room except for the greater amount of water vapor contained in it.

The Wardian case should appeal especially to those who hate the daily chore of watering, because it almost entirely eliminates the need for such attention. Ward had a bottle containing Ferns and Mosses which were in perfect health after eighteen years of confinement without any fresh water. He expressed the opinion that it would be possible to fill a case with Palms and Ferns which would not require additional water for fifty or a hundred years. But this, of course, would be practicable only in a tight case in which the transpired and evaporated water is condensed on the glass and ultimately returned to the soil; and, as previously mentioned, such tight cases are not ordinarily desirable for our purpose.

All sorts of containers have been used in which to grow plants on the principle of the Wardian case. They range from brandy "sniffers" of normal or Gargantuan size through glass teapots and similar whatnots to large fish bowls. Tropical fish fanciers have converted their aquariums into terrariums; and ordinary dirt gardeners have either bought terrariums with gleaming chromium frames or have made their own with less glamorous material. Oversize, hermetically sealed test tubes with Ferns in them, their roots growing in nutrient agar, have been on the market. There are bottle gardens, too, which may be set up in anything from a 2-quart cider jug to an acid carboy with a capacity of 25 gallons. Practically all these containers have one serious defect from the standpoint of the gardener who wishes really to *grow* plants: they have no provision for the escape of surplus soil water. Therefore, most of us prefer to make our own cases.

Construction: The easiest and cheapest way to make a terrarium is to acquire a flat or box about 4 inches deep and of a convenient length and breadth. Unless there are cracks in the bottom, bore about six ½-inch holes to permit water to escape. Then have a glazier cut two pieces of glass about 16 inches wide (this dimension will be the height of the terrarium—it can be varied in accordance with the size of the box so that it is in proportion). These two pieces should be the exact length of the inside dimension of the flat lengthwise. Two more pieces should be cut the same height and the width of the flat *less two thicknesses of the glass.* These are used to make the sides. One additional piece a quarter inch in excess of the inside length and breadth of the flat is cut to serve as a cover. The side and end pieces are fitted vertically in the flat, and soil, which will help to hold the glass in place, is put in. (See illustrations following pages 116 and 120.)

Then the exposed joints of the glass are bound with adhesive tape, the plants are put in, and the top glass rested on the side walls. The final result is an efficient but not especially beautiful case. Unfortunately the flat top may become a repository for books and magazines placed there by unsympathetic members of the household.

A better-looking affair, which does not permit books, et cetera, to repose on it, can be made in the form of a span-roof greenhouse. This is an appropriate shape, because a terrarium in effect is nothing but a miniature greenhouse. A wooden frame holds the glass over the soil container (4 or 5 inches deep, of convenient length and breadth) made of planed boards. The frame is made of strips one inch square planed on all four sides and rabbeted (grooved) on two sides. It is attached to the base by lap joints or by overlapping brass strips fastened to box and frame by screws. If the first method is used, the boards of the soil container should be ½-inch thick; if the latter is used, a thickness of 1 inch is desirable.

The gable ends project about 1½ inches beyond the side walls. Two $3/16$-inch holes, an inch apart, are made in the projection to receive the whittled pegs which prevent the roof glass from sliding. When ventilation is necessary, the pegs are placed in the lowermost holes, allowing the glass to slip down to rest on them. If a completely closed case is desired, the glass is pushed up and held in place by putting the pegs in the upper holes.

Either of these terrariums can be used as a propagating case to raise new plants from cuttings or seeds.

Drainage: Although plants can be grown in cases without any provision for underdrainage, it is much better to have some means for disposal of surplus water. Cases without holes in the bottom are not foolproof because watering has to be done with great care to avoid getting the soil waterlogged; hence there should be from one to several holes in the bottom of the soil container.

In addition, a 1-inch layer of coarse sand or fine gravel should be placed in the bottom, first covering the holes with pieces of broken flowerpot to prevent the sand from sifting through. A thin layer of moss over the drainage is desirable to prevent fine soil from sifting down and clogging it. When the case is thus protected there is much less danger from overwatering. If it is decided to string along with a watertight case, a couple of inches of small pebbles mixed with a few lumps of charcoal will help to overcome the danger of waterlogging. (See Chapter X.)

Soil: An open-textured soil is desirable, especially if the container is undrained. It should not be too rich, because if it is the plants will grow so quickly that they will soon raise the roof. A mixture of two parts fibrous loam, two parts coarse sand, and one part flaky leafmold will suit most of the plants. If acid-soil plants are to be grown, substitute acid peat for leafmold and double the amount.

Planting: Put in the drainage material and fill the box with soil,

One of the original forms of the Wardian case, developed by Nathaniel B. Ward. A sliding panel provides for care of plants and ventilation; plug near base for drainage when necessary. (The mouse, apparently, mistakes the contraption for a cheese box.) Reproduced from: *On the growth of plants in closely glazed cases*, by Nathaniel B. Ward; London, 1842

Foliage pattern made by one of the floating water plants, *Azolla caroliniana*

How to make a terrarium: (1) Bowl, soil mixture, gravel, and plants are assembled

(2) Drainage material and soil are put in place, sloped up one side

(3) Plants, with root balls reduced in size, are carefully inserted

(4) Glass is cleaned with tissue, water applied, and cover put on

A well-planted "bottle" garden—a novel and interesting form of terrarium

but do not pack it down; this last you will do as the plants are set in place. Then, if it is considered desirable to raise the level of one or more parts to give variation of contour, add small, well-shaped, and pleasingly colored rocks and fill in behind them with soil.

The arrangement of the plants is the next item on the program. If the case has a flat top, it is usually better to concentrate the taller plants at either end, giving a sort of valley effect in the middle; if you are dealing with a peaked roof, the taller plants will be spaced down the center where there is more headroom and the completed terrarium turned from time to time to insure an equitable distribution of light.

It is helpful to place and replace the plants within the terrarium without removing them from their pots until you have a rough idea of the kind of arrangement most pleasing to you. Then remove the plants from their pots and scoop holes with the fingers large enough to receive the balls of soil. Press soil firmly around them as you proceed with the planting. Commercial terrariums are planted for immediate effect and almost always are overcrowded and cluttered with "waterfalls" of marble chips, miniature storks, gnomes, and so forth. Unless you dote on fiddle-faddles, it is better to give them the go-by and limit your accessories to Lichen- or Moss-covered rocks of interesting shapes, and give the plants a little room in which to grow.

BOTTLE GARDENS

Planting a garden in a bottle calls for nearly as much skill and patience as that exercised by an old-time sailor constructing a model of a full-rigged ship in a rum bottle. The manipulation of the plants with only a narrow opening through which to work is a delicate operation.

Great care is necessary to avoid spilling soil on the leaves or the inside of the container, because it is not easy to get it off once the plants are inside the bottle. Most, if not all, of the soil must be removed from the roots of the plants to enable them to pass through the opening; this means that the plant is set back to some extent and special care must be taken to spread the roots in the soil; to fill in between and over them, and finally to tamp firmly. The chances of success are improved if the bottle is provided with drainage holes.

You may be able to find a glazier who will drill two or three holes for you.

Obviously a bottle garden cannot be planted without some tools; these, fortunately, can be made at home. A funnel with a wide spout is needed to help get the soil in the bottle; this can be improvised from flexible cardboard fastened into funnel form with a stapler. Three hands are necessary if the job of pouring is to be done without undue exasperation—one to hold the funnel and two to

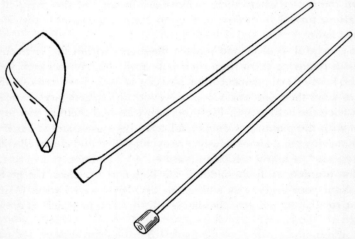

Equipment for making a bottle garden: paper funnel for filling in soil; spatula, whittled from a piece of lath; tamper, constructed from 1-inch section of broom stick, with handle of ¼-inch dowel

manipulate the soil. A spatula to dig holes in the soil to receive the roots can be whittled from a piece of lath or something similar. Be sure to make it long enough to enable you to grasp the projecting portion easily. A tamper can be made by cutting a short section from a broom handle, drilling a hole through it and inserting a thin plant stake or ¼-inch dowel of suitable length.

Long tongs are needed to put the plants in position and hold them there while they are being planted. They can be obtained from dealers in aquarium supplies; or borrow a pair from your garageman—he uses them to fish out broken window glass from automobiles. If it is not possible to locate tongs of suitable size, a makeshift can be improvised from a bamboo plant stake by splitting it lengthwise and inserting a wedge at the upper end of the split to spread the legs. Wind several turns of string and tie tightly near the upper limit of the split to prevent it from going too far.

Procedure: First put drainage material in the bottom. This can consist of coarse sand with the finer particles sieved out, or ⅛- to ¼-inch charcoal obtained from a feed store. The amount to use depends upon the size of the container and whether or not it is provided with drainage holes. Half an inch will be sufficient for a half-gallon bottle if it is drained; otherwise use an inch, or even two inches.

The soil should be funneled in with care to avoid getting it on the sides. Use a mixture of equal parts loam, sand, and leafmold, and put it through a ¼-inch sieve so it will pour easily through the funnel. While the soil should be moist, it should not be wet, lest it clog the machinery. From 2 to 5 inches of soil will be needed, depending on the size of the container. In large bottles it is usually desirable to arrange the soil in a slope (do this with the spatula), which gives a more pleasing effect and provides a greater depth of soil on one side to accommodate the larger plants.

Planting: As with regulation terrariums, it is desirable to arrange the plants outside the container before starting to plant in order to get a rough idea of the spacing. Obviously no plants can be used which are too large to pass through the bottle neck; with this limitation in mind a selection can be made from the lists of plants for terrariums. (Pages 30 to 32.)

The procedure in planting is to turn a plant out of its pot and shake enough soil from its roots to enable it to go through the needle's eye. Then, gauging the extent of the roots, make a hole in the soil large enough to receive them and gently insinuate the plant into the bottle. Hold the plant in position with the tweezers and scrape soil in between and over the roots with the spatula, and make it firm with the tamper. Continue along these lines until planting is completed.

Watering: When all the plants are set they should be watered enough to make the soil moist, at the same time taking advantage of the opportunity to spray off any crumbs of soil that happen to rest on the foliage or the side of the container. This is fairly easy with an ordinary terrarium, but bottle gardens present some difficulty.

Probably the best tool for this purpose is the type of sprayer used for insecticide which has a capacity of about a quart, with the spray nozzle at the end of a flexible rubber tube. The great danger in applying water to terrariums and bottle gardens which have no drainage is that of using so much that the soil becomes waterlogged. To avoid this use no more water in spraying the foliage than is absolutely necessary, and examine the soil the following day to determine whether it was enough to moisten it all through.

CARE OF TERRARIUMS AND BOTTLE GARDENS

If the bathtub can be diverted from its legitimate use for twelve hours or so, a convenient way of dealing with the spraying and watering problems of newly planted terrariums (and established ones too) is to stand them in it, give them a thorough spraying from the bath hose, and let them stand until the surplus water has drained away. This method is permissible only when the container is adequately drained.

The frequency of future watering is determined mainly by the amount of ventilation given. As we have seen, it is possible to keep plants for years in closely glazed cases without adding any water; but when enough ventilation is provided to prevent the condensation which obscures one's view of the plants, occasional watering is needed—it may be six or more months after the initial application.

The need, or otherwise, for watering should be determined after digging into the soil with a spoon, or by screwing an auger into it and pulling it straight up with samples of the lower soil sticking in the grooves. This last is the only convenient method of examining the lower stratum of the soil in bottle gardens. If the soil seems less than moist, it should be watered. When the case is well drained, the soil may have a thorough soaking, but in those which are watertight no more water should be given than is sufficient to make the soil moist. Should too much inadvertently be given, the case must be opened up widely to get rid of the surplus as fast as possible by evaporation.

No plant should be put into a terrarium if it is known to be infested with insects. This is especially important in bottle-fed plants because of the difficulty of getting at the insects to fight them. Fumigation would seem to be the only remedy if you can figure out the correct dosage of calcium cyanide to use and don't mind having so deadly a poison loose in the house. In case you want to work it out (I'm not equal to such high mathematics): seven grams of Cyanogas is sufficient to fumigate 1,000 cubic feet; a cubic foot equals 7½ gallons.

Dead leaves should be picked off and not left to moulder and become a possible source of trouble. Aggressive plants must be pruned; or, if they become too obstreperous, removed entirely lest they smother their neighbors.

Ventilation: Generally the results are better if the cases are ventilated rather freely even though it necessitates watering more frequently. Ventilation is effected by tilting the covering glass or by sliding it down if the terrarium is of the span-roof type. The opening should be large enough to prevent moisture from fogging the glass. The amount of ventilation necessary will be conditioned to some extent by the weather. If the air in the home is not too dry, the side walls are sufficient to insure that little extra humidity and the top can be left off permanently.

Aspect: The kinds of plants grown in the case will in part be determined by where it is placed (see lists of plants for various aspects). Placement in a sunny window where shade is provided by light draperies is generally satisfactory, though exposure to bright sunshine is not necessarily fatal. I have had a Wardian case in a window where it was fully exposed to the sun from noon on, which was unattended for six months and was still in good condition. Some shade is preferable, however, to cut down fogginess of the glass, which is inevitable in bright sun.

PLANTS FOR TERRARIUMS

The furnished terrarium obtained from florists usually contains an indiscriminate mixture of tropical, subtropical and hardy subjects, together with plants of the desert and rain forest, all of which are expected to dwell amicably together. Greater satisfaction may be expected, however, if the plants are selected thoughtfully with the idea of associating those with similar temperature and cultural requirements. The Partridge Berries, Lichens, and Mosses offered for sale in "fish" bowls by florists around Christmastime cannot be expected to thrive permanently in an overheated apartment, though they might do well if kept outside the window instead of in the room. Plants of rapid growth and those which are subject to insect attacks should be rejected. Coleus is an admirable illustration of a plant which belongs in both these categories—it shoots up like Jack's beanstalk and almost invariably is infested with mealybugs.

In the lists below I have made a selection of plants which are suitable for culture in Wardian cases. It may be necessary to shop around in order to obtain all of them.

(For specific information concerning plants in the following lists, refer to Index.)

For ordinary room temperature: Abundant light is desirable but direct sun is not necessary.

Aglaonema commutatum, A. costatum.
Alternanthera amoena varieties. These respond to pruning and
    may be kept to reasonable size.
Anthurium scherzerianum.
Asparagus plumosus var. *nanus* (may need pruning).
Begonia foliosa.
Begonia imperialis.
Begonia imperialis var. *smaragdina.*
Begonia Rex-cultorum, small varieties.
Billbergia nutans.
Calathea illustris.
Calathea roseo-picta.
Calathea zebrina (may grow too large).
Cissus (Vitis) rhombifolia, the Grape-ivy of florists. (For large
    cases only, and even then it will need pruning.)
Codiaeum (Croton) in variety. (Small plants are very attractive
    but they quickly grow too large for small cases. Sunshine is
    necessary to keep their color.)
Cryptanthus bivittatus.
Cryptanthus zonatus.
Dieffenbachia seguine. (Use small plants only—will ultimately
    grow too large.)
Dracaena godseffiana.
Dracaena goldieana.   corn plant
Dracaena sanderiana.

Ficus pumila (*repens*).
Fittonia verschaffelti. (Too vigorous for small cases.)
Fittonia verschaffelti var. *argyroneura*.
Maranta arundinacea var. *variegata*.
Maranta leuconeura var. *kerchoveana*.
Peperomia obtusifolia.
Peperomia obtusifolia var. *variegata*.
Peperomia rotundifolia (*nummularifolia*), a prostrate species rooting at the nodes.
Peperomia sandersi.
Philodendron cordatum.
Philodendron micans.
Pilea microphylla (*muscosa*).
Pilea involucrata ("Panamiga").
Saintpaulia ionantha.
Scindapsus pictus var. *argyraeus* (Pothos).
Selaginella emmeliana.
Selaginella kraussiana var. *browni*.
Syagrus (*Cocos*) *weddeliana*.
Tradescantia fluminensis. Wandering Jew
Zebrina pendula.
FERNS.
Adiantum capillus-veneris.
Adiantum cuneatum. · Maidenhair Fern
Asplenium nidus. — birds nest
Davallia bullata.
Davallia pentaphylla.
Nephrolepis small varieties.
Polystichum tsus-simense.
Pteris cretica varieties.

For the cool room or sun porch, where the winter temperature does not go below 40° or much above 50°:

Acorus gramineus vars. *pusillus* and *variegatus*.
Buxus sempervirens var. *suffruticosa*.
Camellia japonica.
Coprosma baueri variegata.
Daphne odora.
Euonymus fortunei varieties.

Ficus pumila (repens).
Hedera helix var. *argenteo-variegata.*
Hedera helix var. *conglomerata.*
Hedera helix var. "Merion Beauty."
Pittosporum tobira variegata.
Primula obconica.
Primula sinensis.
Pteris cretica.
Rhododendron—Kurume vars., in small sizes.
Saxifraga sarmentosa.

For a case outside a north window, where the temperature may go much below freezing. These plants could also be used in a cool room:

Asplenium platyneuron. ⎫
Asplenium trichomanes. ⎭ Hardy native Ferns.

Buxus sempervirens var. *suffruticosa.*
Chimaphila maculata. ⎫ Hardy native
Chimaphila umbellata (Pipsissewa). ⎬ plants.
Epigaea repens, Trailing Arbutus (acid soil). ⎭

Euonymus fortunei vars.
Gaultheria procumbens, Wintergreen. ⎫ Hardy native
Goodyera repens (Rattlesnake-plantain). ⎭ plants.
Hedera helix. (See list above.)

Hepatica americana (triloba).
Lycopodium in var. (Will stay green over winter ⎫ Hardy native
  but may not permanently thrive.) ⎬ plants.
Mitchella repens.
Polypodium vulgare.
Saxifraga sarmentosa. ⎭

Mosses and Lichens in great variety, small evergreen Ferns, seedling Spruces, Firs, and Hemlocks collected in woods and fields are admirable material for the "hardy" case. But be sure to avoid taking anything you "hadn't oughter."

Lacking a built-in window box, one may get a real window-garden effect by utilizing a portable plant stand, which has the advantage that it can be removed during the summer

Miniature Cactus garden, suitable for hot, dry rooms—
Opuntia, Echeveria, Haworthia, Panda Plant, Echinocactus, and others

Dish garden of florists' plants
Pteris, African-violet, Zebra Plant, Podocarpus, Acorus, Ti Plant, Philoden-
dron, Synogonium, Kalanchoe blossfeldiana, Cliff Brake Fern

CHAPTER V

Small Plant Arrangements

WOMEN, especially, delight in arranging things—whether it be furniture, flowers, or their husbands' mode of living. Another outlet for their energies in this respect is the arrangement of plants in containers. These, when completed, are often known as "dish gardens," a rather horrible term which does not even correctly describe the product which may be an idealization in miniature of a natural scene in woods, bog, swamp, or open meadow; a reproduction of a desert landscape; a section of a garden scene; a model of a formalized garden; or an association of tropical plants.

Dish gardens can, of course, be bought ready-made from the florist, but they may offend the fastidious because frequently they are cluttered up with foolish figures, windmills, wishing wells, bridges, pagodas, and other gimcracks. Culturally, they are seldom all that could be desired because of the association of incongruous materials—desert plants with moisture lovers; tropical plants with hardy kinds, and so on. They are put together to give an immediate effect with the plants jostling each other like people in a subway crowd so that they have no chance whatever for future development. Anyone with the least bit of artistic skill, and perhaps even if he has none at all, is likely to get more satisfaction from a home-made product than from a hand-me-down, plus the pleasure that comes from the actual assembly and the joy of having created something.

Admittedly arrangements of this kind are often ephemeral—their length of life depending in large measure upon the sort of plants used in making them and on the cultural practices. Plants gathered from the North Woods and kept in a dry room with a winter temperature of 75° cannot be expected to last over long. When roots are massacred in the endeavor to jam too many plants into a container that is too small, the outlook is for a short life for the plants and not a very gay one. If plants requiring different soil and growing conditions are given the same quarters, some will survive and others succumb, so the good effect of the arrangement is quickly lost. Then, too, in many cases it is inevitable that some of the plants will grow much faster than others so that the scale and balance of the composition are upset. Even so, an arrangement of living plants is much more lasting than an arrangement of cut flowers; and the fact that it does not endure forever is an advantage in that it gives an excuse for a change in make-up.

Material needed: Receptacles can be as varied as the plant arrangements. Almost any shallow (but not too shallow) container that will hold soil, with room for several plants, can be used. Wooden bowls, wicker or chip hampers lined with moss for temporary use, or a box constructed to fit the window space, are possibilities. Usually, however, pottery receptacles are most in favor. These may be of any shape—round, square, rectangular, or elliptical. They should be at least 3 inches deep—4 is better—and have holes in the bottom to allow surplus water to escape. It is almost impossible to find a piece of pottery with this last feature, so it is usually necessary either to drill the desired holes laboriously, or to rely on ample drainage material, exceptionally porous soil, and careful watering to avoid waterlogging.

Drainage material can consist of flowerpots, soft bricks, or charcoal broken into ½-inch or smaller pieces; coarse sand; fine gravel, cinders, or clinkers of suitable size. To prevent the soil from immediately sifting into the drainage material, which is important when dealing with water-tight containers, it can be covered with a piece of building material of the nature of "sheet rock," with holes bored through it and cut to fit. Sheet Moss obtained from a florist, Moss from the woods, or burlap will provide at least a temporary barrier between soil and drainage.

The character of the soil is of little moment for those arrangements that one knows ahead of time will be only transitory—anything that can be moistened to keep the roots from drying will do— but for those from which some degree of permanence is expected it is necessary to fit the soil to the subject. Woodland plants ordinarily will be dug up with a considerable amount of soil about their roots. This will form the bulk of soil in the container; any additional soil required could well be leafmold with a little sand to make it more porous. For the general run of plants a mixture of sand, loam, and leafmold in equal parts will be suitable, with the addition of another part of broken charcoal for Cacti and succulents.

Accessories for use above ground include small rocks of pleasing form and color, especially those which have Lichens growing on them; pieces of bark or dead branches, which often can be found supporting a growth of interesting Fungi or beautiful Mosses. Colored pebbles or shells, small figures and such, can be obtained from the 5-and-10, if you like them—I don't.

Suitable plants: If you have access to a country roadside (not too well kept), abandoned fields, or woodland areas there is plenty of material that can be gathered during a fall walk that is especially adapted for use in plant arrangements for a cold room or unheated enclosed porch. Be careful to avoid trespassing where you are not wanted, and do not dig up anything that is on the list of plants needing conservation in your region, or any plant that does not occur in fair abundance. Using a stout trowel, dig the plants with as many roots as possible, retaining a ball of earth about each. Wrap the root ball in paper and, when enough plants are gathered, pack them closely together in an upright position in a box or carton. Sprinkle tops and soil with water if they have to be transported to any great distance. And if they have to be carried on the running board of an automobile, use a closed container or wrap tops in paper so that they are not exposed to the drying effect of rapidly moving air.

The woodland will yield many plants of an evergreen nature that are well suited to our purpose. Young Hemlocks, Spruces, or Firs will give the necessary height to the composition. To associate with them a selection can be made from Hepatica, Rattlesnake-plantain, Pipsissewa, Partridge Berry, Tea Berry, small Ferns, Club Mosses, and true Mosses. If the scale is small, one or other of the Club Mosses (*Lycopodium*) can be used instead of the young trees, in which case still smaller material—Tea Berry, Partridge Berry, sporeling Ferns, and Mosses will form the "undergrowth."

From roadsides and sunny abandoned fields one may be able to gather young Red Cedars, Common Juniper, and Ferns such as

the Ebony Spleenwort, which provide an effective contrast with
the low gray rosettes of Pussy Toes (*Antennaria*). A touch of color
is given by that grayish Lichen (*Cladonia*) with bright crimson
apothecia (fruiting bodies), and other Lichens on rocks or wood
can be included for variety. With this and the preceding type of
arrangement it is perhaps permissible, though it does savor somewhat of fakery, to make use of cut sprays of evergreens, which will
last a considerable time when stuck into moist earth, especially if
kept cool; and twiggy branches, which can be made to simulate
deciduous trees—the twiggy branches of Bridal Wreath can, by a
stretch of the imagination, be likened to the branch system of
an Elm.

Shoots of Boxwood, Retinospora, Arborvitae, evergreen Barberries, can be arranged in a gardenesque composition with considerable ease because all that needs to be done is to stick the sprigs in
the moistened earth, or sand in this case, in the container. This
phase is perhaps more nearly akin to flower arranging than the
making of a dish garden.

One aspect of small-plant arrangements which more nearly approaches the garden idea is the construction of model gardens. For
years these have been in evidence at flower shows (I remember seeing them as a boy at English flower shows where, to me, they were
the most appealing feature). Usually the plants are artifically represented by pieces of sponge cut to shape, colored, and fastened to
small sticks to simulate trees, Turkish toweling dyed green is used
for the lawn, and so on; but sometimes natural material—used in
the form of cut sprays—serves as trees and shrubs; while small,
brightly colored flowers are dibbled in to represent flower borders.
Those in which artificial material is used do not concern us here;
and the kind which makes use of cut flowers is too ephemeral for
most of us.

Model gardens of this kind, however, can be utilitarian in giving
us a better idea of what a proposed garden will look like than can
be gained from the most elaborate paper plan. Such a model could,
for instance, represent a Tudor "knot" laid out in the intricate pattern beloved of Elizabethan gardeners, with sprigs of Juniper, Red
Cedar, et cetera, representing the Boxwood, Lavender-cotton, Ger-
mander, and Rosemary used in the actual planting. In the knot
gardens of Elizabethan times the spaces between the lines of plants

forming the pattern often were surfaced with colored material which might be crushed brick for red; coal for black; sand for yellow or white. In making these models the surfacing material can be provided by mixing fine sand with dry colors obtained from a paint store. While these gardens of cut sprays are far from being permanent, they are fun to make; and, if the tougher evergreens are used, they may last in good condition for several weeks.

The most enduring and in many ways the most satisfactory dish gardens are those in which Cacti and succulents are used. Under these conditions they are usually slow-growing, so that the composition does not quickly become unbalanced; the plants are adapted to the dry air of the living room; they can get along, as they have to do in a dish garden, without much soil about their roots; and there is sufficient variety in their appearance to permit making up interesting compositions. *Opuntia ramosissima denudata,* when no more than 6 or 8 inches high, may resemble a branching Sahuaro and can be used as such along with much smaller Cacti in an arrangement suggested by a scene in the Arizona desert. Cactus specialists can supply small plants in an infinite variety of form and color; and an acceptable enough arrangement can be made up from Cacti collected in the Southwest and offered at an amazingly low rate in advertisements in horticultural publications and in the garden pages of the lay press. It should be remembered, however, that these collected plants are much more difficult to establish than greenhouse-grown specimens, especially under house conditions.

Succulents are just about as enduring as the Cacti and may be had in all shapes, sizes, and colors, ranging from the dowdy, uninteresting Jade Plant to the intriguing Panda Plant with its fuzzy leaves tipped with tufts of rust-colored hairs which become dark brown with age. Relatives of the Jade Plant, such as the Necklace Vine, with each pair of leaves threaded on the stem; and *Crassula lycopodioides,* which looks like a Club Moss, are effective in contrast. The plushlike leaves of the Mexican Firecracker; the blue-gray rosettes of other Echeverias; the mottled leaves of some of the Kalanchoes, Gasterias, and Aloes, provide material of exceptional interest. These Cacti and succulents are grown mainly for the beauty of the stems, spines, and leaves, but sometimes they give an extra dividend of occasional flowers, often brilliantly colored.

Another type of arrangement is that made up of tropical ma-

terial which includes the variegated Ti Plant and the Gold Dust
Dracaena; any Bromeliads that may be available; small Philodendrons; and Variegated Wax-plant. Most of these are grown for their
colored foliage; for flowers African-violets, *Kalanchoe blossfeldiana,*
and Wax Begonias can be used. For green leaves the dwarf, small-
leaved varieties of English Ivy (even though not tropical) can be
included, and that tufted mosslike Selaginella of brightest possible
green known as *S. browni.* Many of these plants and others suitable
for the purpose can be picked up at the neighborhood florists or
at 5-and-10-cent stores. Do not, however, make the mistake of buying plants in large pots—the containers used for dish gardens usually
are not big enough to hold them. Plants from 2- to 4-inch pot sizes
are generally preferable.

As the days begin to lengthen small pots of Azalea, Begonia, Marigold, and other plants in full bloom begin to make their appearance
in stores. These can be combined with cut sprays of Boxwood and
other evergreens to make effective temporary dish gardens. By the
time the flowers have faded, weather conditions may be such that it
will be possible to remove the plants from the container and plant
them separately outdoors.

Often the dish gardener has to be an opportunist and secure
plants when they are offered for sale. He may combine them, even
though they do not entirely fulfill the ideal of using none but con-
gruous plants in a container, thinking that any kind of dish garden
is better than none at all; or hold them as pot plants until he is able
to assemble enough of the right kind of material for the ideal in
mind.

How they are put together: First gather all materials needed—
plants, container, soil, drainage, et cetera—on a work table or bench
large enough to permit comfortable working. Before removing plants
from their pots, arrange them in the container to get a rough idea of
how they can best be placed to make an artistic composition. It will
save time when it comes to actual planting if it is known in a general
way where the plants are to go. Then remove the plants and put
drainage material in the bottom of the container. If it is so shallow
that there is not much room for soil, and if it is provided with
drainage holes, a piece of broken flowerpot over each hole to prevent soil from sifting through will be sufficient. If, however, it has
no provision for the escape of surplus water, and if it is 3 inches or

more in depth, put in ½ to 1 inch (or even more for deep dishes) of broken pots, bricks, or something similar. This should be covered with burlap, Moss, or sheet rock to keep the soil from immediately clogging the drainage. Then fill the container with soil, *without pressing it down.*

The plants are removed from their pots by placing the fingers of one hand on the soil and turning the pots upside down and tapping the rims on the edge of the bench. Knowing just about where they are to go, it is easy to dig a hole in the soft soil with the fingers to receive the roots. If, as often happens, the ball of soil is too deep for the container, carefully tease out the roots until enough soil can be removed to make it fit. As the plants are set in place, pack the surrounding soil, which should be moderately moist, firmly about their roots.

When all the plants are placed, it is time to think about watering. This is a ticklish operation if the dish is watertight, and one where nice judgment must be exercised to give enough water to moisten the soil all the way through but not so much that it stands free in the soil. It is best to put on less than you think is necessary and then, the following day, dig down to the bottom of the soil with a kitchen spoon and notice its condition, and give more water if need be. Containers with adequate drainage holes can be soaked until water runs through the bottom.

Subsequent care consists of placing the arrangement in the aspect most suited to it—a south window for Cacti and succulents; an east or west window for the general run of plants; and a north window or a table or mantel away from direct sun for Ferns and others which object to too much light. Winter-hardy plants should be kept in a cold room or unheated porch.

Watering must be done thoughtfully. Except for Cacti and succulents, most of which will not object if the soil becomes dry from time to time during the winter months, the plants demand moist soil. At first, comparatively little water will be required after the initial watering, but when the plants are established and the soil becomes filled with roots, more and more will be needed. It is a good plan to keep that kitchen spoon handy and dig down into the soil whenever there is any doubt as to its need for water.

When some of the plants become overgrown, rip the arrangement apart and start all over again, reusing those which are suitable, and supplementing them with new material. Discard the unpresentable ones, and pot up those which are healthy but too large.

SUBMERGED GARDENS

Fifteen or twenty years ago it seemed that nearly every home maintained an aquarium furnished with guppies and other tropical fish, with plants as incidentals. The natural outcome of this activity on the part of the pisciculturists was that horticulturists, seeing the splendid opportunities offered by the decorative arrangement of plants in submerged gardens, took over to such an extent that the Federated Garden Clubs of New York State felt warranted in featuring planted aquariums in their section in the International Flower Show. This brought out arrangements of such breath-taking beauty that the making of gardens in aquariums became very popular. Nowadays the culture of aquatics indoors is in a state akin to eclipse, but it will come back, so no apologies are offered for discussing it here.

In order to get the best results from an aquarium it is necessary to combine two hobbies—plants and fish. These live together in a co-operative relationship, each contributing to the other's welfare. The submerged plants give off oxygen which enables the fish to breathe, while the carbon dioxide given off by the fish and their excrement provides the nutrients necessary for the welfare of the plants. By securing a proper balance between plant and animal life it is possible to set up an aquarium which will remain in good condition for years by merely adding water to replace that lost by evaporation.

Plants: An ardent fish fancier of my acquaintance used to annoy me exceedingly by lumping together all the plants under the generic term "Grass." Actually no true Grasses are ordinarily used in planting aquariums, though some of the plants are Grasslike in appearance. One of the best of these is *Vallisneria spiralis,* known as Eel-grass or Tape-grass, though it is not related to the true Grasses. It is suited only for large aquariums because its pale green translucent leaves may attain a length of 2 or 3 feet. It is easy to grow and is particularly valuable for framing the planting. If a few plants are set at each end of the aquarium, the leaves will arch over and meet in the center.

Other plants of similar appearance include submerged forms of various Arrowheads or *Sagittaria*. The one listed as *S. sinensis* (*graminea*) grows a foot or more high and can be used at the back of the aquarium in between the Vallisneria; or as end plants in smaller aquariums. The Ribbon Arrowhead has small, narrow leaves; while the Awl-leaf Arrowhead (*S. subulata*) is still smaller, seldom exceeding 6 inches in height.

Then there is a group characterized by finely divided leaves arranged on the stems to give a plume-like effect. The most popular is *Cabomba caroliniana,* Fish Grass, whose fanlike leaves are so brittle that they are broken if the fish get too rough with it. This is commonly offered for sale in pet stores and in the 5-and-10. *Myriophyllum,* Water Milfoil, is of similar habit and is said to be a favorite spawning ground for certain types of fish. Ditch-moss (*Anacharis canadensis*), which may make shoots 3 feet long if the water is of sufficient depth, has undivided leaves arranged, usually in fours, along the stem and gives much the same effect as the preceding. This is another easy doer and is the plant known in England as "Babington's Curse" because it was introduced from America by a professor of botany of that name at Cambridge University. For a time it grew so rampantly as to impede navigation on some of the waterways.

All of the plants mentioned are good oxygenators and hence are in great favor with the fish fanciers. They all have comparatively narrow leaves, however, and the plant lover will want to introduce subjects of different appearance to provide variety. One of these is *Ludwigia,* which belongs in the same family as Evening Primrose, though of entirely different appearance. It has small, roundish leaves which are green above with pinkish undersides, providing a different color note. The Southern Spatterdock has large, broad, light green leaves which are very effective when light shines through them. It is a particularly good oxygenator.

The above are grown solely for the effect of their foliage. If good light is available, a few aquatics with conspicuous flowers are worth a trial. These grow with their roots in sand or mud and float their leaves on the surface. They include Floating Heart (*Nymphoides peltatum*) and Water-poppy (*Hydrocleis nymphoides*) with yellow flowers; and Water Snowflake (*Nymphoides indicum*), which, as its name implies, has white flowers.

These plants need to have their roots planted in sand or soil; there are some which will grow floating on the surface or partially submerged. One of the most interesting of these is Bladderwort (*Utricularia* spp.), an insectivorous plant with tiny bladders on its leaves equipped with an ingenious mechanism for trapping minute aquatic animals. The working of these is described in detail in Darwin's book on insectivorous plants. Bladderworts grow wholly or partially submerged in the water, and while they do not add greatly to the appearance of the aquarium, do provide a talking point of interest.

Those plants which grow floating free on the surface are for the most part Ferns or their allies, such as *Ceratopteris* (Water Fern), *Salvinia,* and *Azolla,* which last has been compared to floating branchlets of Arborvitae. It is beautiful when examined under a magnifying glass. The easiest of the floaters to grow is Duckweed, but it is messy-looking and unworthy of a place in the aquarium except as fish food. One of the most beautiful floating species is Shell-flower or Water-lettuce (*Pistia*), a relative of the Calla-lily, which has rosettes of fluted leaves 2 or 3 inches across, but it is not easy to grow.

Among aquarium plants those most likely to grow well and give the most satisfaction are the rooting, submerged plants. They can be obtained in great variety from water-garden and fish specialists, from pet stores (though usually in not so great a variety), and from 5-and-10-cent stores.

Planting: When you have obtained plants from friends or dealers, spread them out in a large shallow pan of water, for their leaves are injured if exposed to air. Place from 1 to 2 inches of coarse, washed sand in the bottom of the aquarium and slope it to provide interesting contours. A small rock or two will help in achieving this end. Submerged wrecks, castles, et cetera, are not necessary. To avoid disturbing the sand, place a piece of wrapping paper over it before gently pouring in 3 or 4 inches of water.

The stronger-growing plants should be set at the rear and ends of the aquarium. Plant the rooted specimens first by making holes of sufficient size with a teaspoon to receive the roots and scraping the sand over to cover them. Some of the plants will be received as unrooted cuttings. These should be bundled in groups of 3 to 5 and their bases weighted by winding a piece of lead wire or a thin lead strip around them. They are then pushed gently into the sand. When all the plants are in place add enough water to fill the aquarium, pouring very gently to avoid loosening the plants.

Do not use too many plants—they increase so quickly that if they are planted thickly you will soon be "unable to see the woods for the trees." When they begin to crowd each other a certain amount of pruning is necessary. Whenever it is possible to do so without spoiling the artistry of the arrangement, the older portions of the plants should be selected for removal, leaving the young, vigorous shoots to carry on. A sharp wood chisel is a handy tool for cutting off the roots of the portion to be removed and the runners connecting old and new clumps; or you can purchase what are known as "plant snips" from a dealer in aquarium supplies.

Weeds are always with us, even in aquariums. Certain objectionable Algae make their appearance, growing either on the glass or free in the water. When this happens, the number of "scavengers" (such as snails) should be increased and the aquarium placed where the light is more subdued. Meanwhile the Algae adhering to the glass can be scraped off by a safety razor blade affixed to a suitable holder; and much of that which is floating in the water can be removed by gently twirling something in the nature of a swizzle stick in among it.

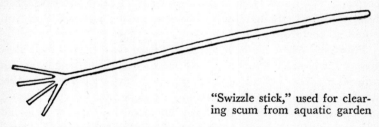

"Swizzle stick," used for clearing scum from aquatic garden

It is not possible to go fully into the ins and outs of the culture of aquatics in a book on house plants, involving as it does fish culture also. Those who are specially interested should consult a book such as *Goldfish Varieties and Tropical Aquarium Fishes,* by W. I. Innes, which deals with plants as well as fishes.

Introduction

FOR successful growth, house plants must have proper care, and this involves regular attention to their requirements. It does not imply that they cannot be left untended for a day or two if proper precautions are taken, but it does mean that, whenever possible, they should be looked over carefully with an eagle eye every day to be sure that all their needs are supplied. The plants should be studied and those which require a rest period provided for; watering must be done thoughtfully; temperature, humidity, ventilation, and gas leaks attended to. If you are one of those who are able to keep plants growing healthily year after year, repotting must be done in proper soil whenever it is needed, and fertilizers supplied at the right time.

Provision must be made for summer care; and pruning, pinching, and propagating carried out at the right seasons. Remember to watch out for insect pests! If you can catch them in their early stages, life will be much simpler both for you and the plants.

All these subjects are considered in detail in the pages which follow; but first acquire the right philosophical attitude toward your plants. Inevitably some will languish and reach a stage when they are no longer useful, beautiful, or interesting. When this happens, throw them out without any compunction, for a plant which becomes debilitated under house conditions seldom can be restored even if the unfavorable factors are rectified; it is better to start with a new healthy plant if you are determined to grow that particular species.

I have a friend who refuses to keep dogs because she becomes so attached to them that when the time for parting comes (a dog's life being not so very full of years) she is so anguished that her life seems unbearable. This is a timorous attitude which deprives one of much of the joy of living. Remember that hackneyed old quotation, "It's better to have loved and lost . . . !" So, with plants, reconcile yourself to an occasional loss and take pleasure in those which thrive.

CHAPTER VI

Soils

PLANTS in the home should be grown in containers as small as possible consistent with maintaining them in a vigorous, healthy condition. Large pots filled with soil are heavy and a nuisance to handle; and their weight may prohibit the transportation of the plants to the bathtub for that desirable weekly spraying. Plants which are overpotted usually are unhealthy because of waterlogged soil that is difficult to avoid when there are not enough roots to use quickly the water supplied by an overzealous gardener. A plant in a pot too large for it is evidence of poor culture, and distressing to look at because of lack of balance. But small pots entail a restricted root run and a small bulk of soil, consequently the latter, for most plants, must be abundantly supplied with nutrients. The uninitiated might think that these could easily be supplied by mixing liberal quantities of concentrated fertilizer with any kind of soil. This will not do, though, because some, or all, of the fertilizing ingredients are "quickly available" and when used too freely go into solution at a strength that "burns" the roots in contact with them. Then, too, the soil must be in *the right physical condition*—sufficiently porous to allow water to pass through it freely, and well supplied with decayed organic matter which will hold some moisture and at the same time help keep the soil open so that it is well aerated.

While it must not be thought that a special soil mixture has to be made up for each species, plants do vary in their soil requirements, and the successful cultivator does his utmost to supply their needs. Some grow best in a rather heavy clay loam; others need an open sandy soil; some cannot thrive unless the mixture consists largely of decayed organic matter—which must have an acid reaction for certain types and be neutral for others. While some house plants will thrive in soil used just as it is dug from the vegetable or flower garden, many of them will not; and in some regions the soil is utterly unsuited as a potting medium without amelioration of some kind, either because it packs down too hard in the pots, or has other objectionable features.

For these reasons the grower of house plants should follow the practice of the professional grower of pot plants and keep on hand various ingredients which can be combined to make the right kind of soil for different plants and purposes. He will also need drainage material to facilitate the escape of surplus water from the pots— pieces of broken pot to put over the hole in the bottom, with smaller pieces, cinders, or clinkers, for a covering layer ½ to 1 inch deep, depending on the size of the pot.

The base for most potting mixtures is **loam,** which is a naturally occurring mixture of clay (20 per cent or less), silt (30 to 50 per cent), and sand. When sand predominates, it is known as sandy loam. When making up a potting mixture with clay loam more sand must be added to give the necessary porosity than would be needed with a sandy loam. When the loam is very sandy it is unnecessary to add sand for most plants.

Gardeners prefer to get their loam from a fertile pasture by cutting slabs 4 to 5 inches thick from the surface. These are stacked upside down in a neat pile with a layer of cow manure about 2 inches thick between each layer of sods. If the stack is made in the spring, it should be in excellent condition for use in the fall. This is the "fibrous loam," beloved of professional gardeners and occurring frequently in their soil-mixture formulas. (Recent investigations, however, cast doubt on the value of fiber in potting mixtures.) The small amount needed for home potting can conveniently be handled by placing the sods in a slatted crate of suitable size rather than in an open pile. If the cow pasture is far away and transportation is difficult, it may be necessary to fall back on loam stolen from the vegetable garden, with dehydrated cow manure as a filling for the sandwich, at one fourth the rate suggested above.

To provide the necessary organic matter flaky **leafmold** is preferred for most plants. This consists of leaves in which decay is sufficiently advanced so that the integral parts crumble easily, but in

*Small dish garden of native plants—Hemlock
seedling, Ferns, Partridge Berry, Rattlesnake
Plantain, Pipsissewa, Hepatica, et cetera*

*Miniature landscape ar-
ranged in a decorated box
—Red-cedar seedlings,
Common Juniper, Wild
Strawberry, Hawkweed
(winter rosette), Mosses,
Lichens, Fungi*

Preparing for winter bloom indoors
Geranium plant is carefully "lifted" and pruned back severely for potting.
Removed portions can be used for cuttings

which the texture is flaky rather than powdery. Leafmold can be prepared on a small scale by gathering tree leaves in the fall and packing them wet in a crate so that air has access to the pile. Maple leaves will be ready for use in about a year; Oak leaves take longer to decay. A leafmold crate can be kept in perpetual operation (until the wood rots) by raking out the leafmold from the bottom (remove the lowermost slat to make this possible) and adding fresh leaves to the top whenever they are available and there is room. Or the contents of the crate may be turned out and that which will pass through a coarse screen (½ to ¾ inches) put aside for immediate use while the remainder is returned to decay further.

Leafmold from Oak leaves or Pine needles is good for plants which require an acid soil; or peatmoss can be used. If these sources of humus-forming materials have to be used for sweet-soil plants, and the base soil also is acid, pulverized limestone should be added to the mixture. About ½ pound of pulverized limestone should be sufficient to neutralize the acidity of a bushel of peatmoss.

When none of these forms of organic matter is available one can fall back on commercial humus obtainable at seed and hardware stores—sometimes at fancy prices.

Coarse river or bank sand is used to give the desired porous texture. Sea sand often is of too fine a texture and must be washed before using to remove salt. This is not difficult to do, and the presence of salt should not deter anyone from using sea sand provided it is sufficiently coarse. All that has to be done is to put the business end of a hose in the bottom of a bucket, fill the bucket with sand, and then turn on the water and let it run for ten minutes or so, occasionally stirring the sand. This will also get rid of clay or silt if any is present. Builders' sand, obtained in New York and possibly other coast cities, is sometimes washed with sea water to remove silt. Such sand also should have a stream of fresh water passed through it before using it for plants.

Fertility can be added to the soil by using organic **manures.** These are preferable because their fertilizing constituents are slowly liberated. Dried cow manure gathered from a pasture is the ideal material; or you can use thoroughly rotted horse manure. If the processed commercial product is all that is available, use at half the rate recommended for that collected from a pasture.

Bonemeal, although it contains a small percentage of nitrogen, is used mainly to augment the supply of phosphorus in the mixture. Coarse meal releases its nutrients slowly and is desirable when plants are to be kept in the same pots over a period of years. Fine bone flour is used when quicker action is needed. Raw bone meal contains a slightly higher percentage of nitrogen (2 to 4 per cent) and less phosphoric acid (20 to 25 per cent) than steamed bonemeal (1.65 to 2.50 per cent nitrogen; 20 to 30 per cent phosphoric acid). The latter is more quickly available than the former and might be preferred when it is undesirable to add greatly to the nitrogen supply. However, the differences between the two forms are so slight that no one is justified in worrying to the extent of losing sleep over which kind to use.

To aid in making the soil right for those plants which demand a light, very porous mixture, we can use the following: mortar rubble, broken into pieces ¼ inch in diameter and smaller, for those Cacti and other plants which need lime as well as porosity in their soils; broken flowerpots or soft bricks similarly hammered into small pieces for acid-soil plants; and broken charcoal (obtainable from "feed" stores) especially for Bromeliads, Orchid Cacti, Anthuriums, Orchids, et cetera.

Here are some mixtures that can be used for various purposes and types of plants. There is nothing sacred about them to prevent anyone from making any change that seems according to common sense. The variability of the ingredients in different sections of the country precludes any hard-and-fast recommendations. It would be as well, however, not to increase greatly the amount of manure or bonemeal without first trying it out on a small scale.

For seed sowing, and potting cuttings just removed from sand bed: Equal parts of loam, leafmold, and sand passed through a ½-inch sieve and thoroughly mixed will serve for most plants. If loam is sandy, reduce the proportion of sand; if of a clayey nature, increase it so that a handful of the moist mixture when squeezed into a ball readily falls apart when pressure is released. For acid-soil plants, such as Azaleas—though house-plant growers are not likely to be raising them from seed—substitute peatmoss for leafmold and double the amount. For those which require a soil rich in humus but not especially acid—African-violet, Begonia, Gloxinia—double the amount of leafmold.

For transplanting seedlings: Same as the above, with the addition of bonemeal, ¼ cupful to a peck, plus 1½ cups of dried cow manure. For acid-soil plants omit bonemeal (because of its lime content) and increase organic matter as indicated above.

MIXTURES FOR POTTING ESTABLISHED PLANTS

When transferred from one pot to another of larger size without root disturbance:

General purpose mixture: Chrysanthemums, Fuchsias, Geraniums, Palms, Screw Pines and similar plants: Four parts loam, 2 parts sand, 1½ parts dried cow manure, 2 parts leafmold with ½ cup bonemeal to each peck of mixture. If loam is clayey, increase quantity of sand; if sandy, reduce it. Loam—taken from a sod pile which is reasonably free from stones—does not need sifting. Chop up the lumps with a spade into pieces of walnut size. If put through a screen, much of the desirable fibrous material will be held back by the sieve. The leafmold should be passed through a ½-inch sieve for small pots; a 1-inch sieve for pots 6 inches and over. This is to remove sticks and stones. The manure should be rubbed through a ¼-inch mesh sieve.

For bulbs: Daffodils, Hyacinths, Tulips: Six parts loam, 4 parts sand, 3 parts leafmold with ½ cup bonemeal to each peck. For Amaryllis, Lachenalia, Veltheimia, and the like add 1 part thoroughly rotted manure to the mixture.

For plants requiring a humusy mixture: African-violets, Begonias, Ferns, et cetera: Four parts loam, 4 parts leafmold, 2 parts sand, 2 parts dried manure; with ½ cup bonemeal and 2 cups broken charcoal (¼ inch and smaller) to each peck of mixture. The last item is not essential, but does help make the mixture light and well aerated, which is desirable.

For acid-soil plants: Azaleas, Camellias, Gardenias, et cetera: Four parts loam, 3 parts sand, 3 parts peatmoss, 1 part leafmold, 1 part thoroughly rotted manure.

For Cacti and succulents: Equal parts loam, sand, leafmold, mortar rubble (or broken bricks, or flowerpot chips) with ½ cupful of bonemeal to each peck. One successful grower of Cacti uses double the amount of leafmold.

For Christmas Cactus, Orchid Cactus: Four parts loam, 2 parts sand, 3 parts peatmoss, 1 part leafmold, 1 part thoroughly rotted manure, 1 part mortar rubble, 1 part broken charcoal.

For most Bromeliads, many Orchids, and *Anthurium scherzerianum*: Pot should be ⅓ full of drainage material. For potting, use Osmunda fiber 6 parts, ½ inch charcoal 1 part. If Osmunda is unobtainable, try equal parts peatmoss, sand, and granulated charcoal.

A sufficient supply of soil for immediate needs should be kept under cover at all times so that necessary potting is not held up by rain, preventing soil from being brought in. (One might very well find it convenient to catch up with potting on a rainy day.) In the fall enough soil should be brought indoors to last through the winter. It will be needed for seed sowing and potting in late winter when it is impossible, because of snow or frozen ground, to bring in soil from outdoors.

Country dwellers find it easy to obtain the necessary ingredients to make up various soil mixtures. Those who live in small towns or suburban areas may not have convenient access to a cow pasture but they might be able to strip sods from part of the lawn area to make a loam pile (replace the sods with soil taken from the vegetable garden), and should have no difficulty in gathering a sufficient supply of leaves to rot down into leafmold, if it is not possible to obtain leafmold ready made from nearby woods. The city slicker is rather up against it. He might be able to get soil from the neighborhood florist; or he can purchase it from a horticultural supply store at a price that will make him think he is buying Manhattan real estate, but as usually only a small quantity is required it will not make too large a dent in the pocketbook. He can also save the soil from the pots of defunct gift plants unsuited for house culture. This soil, while not ideal, is better than none and can be pepped up with manure and bonemeal to make an acceptable dish for most plants.

CHAPTER VII

Fertilizers

SOME house plants, such as Bromeliads and Cacti, thrive on what a vegetable grower would consider a very inadequate supply of nutrients; others, like the Chinese Evergreen, can get along very well indeed for long periods on just plain water and air; but most of them require a goodly ration of mineral nutrients. These are supplied initially by the soil in which the plants are potted—when water is applied and the minerals are slowly dissolved, forming what is known as the soil solution. But usually there comes a time when the available nutrients become depleted, or are present in insufficient quantity, so that something must be done to keep the plants well fed and happy. This something means either repotting in new soil or in a larger container, or the addition of fertilizers to the soil. Often the latter is preferable because of the undesirability of using excessively large pots under house conditions.

It must be recognized, however, that fertilizers are not a cure-all, and improperly used may do more harm than good. Do not get the notion that because a teaspoonful is beneficial a tablespoonful will be three times as effective. If the first amount is the optimum for a particular plant in, say, a 6-inch pot, tripling the amount is likely to result in a concentration of salts in the soil solution in sufficient amount to "burn" the roots. If any erring is done, let it be on the side of too little rather than too much.

Never give fertilizer to a plant which is suffering because of waterlogged soil; it is in no shape to make use of additional nutrients which, if supplied, will only accentuate the trouble.

Do not attempt to force a plant to grow by giving fertilizer during its resting period.

Remember that a plant potted in fertile soil will not need additional fertilizer until the pot becomes crowded with roots. This can be determined by turning the plant upside down and tapping the rim of the pot on a bench or table, holding the ball of soil with one hand so it does not fall to the floor. If the ball is covered with a network of roots, you can assume that fertilizer will not be harmful.

If most or all of the leaves of the plant are yellowish, if it is not making vigorous growth during the season it should be active, and if its poor health is not attributable to unsuitable growing conditions (too hot, too cold, insufficient light, waterlogged soil, dryness at roots, or desiccated air), then, in any of these circumstances, giving it additional fertilizer may be very helpful.

WHAT TYPE TO USE?

In order to use fertilizers intelligently it is desirable to know something of the role played by the various ingredients. There are many soil elements necessary for plant growth. They include: nitrogen, phosphorus, potash, calcium, sulphur, magnesium, iron, copper, zinc, boron, manganese, sodium, aluminum, and others. The merest trace of some of these is enough, and with the exception of the three first named, they occur in sufficient quantity in most soils. It is with nitrogen, phosphorus, and potash, therefore, that we are most concerned.

Nitrogen promotes strong growth of shoots and leaves and it is an essential constituent of the green coloring matter (chlorophyll) of plants. An excess of nitrogen, especially if associated with a deficiency of phosphorous and potash, may result in growth of leaves and shoots to an extent which prevents flower production; also it is believed that such an excess results in a flimsy development of cell walls which makes them an easy mark for invading fungous enemies. Fertilizers rich in nitrogen can be used to advantage for those plants which we grow primarily for their leaves—Palms, Ferns, et cetera; and for flowering plants whose leaves are yellowish and whose shoot growth is weak.

Phosphorus is concerned in flowering and the production of fruits and seeds; it promotes strong root development; stiffens plant stems and makes them more woody.

Potash also has a stiffening influence on the stems of plants and may help them to resist disease. In common with phosphorus it helps to prevent the characteristic rank growth likely to ensue when there is an overbalance of nitrogen. Usually there is no deficiency of potash in soils abundantly supplied with organic matter.

SOURCES OF SUPPLY

Giving an excess of one fertilizing element will not make up for a deficiency of any of the others, therefore it usually is best to use what is known as a "complete" fertilizer—one containing nitrogen, phosphorus, and potash. Animal excrement is complete in the sense that it contains these three elements, but they are not well balanced because of insufficient phosphorus. Nevertheless, a valuable liquid manure can be made by steeping a bag of cow manure in water and diluting the liquor to a pale amber color before using it about every two weeks during the period of active growth. It usually is satisfactory if bonemeal (which slowly liberates phosphorus) is mixed with the potting soil.

There are, however, obvious objections to the use of animal manures in the home. Many do not have a convenient place in which to store the brew, and some squeamish souls object to the odor in the living room. Animal manures used in a dry state have the same disadvantages, perhaps in lesser degree; but if you are willing to overlook them, dried and pulverized cattle and sheep manure can be used at the rate of a level tablespoon to a 6-inch pot, scratched into the surface and watered in. Use poultry manure at half this rate.

Cottonseed meal is a complete fertilizer of vegetable origin with only small proportions of phosphorus and potash. It is used at the rate of a teaspoonful for a plant in a 6-inch pot. It has an acid reaction and is useful for fertilizing Azaleas and similar acid-soil plants.

Commercial fertilizers are a convenient means of supplying additional nutrient to the soil of potted plants. Those in which nitrogen, phosphorus, and potash occur in the ratio of 1-2-1 are good general-purpose types. If extra phosphorus is needed, one with a ratio of 1-3-1 would be desirable. Fertilizers commonly offered for sale with these ratios will be recognized as those with an analysis of 5 per cent nitrogen, 10 per cent phosphorus, 5 per cent potash; and 4 per cent nitrogen, 12 per cent phosphorus, and 4 per cent potash, respectively. These can be used dry at the rate of a level teaspoonful to a 6-inch pot; or in liquid form made by stirring 2 tablespoonfuls in a gallon of water. Application may be made every four to six weeks when the plant is actively growing. Fertilizers more concentrated than these, such as 15-30-15, are available. If these are used, the rate of application must be correspondingly reduced. For making liquid fertilizers, completely soluble forms of dry fertilizers, obtainable from large seed stores, are preferred.

When fertilizing acid-soil plants, the nitrogen carrier should be acid in reaction (such as sulphate of ammonia rather than nitrate of soda); and for Azaleas and Rhododendrons use half the rate. Personally, I prefer to use a thin layer of a 50-50 mixture of rotted manure and acid peatmoss for plants of this nature, plus a level teaspoonful of cottonseed meal to a 6-inch pot.

Those gardeners who also run an outdoor garden probably will have fertilizers on hand suitable for use on house plants, but those whose gardening is restricted to the home may find it inconvenient to buy ordinary commercial fertilizers in sufficiently small quantities. For such, there are those put up in convenient tablet form. These vary in their nutrient content according to the brand, and usually the best plan is to follow directions on the package.

When nitrogen only is considered desirable, either nitrate of soda or sulphate of ammonia can be used at the rate of a tablespoonful to a gallon of water.

Phosphorus can be supplied through the medium of 20 per cent superphosphate at the rate of $1\frac{1}{2}$ tablespoonfuls to a gallon.

Wood ashes can be used to supply potash to plants which do not require an acid soil; they contain lime which has an alkalinizing action. The potash content is variable (2 per cent to 10 per cent), which makes it difficult to give specific rates of application, but 2 tablespoonfuls to a gallon of water should be about right. For acid-soil plants muriate of potash (about 45 per cent potash) can be used—1 teaspoonful to a gallon of water.

Not so long ago many amateurs and some professionals were all hot and bothered over Vitamin B_1. Plants are able to make their own supply of this, and in most soils it is a waste of time and money to use Vitamin B_1 tablets as fertilizers. Several enthusiasts have written to me concerning the wonderful results accruing from their use; but, when queried, they admitted that they had no untreated check plants with which to compare those which had been dosed. The hard-boiled reaction to claims of this nature is that the interest of the grower in B_1 prompted better care than normal, with the result that the plant reacted favorably. I have tried at least two forms of Vitamin B_1 on many varieties of plants, with untreated check plants of the same size and variety with which to compare them. The only differences visible were, if anything, in favor of the untreated plants.

It is impossible to lay down hard-and-fast rules as to the time and frequency of application of fertilizers. Good gardeners, by observing the plant, can tell when to start using them and, just as important, when to stop. If a plant is growing satisfactorily, leave well enough alone, and refrain from taking a chance of upsetting the apple cart by overfertilizing. Much depends on the potting soil—if it was good initially and slowly gives up its nutrients over a long period, little or no additional fertilizer may be needed.

CHAPTER VIII

Growing Plants Without Soil

IT HAS always seemed to me that growing plants without soil by using nutrient solutions is more trouble than growing them in soil by the old-fashioned method. But hydroponics ("slop culture" or "bathtub" gardening) may offer a solution (no pun intended) to those who have difficulty in securing acceptable soil, and may appeal to those who get a kick from mixing chemicals.

Growing plants in nutrient solutions is no new thing, but only within the last fifteen years has it been used extensively in commercial practice. For a while it became a fad for amateur gardeners. Some plants thrive exceedingly well when grown directly in the solution; and it will surprise many to learn that certain Cacti, which we ordinarily think of as resenting wet feet, will grow with their roots constantly immersed in liquid. Many plants grow better when their roots are in sand, gravel, or cinders watered with the solution.

Other advantages claimed for this method of culture are that it eliminates soil-borne insect pests and diseases, and that it enables one to control the kind and quantity of nutrients offered to the plants. Considerable knowledge of a plant's requirements are necessary, however, before one does much monkeying with the standard solution. Also, the solution provides a mild fertilizer which can be used at weekly intervals to water plants in soil.

Among the drawbacks when growing plants directly in the solution are: the necessity for aerating the solution twice daily by pumping air through it (develop your biceps by using a bicycle pump!); changing the solution every three weeks to obviate the danger of a concentration of salts in excessive quantity due to evaporation of liquid, and to insure that no element is lacking; and the difficulty of supporting certain plants in a sightly manner. There are some, such as Chinese Evergreen, Dieffenbachia, English Ivy, and Wandering Jew, which need no special support; but others, such as Ferns and plants of similar habit, must be held up by excelsior or something of a similar nature packed around the base of the plant and confined within a hardware cloth cage made to fit over the solu-

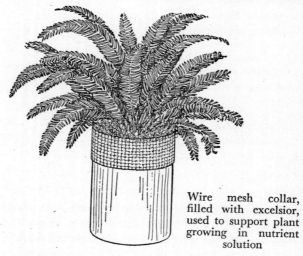

Wire mesh collar, filled with excelsior, used to support plant growing in nutrient solution

tion container. And then there is the necessity for frequently testing the solution with a soil indicator to determine whether it is too acid or too alkaline.

When growing plants in a supporting medium such as sand, gravel, or moss, which usually is the best method for the home gardener, the medium should be flushed at weekly intervals with plain water to remove any possible accumulation of excess salts.

Solutions: The easiest way to indulge in hydroponics is to buy the necessary chemicals ready mixed and needing nothing more than the addition of water according to the directions on the package. During the height of the soilless culture fad these were obtainable from seed and hardware stores under more brand names than you could shake a stick at; nowadays they are not so plentiful, but some are stocked by most horticultural supply firms.

Dr. Connors (one of the pioneers in modern soilless culture) and

Dr. Tiedjens, in their book *Chemical Gardening for the Amateur,* suggest, in addition to many other formulas, one in which the necessary materials can be obtained by rummaging around the kitchen (and bathroom). Here it is:

Saltpeter	1 teaspoonful
Epsom salts	1 teaspoonful
Baking powder (a brand which does not contain alum)	2 teaspoonfuls
Washing ammonia	1 to 4 teaspoonfuls
Water	1 gallon

A formula suggested years ago by Dr. Shive, which I have used successfully, is made with salts of the ordinary fertilizer grade, as follows:

Nitrate of soda	1 teaspoonful
Superphosphate	2 teaspoonfuls
Epsom salts	3 teaspoonfuls
Muriate of potash	1 teaspoonful
Water	5 gallons

The ingredients are dissolved separately by shaking each in a pint or so of water. Allow the sediment to settle, pour off, mix the clear liquids, and add enough water to make 5 gallons.

Certain minor elements are needed by plants in very small quantities. These are likely to be present in fertilizer grade chemicals, but to make sure, 1 teaspoonful (half the usual rate) of trace element stock solution, made up as follows, can be added to 5 gallons of culture solution:

Ferrous sulphate	½ teaspoonful
Boric acid	¼ teaspoonful
Manganese sulphate	¼ teaspoonful
Zinc sulphate	¼ teaspoonful
Water	1 pint

There are many variants of culture solutions, using different salts to supply the necessary nitrogen, phosphorus, potash, et cetera; if you want to go more fully into this, a book on soilless culture, such as the one mentioned above, is what you need.

Techniques: Plants with fairly stiff stems, of the nature of Philodendron, Dieffenbachia, and Chinese Evergreen, can be supported directly in the solution contained in glass or pottery vases, or preserving jars if your tastes are not too fancy. On the theory that roots, like those whose deeds are evil, prefer darkness, the containers should be opaque, but I notice that the roots on Ivy shoots growing in water in a clear glass container are just as abundant and apparently as healthy as those near by in a crockery marmalade jar. It should be remembered in this connection that the roots are sometimes decorative and it is interesting to watch them grow.

While some plants grow satisfactorily in a solution which is not artificially aerated, it is considered desirable to bubble air through the solution daily for all plants thus grown. For most plants, the solution should be slightly acid, showing between pH 5 and pH 6.5. To make sure it is not too acid or too alkaline, it should be tested occasionally with a soil indicator. If above pH 6.5, showing too much alkalinity, add a few drops of vinegar until the correct reaction is reached. If below pH 5, indicating that the solution is too acid, add a few drops of a solution of bicarbonate of soda. Discard the solution every three weeks and use a fresh mix. If you are a thrifty soul and do not like to see fertilizer go to waste, pour the rejected solution on lawn or garden soil.

For most house plants it will be desirable to use a more substantial medium than water to support the plants. This can be sand, gravel, fine cinders, or Sphagnum Moss. The three first named dry out rather quickly and consequently need frequent application of solution; Sphagnum dries out slowly, does not perhaps provide such good aeration, is a difficult medium in which to pot the plant without injuring or bunching the roots, and not all plants grow well in it.

The containers used should be of non-porous material with drainage holes in the bottom—glazed flowerpots are satisfactory. Soil should be carefully washed from the roots to avoid injuring them before potting the plants in the selected supporting medium. Sand is the easiest material to work in between and over the roots. Flood with water and jar the pot on the bench to settle the sand firmly around the roots.

Future watering will be done with nutrient solution. It can be poured from a watering can or teapot in the usual manner of watering; the surplus which runs through the drainage holes can be collected from the drip saucers beneath the pots and used over again.

In the "continuous-drip" method the solution is applied drop by drop by means of a mechanical contrivance. This is excellent from the standpoint of results, but it involves the use of three containers per plant instead of the usual two—one to contain solution, one to hold the plant, and one to catch the drips from the plant container. Personally, I wouldn't want too many such contraptions around.

Continuous-drip method of growing plant in gravel or sand, with nutrient solution. Solution caught in receptacle under pot is returned to upper tank to be used over again

At weekly intervals the sand should be flushed with clear water to prevent accumulation of excess salts. A convenient way to do this is to stand the plants in the bathtub (leave the drain open!) and apply a copious amount of water to the sand from the sprinkler nozzle on the bath hose.

Growing plants in nutrient solutions has definite possibilities of interest and the production of first-class plants. It does not eliminate the necessity of observing other rules of good cultivation—the provision of correct temperature, ample light, and keeping the plants free from insect and fungous pests. The editorial writer of one of the New York newspapers who, when the fad was at its height, said something to the effect that the time was coming when every housewife could grow all the vegetables she needed in nutrient solutions on a closet shelf, was wide of the mark indeed.

Plants in water: There are a number of plants capable of forming roots and thriving for long periods when their stems are kept in ordinary water from the faucet. The most familiar examples are Chinese Evergreen and English Ivy varieties (the best one seems to be the one most commonly sold by florists under this name which, however, is actually *Hedera helix hibernica,* Irish Ivy). Others that can be used are Wandering Jew in several varieties; various members of the Jack-in-the-pulpit Family such as Philodendron, Dieffenbachia, Syngonium, and Pothos.

There are various woody evergreens, the shoots of which last a long time if their bases are kept in water, and which can be used to advantage in wall vases and similar containers. Some of them will form roots when so treated and may then be potted in soil to become permanent occupants of the home. Among those amenable to this treatment are Conifers such as the Giant Arborvitae (*Thuja plicata*), Redwood burls (*Sequoia sempervirens*), both from the Pacific states. The last named should be set in a shallow bowl of water. Then there are shrubs such as Boxwood (*Buxus*), Oleander (*Nerium*), Rhododendron, and the so-called Huckleberry (*Vaccinium ovatum*).

Certain bulbs can be brought to the flowering stage in water. See pages 184 and 186.

VEGETABLES AS HOUSE PLANTS

A raid on the vegetable bin in January will yield material with decorative and interesting qualities which will grow when placed in water.

A sweet-potato vine will remain in good condition for many months and its culture is simplicity itself. Just obtain a fat, sound, unblemished tuber and insert it in a suitable container—a good-looking pickle jar, a quart-size Mason jar, or something fancier.

The Potato should lodge half in and half out of the bottle neck. If the opening is too large, your ingenuity will enable you to devise a means of wedging the tuber in the right position. Whenever there is any doubt as to which end should be upward (usually it is the fatter part), lay the tuber on a bed of moist moss, or peat, in a warm place. This will cause growth to start and enable you to determine how to place it.

I am told that many of the Sweet-potatoes sold in grocery and vegetable stores are kiln-cured and incapable of growth; so either use home-grown stock or pick out a specimen which is showing

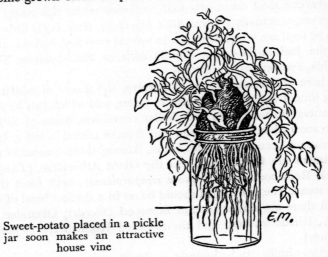

Sweet-potato placed in a pickle jar soon makes an attractive house vine

signs of life. The water in the container, in which a lump of charcoal is placed, should touch the base of the Potato. Water added to replace that used by the plant and lost by evaporation should be of room temperature or a little warmer. The shoots should be a foot or more long in six weeks or so, and after a while they may attain a length of 6 feet. Probably too many shoots will grow, and you will want to remove all but three or four of the strongest ones, which should be done while they are still small.

Top cut from Carrot and placed in moist pebbles quickly produces a nice green "fern"

Beet roots may be treated in the same way as Sweet-potatoes, but Carrot and Rutabaga should be sliced off with a horizontal cut 2 or 3 inches from the top and stood in a saucer of water. Or you may prefer to embed them in pebbles in a water-holding bowl, which makes a more stable arrangement.

CHAPTER IX

Pots and Potting

PLANTS can be, and are, grown in any kind of container that will hold a sufficient quantity of soil, but some are preferred over others for certain purposes. Those most generally used are the standard clay pots, which are pinkish in color and somewhat porous. These are made by the million and are easily obtainable in normal times, and are inexpensive. While not decorative they are inoffensive and do not distract attention from the plants they contain. The standard pot is as broad as it is long; the height of Cyclamen pots is about four fifths their diameter; Azalea pots are three fourths; bulb and seed pans are about half as tall as they are broad; fillers for Fern dishes may be a little lower in proportion; while "long Toms," used for potting young Roses are, as the name implies, deeper than their width. Standard pots are obtainable in sizes ranging from 1½ to 24 inches, but these extremes are seldom seen. Sometimes earthenware pots are made with holes around the sides or extra holes in the bottom in addition to the usual drainage hole. These are for plants such as some Orchids and Bromeliads which require an exceptionally well-aerated rooting medium.

There has been some controversy recently concerning the merits of porous pots *vs.* glazed and glass pots. The advocates of porous pots point out that the soil is likely to be better aerated; there is less danger of the soil becoming waterlogged; and, under house conditions, the loss of moisture from the sides of the pots is an advantage in helping to humidify the air. Their opponents maintain that the need for frequent watering is diminished by the use of impervious pots and that plants grow better in them. In those regions where the

climate is hot and dry—California and South Africa, for example—
tin cans with holes punched in them for drainage—which of course
are impervious but aesthetically leave much to be desired—seem to
be preferred as plant containers. Plants can be grown well in both
types, but when the air is dry perhaps glazed pots are better.

If your tastes run that way you can use fancy decorative pots,
but don't get the impression that because they are expensive they
are superior to the ordinary clay pot as a growing medium. In any
case, make sure they have a hole in the bottom to allow surplus
water to escape. Plants can be grown in watertight containers but
their use involves extra care to avoid waterlogging the soil.

In the tropics, sections of Bamboo 2 or 3 inches in diameter, each
containing a node, are commonly used as flowerpots. Some years
ago in Trinidad I was interested to see a coolie industriously chopping off the growth bud from the base of each section. Inquiry
elicited the fact that this was done to prevent the pot from growing!

Hollowed-out logs, wicker baskets, and, for Orchids, wooden
"baskets," are sometimes used to hold soil; but except for the square
or round wooden plant tubs which are preferable for plants of large
size, the good old earthenware pot is the real standby.

"Strawberry pots" made of earthenware and equipped with
"pockets" on the sides to hold soil which is in contact with that in

Small collection of
Cacti and succulents
in old-fashioned
strawberry jar

the body of the pot are much used, suitably planted, for patio deco-ration in California. They also have possibilities for home decoration provided a size is chosen that is in proportion with the space avail-able for it. There is at least one firm which sells these containers together with a selection of suitable plants to fill them. The usual practice, and it is a good one, is to use at least a few plants of trail-ing or semi-trailing habit in the side pockets.

Containers for suspended plants: In greenhouses, hanging bas-kets made of wire and lined with sheet Moss, obtained from a florist or from logs in the woods, are commonly used. They are not satis-factory for home use because of the difficulty of keeping the soil moist, which involves much sloshing of water around, and a flood on the floor. If your decorative scheme calls for hanging plants, use pottery containers furnished with a saucer to catch any water that may run through the drainage hole; or use a hanging jardiniere in which an ordinary flowerpot is placed—but watch out that water does not collect in the bottom of it.

Pots not in use should be stacked neatly according to size, indoors or out. If they are dirty, they should be washed with water and a scrubbing brush and allowed to dry before using.

HOW TO POT AND REPOT

I still remember the thrill that came to me when I was first al-lowed, officially, to repot a plant. This occurred only after spending about two years in the humble but important job as crock boy, whose responsibility was "crocking" the pots—putting in drainage material —for the journeyman gardeners who did the actual job of potting. Since that time (more than forty years ago, bigosh!) I have come to realize that potting plants is not a mysterious process which can safely be revealed only to those who have undergone an extensive apprenticeship.

Actually, it is far more difficult to learn *when* to pot than *how* to do it. Generally speaking, the best time to transfer ("shift" is the technical term) those plants which are permanently grown in pots is at the close of the resting season, usually in late winter. Young plants which are actively growing (as in the case of those raised from seeds or cuttings, or small plants dug from the flower border

Begonia semperflorens, the most constant flowering of winter house plants.
As the root ball is large, soil around it in pot is firmed with a tamping stick

After Begonia is potted, it is trimmed back to induce new growth and make a more compact plant

Trimmings provide cuttings, which are inserted in pan of moist sand to root

in the fall) should be transferred to larger pots at any season whenever the roots become so crowded that growth is likely to be checked.

Therefore, keep a close watch on your plants at all times, especially in winter when the lengthening of the days brings about a recrudescence of activity. When new leaves are beginning to form near the soil level, as in the case of Ferns and Aspidistra; or new shoots start at the tips of the branches of the shrubby plants; or new leaves push forth with greater vigor on the Dracaena—in other words,

How to remove plant from pot. With left hand holding plant securely, rim of pot is jarred sharply against edge of bench or table

whenever there are signs of renewed activity after a period of quiescence—examine the plants to determine whether or not repotting is necessary. This is done by turning the plant upside down and, putting the fingers of one hand on the surface soil, tapping the rim of the pot on bench or table to remove the ball of roots—not by holding the pot with one hand and yanking at the plant with the other! If the roots are matted together and obviously crowded, a shift into a larger pot is probably needed.

Sometimes, however, it is desirable to repot into a smaller container than a larger one. This situation occurs when roots are unhealthy and do not fully occupy the soil, a condition brought about by previous overpotting coupled with too much water, and possibly the presence of earthworms which clogged the drainage. Whether or not to spend time on such a plant in an attempt to save it depends upon its condition, its value (sentimental or otherwise), and whether you get pleasure from nursing sick plants and restoring them to health. If the plant's efforts at making new growth are feeble, it is better to put it in the garbage pail and forget about it; but if it seems to be making a real attempt at growing, and there is a possibility that it may regain its vigor, this is what should be done:

Carefully shake all soil away from the roots, taking pains to avoid injuring any which show signs of vigor. With a sharp knife remove dead and injured roots, making the cut through healthy tissue back of the injured portion. Select a pot large enough to contain the roots without overcrowding and prepare it by putting at least an inch of flowerpot chips in the bottom to insure free drainage. Put the roots in the pot, hold the plant at the right level with one hand and sift the soil in between the roots with the other. Jiggle the roots as you are putting in the soil to avoid bunching them, using a lean mixture of equal parts sand, soil, and leafmold sifted through a ¼-inch sieve. When the pot is filled to the rim with soil, jar it on the bench and then press the soil down with the fingers. This will leave just about enough room for watering, which should be sufficient to soak the soil thoroughly; then do not water again until the soil is nearly dry. Ample air is necessary for free root action, so subsequent watering should be aimed at keeping the soil no more than moist until plenty of new roots are formed, at which time normal watering may be resumed.

Plants need repotting when the pot is crowded with roots and the available plant-food nutrients in the soil are exhausted, but in the case of house plants, where small pots are desired because of the ease of handling them, it is worth while to consider, first, whether the plant cannot be kept in health by an operation known to the gardener as "top-dressing." This merely requires the loosening and removal of soil on the surface and replacing it with a 50-50 mixture of loam and rotted manure, to which bonemeal has been added at the rate of 1 tablespoon to a 6-inch pot of soil. Before the top-dressing is added, the plant can be removed from its pot and if the drainage has become clogged the trouble remedied before returning the plant to the pot. Subsequent supplementary feedings with liquid nutrients (fertilizers dissolved in water) usually are desirable for potbound plants. If, however, the pot is so full of roots that no soil can be removed from the surface, then one can be reasonably sure that a shift into a larger pot is in order.

A modification of the top-dressing procedure is to remove a good deal of the old soil and to replace the plant in a pot of the same size. Only the experienced plantsman can surely tell whether this should or should not be done: knowing which plants can endure the inevitable root injury and respond to the treatment comes only from extensive handling of plants over several years. The plant to be operated upon is turned out of its pot, the drainage material is removed, and, with gentle pinching, kneading, and rubbing motions,

Flowerpot, with crock over drainage hole, layer of drainage material, and coarse material (such as Sphagnum Moss, coarse leafmold, or soil siftings) to prevent soil from washing down into drainage material

the soil ball is reduced until it is small enough to go back into the pot with enough room between it and the pot to permit new soil to be packed around it with the potting stick.

The first step in repotting proper is to provide clean pots of suitable size. If new pots are used, it is best to soak them for ten minutes in water and then allow them to dry before using. The pot into which the plant is to be shifted should not be much larger than the old one. Usually ½ to 1½ inches of clearance between the ball of earth and the side of the new pot is sufficient. The use of too large a pot results in the soil's remaining too wet and less thorough aeration. Adequate drainage is secured by covering the hole on the bottom of the pot with a piece of broken flowerpot with the concave side downward; this in turn is covered with a layer ½ to 1 inch thick of flowerpot chips, small clinkers, or something similar. On top of this organic materials such as Moss, flaky leafmold, or coarser parts of the compost are placed to a depth of ¼ inch. This is to prevent fine soil from sifting through and clogging drainage. Professional gardeners, especially commercial ones, often make only sketchy provision for drainage, but good drainage is an insurance against waterlogging that the novice cannot afford to neglect.

The next step is to take the plant from its pot, rub off the loose surface soil, and remove the old drainage material if the latter is not too firmly embedded in the crowded roots. Place the plant in the new pot, first putting in a little soil, tamped down on the drainage, if it is necessary to bring the old ball of earth to the correct height. This should be about 1 inch below the rim, more or less, depending on the size of the pot, to provide for convenient watering.

Having set the plant at the correct level, soil is filled in around the roots and settled somewhat by jarring the pot on the bench. It is desirable that the new earth should be packed to the same density as that in the old ball. This is done by means of a "potting stick"—a 12-inch label, a portion of a lath, or something similar. When the soil is uniformly packed with the potting stick, finish off by pressing down the surface soil and leveling it with the tips of the fingers; after which give the pot a slight jar on the bench to smooth the surface.

When potting Cacti and other plants of a spiny nature handle them with ice-cube tongs, being careful to avoid bruising; or make cornucopias of stiff paper and slip them over the thumb and finger, holding them in place with a dab of quick-setting mucilage.

After potting is completed, thoroughly soak the soil with water applied by means of a watering can with a fine rose. Do not water again until the soil shows signs of becoming dry. Great care should be taken to avoid overwatering until new roots grow.

Repotting plants which have to be divided seems more nearly akin to plant propagation under which subject it is discussed.

Loose-root potting: When potting seedlings removed from a flat or seed pan, the technique is somewhat different. Usually these go into comparatively small pots and a single piece of broken pot over the hole on the bottom provides sufficient drainage. The pot is filled to the rim with soil. Then, with a dibber or with a finger, make a hole large enough to accommodate the roots; set the roots in it; jar the pot and press down the soil with the fingers. When repotting rooted cuttings (which are likely to have a larger root system which

A small portable potting bench is a great convenience in the care of house plants

Above, potting off a seedling; *Below,* potting a rooted cutting

SIX STEPS IN REPOTTING

(1) With fingers of left hand held about base of plant, pot is tapped against edge of bench to remove root ball

(2) The soil is gently loosened and some earth removed in order to reduce the size of the old root ball

(3) Old crocking material (broken pieces of flowerpots) is removed from the root ball, and the roots loosened up

(4) Root ball is placed in new pot, which has been "crocked" and had drainage material and soil placed in bottom

(5) More soil is poured in between the root ball and sides of pot and packed firmly into place with a thin tamper

(6) Cross-section of pot, showing crocking, drainage material, old root-ball, and fresh, tamped soil in place

A real garden indoors, with watertight tray to hold moist gravel, on which potted plants stand

cannot easily be "dibbled" in), the technique is similar to that of repotting into smaller pots previously described. A little soil is placed over the drainage, then the plant is set in place. Fine soil is sifted between and over the roots with a throwing motion of the hand, and, when the pot is filled to the rim, the soil is pressed down with the fingers in such a way that it is made firm *about the roots*—not just on the surface.

When the soil surface becomes packed and hard as a result of overhead watering or covered with a growth of Mosses or Algae, it should be loosened with a pointed stick or dinner fork.

There is a widespread notion among amateur gardeners that repotting into a larger pot is a panacea for all the ills that befall potted plants. This is not so, and if a plant fails to thrive because of overwatering, poor drainage, or unsuitable soil, repotting it into a larger pot only accentuates the trouble.

CHAPTER X

Watering

THE QUESTION, "How often should I water my house plants?" is one most frequently asked and most difficult to answer because so many different factors are involved. Among these are:

1. The nature of the plant. For example, Cacti, succulents, and other desert plants need less water than Palms, Ferns, Hydrangeas, Paris Daisies, et cetera.
2. When growth is active, more water is needed than when the plant is at rest.
3. If the pot is filled with roots, all absorbing moisture, the soil dries out more quickly than when roots are few compared with the bulk of soil, as, for instance, in the case of newly potted plants.
4. Some soils are able to hold more moisture than others and in consequence are slower in drying. A plant in sandy soil, therefore, other things being equal, will need watering with greater frequency than one in heavy loam with plenty of humus mixed with it.
5. Ordinary flowerpots are porous, and the soil loses its moisture through their sides as well as from the surface; therefore it dries out more rapidly in them than it does in glazed pots or tin cans which are impervious to moisture.
6. Humidity of the air, which is influenced by conditions outdoors as well as those within the house, affects the need for water; less is called for when the air is moist.
7. Sunshine and shade. Plants transpire more moisture when exposed to sunshine; therefore more is needed at their roots.

8. Temperature. Plants growing in a cool room need less water than those grown in a warm room because the moisture-holding capacity of cool air is less than that of heated air, and the loss of moisture by evaporation from the soil and by transpiration from the leaves is consequently reduced.

9. Low temperatures outdoors in winter often are accompanied by low humidity. The use of artificial heat to raise the temperature indoors reduces the relative amount of moisture of the indoor air still more and increases the need for copious watering.

With all these points in mind it can readily be seen that plants cannot be watered properly in measured amounts by clock or calendar but only by applying water when they need it. Some may require watering two or three times a day under certain weather conditions; others two or three times a week; while some can be left for a month or even longer without watering. The important thing is to give the plants daily attention and water those which call for it.

WHEN DO PLANTS NEED WATERING?

The good professional gardener uses the senses of sight, touch, and hearing to determine whether his plants need watering. If he sees that the plant is wilting, he is reasonably sure that moisture is lacking; a glance at the soil surface may confirm the diagnosis—it will be lighter in color when dry. It is not wise to let the plants get to the wilting point before watering them, so before this happens the soil is examined by looking at it and by touching it. If it looks moist and feels moist probably no watering is required, but sometimes if the soil did not get a good soaking at its previous watering it may be moist on top and bone-dry below. This is where the sense of hearing comes into play. Tap the pot; if the sound is dull, no water is needed. But if the pot gives off a ringing note, the soil below is likely to be dry. This can be confirmed or disproved by turning the plant out of its pot and examining the soil with the eyes. Don't get the notion it is necessary to evict every plant every day! A look at the root ball once or twice during the season is likely to be sufficient to give you the hang of things, so that you have a good idea of the moisture conditions of your soil, with your plants, under your system of watering.

Tapping the pots can be done with the knuckles or with a small wooden mallet. When I was a journeyman gardener, we thought it savored of sissiness to use anything but the knuckles, but anyone in fear of developing calluses on them can easily make a mallet by cutting 2 inches off the end of a broom handle and boring a ¼-inch hole through it to receive a small plant stake about 18 inches long to serve as a handle.

Experienced gardeners can tell from the weight of a lifted pot whether or not water is needed—it is heavy when wet, light when dry.

All this sounds like an awful lot of bother but it really is not so bad. After you have been watering the plants for a few days you quickly learn which are the habitually thirsty ones and water them accordingly. You will also learn to take into account weather conditions outdoors, knowing that less watering is needed on dull, humid days than on bright, sunshiny ones. Temperature will also be considered and less water given when it is low and little or no artificial heat is being used.

WHEN AND HOW TO WATER

In general, watering should be done in the morning when the temperature is rising, because transpiration is more rapid during the hours of daylight and the need for water is greater in consequence; furthermore, it is considered undesirable for plants or soil to be too wet when the temperature is falling. This, however, should not deter anyone from watering a plant at any hour if it is obviously suffering from a lack of water.

While millions of plants are successfully grown in greenhouses using water which may be many degrees lower than the air temperature, just as it comes from the hose, it would seem to be desirable for the water to be of room temperature or a few degrees higher to avoid chilling the roots. Although there seems to be no clear-cut evidence that watering with cold water is harmful to plants in general we do know that ring-spot of African-violets is caused by water of lower temperature than the air coming in contact with

The "Calla" Begonia, curious and attractive, but in many sections difficult to grow; an old New England favorite

Kalanchoe uniflora, *little known, but a good trailing plant for a sunny window; attractive and easily grown*

African-violets, among the most popular of all house plants, are noted for their finicky dispositions. Rich soil, extra thorough drainage, fertilizing, no water on the leaves, and shade from direct sun tend to keep them happy. Blue Boy (above) *and Pink Beauty*

the leaves. Some growers of house plants attribute their success to the practice of using the tea left over from breakfast for watering purposes. One can congratulate them on their success, express commiseration for their inability to drink coffee or their lack of liking for it, and wonder whether the tempered liquid or the tannic acid contained in it is responsible for the good growth of the plants! If the water from the faucet is "hard," it is desirable to use rain water for acid-soil plants.

Many people ask whether plants should be watered from the surface or from below. The answer is that the good grower is likely at times, under certain circumstances, to use both methods. Surface watering is easier and in general satisfactory provided there is sufficient room between the surface of the soil and the rim of the pot to hold enough water to moisten the soil throughout. Unfortunately there is a tendency among amateurs to fill the pot too full of soil when repotting so that the only way to do an adequate job of watering is to apply water to the surface several times until it runs through the drainage hole in the bottom; or submerge the pot for half its depth in a vessel of water and leave it there until moisture shows on the surface. Even when there seems to be sufficient room to water satisfactorily from above, it is a good plan, in the case of potbound plants, to subirrigate them, say once a week, to insure thorough soaking of the ball.

Waterlogging: Most plants cannot thrive in a waterlogged soil which, because the pore spaces are constantly filled with water instead of air, deprives the roots of the oxygen they need to function.

Adequate drainage material in the bottom of the pot and the prompt eviction of earthworms which may clog the drainage are among the means of avoiding a waterlogged soil; careful watering is another. Standing flowerpots in watertight jardinieres is a source of danger unless great care is taken to make sure that water does not collect in the container and partially submerge the flowerpot. It is very difficult to maintain the correct moisture conditions in flowerpots without drainage holes. This type is usually of glass or glazed pottery, which makes matters worse because there is no loss of moisture except from the surface of the soil. Consequently a single overwatering may be sufficient to cause ill-health or death of the plants because there is no way whereby the surplus water can be removed quickly. Of course the pot could be stood upside down for an hour or two, but this is not always convenient; and often the grower does not realize in time that the soil is waterlogged.

Wick-watering: This is a method whereby water is conducted by capillarity from a reservoir through a wick, preferably of glass fabric, to the soil. Wicks of various sizes for use with different-size pots are obtainable from firms dealing in garden supplies and possibly elsewhere. The wick is cut long enough to permit the end to be teased out so that it will approximately cover the bottom of

"Wick-watering" keeps soil evenly moist for a long period from one application. Water is drawn up through wick, pushed through drainage hole, and unraveled to cover bottom of pot

the inside of the pot and reach the water in the container below. It is easier to install the wicks when repotting is done (no drainage material is necessary or desirable), but they can be supplied to plants already potted by turning them out of their pots, removing the drainage material, replacing it with soil, inserting the wick through the drainage hole, spreading it out, and replacing the plant.

One method of supporting the plant over the water reservoir on a metal plate resting on a flanged saucer is shown in the drawing. Other devices will occur to everyone. I have used a ¼-pound butter dish which supports, though on a rather insecure base, an African-violet in a 4½-inch pot. By raiding the kitchen I was able to obtain an enameled baking pan and a metal contraption for the bottom of a roasting pan which is perforated with ½-inch holes through which the wicks are passed. By resting this on the baking pan four or five 3- to 4-inch pots can be accommodated. The corner cut away from the metal doodingus to allow gravy to be scooped up for basting enables me to see when the reservoir needs replenishing.

When wick-watering first came into the limelight, I thought that perhaps it might be the foolproof method we were looking for, but now it does not seem that way—at least not to me. When dealing with a variety of plants of different sizes it is difficult to fit them with wicks of the right capacity to deliver just the amount of water needed. I found that some of mine were getting too much water, especially during dull weather. Of course this can be adjusted by omitting to fill the reservoir when each plant has a separate source of supply, but when a variety of plants is supported over one reservoir this cannot be done. Occasionally the wick does not deliver enough water, and the supply has to be supplemented by ordinary surface watering, so even with a wick device you have to use your head.

The method is well adapted for use with plants such as Gloxinia and African-violet whose leaves are better kept dry; and undoubtedly some plants, especially those which need to be kept constantly moist, thrive better when watered by capillarity. I have a wick-watered Picka-back Plant, growing in a 3-inch pot, which has attained a diameter of 15 inches. I doubt if it would have reached this size with ordinary watering. The wick method also affords a means of applying nutrient solutions to the sand or other media in which the roots are growing.

Even with this method of watering the plants need fairly frequent attention to replenish the water in the reservoirs, unless they are large and cumbersome. I find that the African-violet in a 4½-inch pot normally uses up a butter dish (¾ cup—6 ounces) full of water every two days.

The so-called "self-watering" window box works on much the same principle and is satisfactory if care is taken to avoid getting the soil too wet. The water-holding part beneath the false bottom should be allowed to dry up from time to time.

The practice of occasionally standing house plants outdoors when it is raining is a good one *provided* the temperature is not much lower than it is in the house.

To do a real job, watering must be done thoughtfully, taking into consideration the weather, the kind of plant, and whether or not it is undergoing its resting period. (See page 87.) It might seem that with all this meticulous attention the care of plants would tie one down as much as keeping a cow. However, it is not quite so bad as all that. They can be left without attention over week ends if all are well watered before departing at noon on Friday and the really thirsty ones are "bedded down" in the pebble-laden water-tight trays, plunged in peatmoss in a window box, provided with fairly large drip saucers filled with water, or watered by the wick method.

CHAPTER XI

Environment: Light, Air, and the Like

MOST amateurs fail to realize that their rooms are too hot, not too cold, for the great majority of plants suited to house culture. This is probably not so much a matter of temperature, as such, as it is of humidity, which is lowered whenever the air temperature is raised by artificial heat, unless the furnace is equipped with an extraordinarily efficient humidifying device. Even tropical plants, which we think of as delighting in heat, get along better in a bedroom (if the thermometer falls no lower than 50°), where the relative humidity is higher because of the lowered temperature, than they do in a living room consistently maintained at 70°, or higher, with consequent aridity. Thus it seems they accept the lowered temperature as the lesser of two evils. Therefore, if you want to succeed with house plants, keep the temperature as low as possible, consistent with your own comfort. Try to avoid letting the thermometer go above 72°, and allow the temperature to drop 10° or 15° at night.

Of course care must be taken not to overdo things. In those sections where winter readings of zero and below are commonplace, the temperature of the air *near the windows* where the plants are kept may fall dangerously low at night. To avoid damage, supplementary heating devices should be used as suggested on page 83; or newspapers may be slipped in between the plants and the window glass; or the plants may be temporarily transferred to a warmer part of the room.

There are a few plants which are likely to suffer or not grow so well if the temperature falls below 60°. Poinsettias may drop their leaves, African-violets stop blooming, and the leaves of the florists' Gardenia become yellowish if kept too cool.

When growing plants that need really cool conditions during the winter (40° to 50°), keep them in a non-heated room or sun porch, bringing them into the living room only occasionally or when they are in bloom. Doing this will take care of their temperature and humidity requirements most of the time; and the plants should not be greatly harmed by deviations from this procedure during the short periods they are on display.

HOW TO MAKE THE AIR HUMID

Plants transpire an enormous amount of moisture, and the sides of the pots (if they are of the porous kind) and the surface of the soil give up their quota of water vapor. So the more plants you grow the more humid the air becomes and the easier it is to grow more plants.

If you can do so without injuring curtains, drapes, and furniture, spray the leaves (except the fuzzy ones) with water at least once a day. Provide watertight trays in which to stand the plants. I use

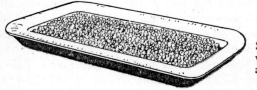

Shallow pan, filled with gravel, used as a base on which to set flowerpots

shallow rectangular enameled trays which are a component of broiler equipment. If you wish a more fancy arrangement you can have metal trays constructed to fit the window space. Place water in them and then fill with pebbles to support the pots so that the plants do not stand directly in the water. Or use plant saucers with pebbles and water in the same way.

If your house is heated by steam or hot water, place evaporating pans on the radiators and *keep them filled with water* whenever the heating plant is operating. If the house is heated by a hot-air furnace, be sure that the humidifying device with which it is equipped is in working order. I have a quart-size insecticide sprayer which delivers a mistlike spray. This I keep filled with water and spray the plants with it on sunny dry days. It provokes acid comments from my good wife anent the appearance of the window curtains, but it does benefit the plants.

Growing plants in closed glass cases offers a means whereby those plants which demand high humidity can be successfully managed. (See section on Terrariums.) Using a glass screen to enclose, or partially enclose, a bay window is an extension and modification of this method. If this is done, care must be taken during cold snaps to avoid letting the temperature fall too low. Keep a thermometer in the enclosed space and if the mercury approaches the critical point, start up a small electric stove, with a pan of water on it; or even keep a few light bulbs operating to raise the temperature.

VENTILATION

"Fresh" air is not essential for plants in the same way that it is for human beings. I have before me a plant of Wandering Jew growing happily in a quart Mason jar in which it was "canned" six months ago. Since its incarceration it has grown to more than ten times its original size and looks much healthier—a good indication that some plants, at any rate, can get along without a "change of air." Even so, it is desirable to admit outside air to the rooms in which plants are growing as freely as possible, whenever the weather permits it.

During the months when artificial heat is used the air indoors is usually drier than that outside, so free ventilation may help to maintain the humidity that is desirable. It is also a measure of insurance against harmful concentrations of coal gas or artificial gas within the home and likely to improve the health of the human occupants as well as that of the plants. Avoid, however, admitting air in such a way that cold blasts blow directly on the plants. Sometimes this can be done by opening windows from the top, or a window well away from the plants, or even one in another room if the communicating door is opened.

Artificial gas and coal gas have injurious effects on most plants. African-violets refuse to bloom, Jerusalem-cherries drop their fruit and leaves, and some kinds just look unwell. I have a Wax Begonia, a chance seedling dug up and potted in early fall, which grew beautifully until the heat was turned on. Then the leaves gradually began to fall until now, after a cold spell necessitating considerable heat (gas-furnace), it looks like a half-plucked chicken. Of course it may be dry air that did it, but I don't think so. The "humidometer" in the living room seldom registers below 40° humidity (is the gadget lying?), and the room in which the Begonia is dying must be even more humid because it is kept at a lower temperature, has lots of plants in it standing on wet pebbles in watertight trays which usually (yes, I slip up occasionally) have water in them, and the foliage is sprayed daily.

There is no "possible, probable, shadow of doubt" concerning the reason for the demise of a fine pot of Helxine which was kept on the dining table. I came down one morning and found all the leaves blackened. Scouting around for the cause, I discovered that the pilot light on the gas stove in the kitchen had been blown out (not deliberately by a member of the family, I hasten to add, but by the draft caused by a slamming door, or something), and though no odor of gas was perceptible in the dining room, there was enough present to account for the passing away of Helxine. So gas has to be reckoned with.

Commercial growers whose greenhouses are located near gas mains sometimes keep a few Tomato plants among their crops so that by observing them the presence of gas may be detected and steps taken before it occurs in sufficient quantity to be injurious to the crop. When gas is suspected of being the cause of ill-health of plants in the home, it might be well to bring in a healthy potted Tomato plant. If gas is present, the leaves will turn downward and discolor long before the gas is perceptible to the human nose.

Another method of determining the presence of gas is to bring into the room a few fresh-cut Carnation flowers. Gas will cause them "to go to sleep" within a few hours—that is, the petals will curl inward so that the flowers look only half alive.

Experiences of those who grow plants in homes where artificial gas is used are somewhat contradictory—some have fair success, others fail completely. Natural gas, apparently, is much less injurious because it does not contain the substances harmful to vegetation.

Doubtless there are other factors besides gas to account for these differences, such as: temperature, humidity, light, ventilation, and cultural skill. But most important, probably, are variations in the efficiency and use of the equipment in different homes. If gas is turned on and allowed to escape into the air before lighting it, if leaks are not promptly attended to, and if there are no flues to carry off incompletely consumed gas, one can expect to run into trouble. Generous ventilation of the rooms, by reducing the concentration of gas, is helpful, but a better way of solving the problem is to grow those plants which are fairly tolerant.

I don't want to stick my neck out too far, but, on the basis of my own observations, the following are among the plants that can endure a small amount of gas in the air: Bromeliads in general; Cacti and succulents; *Begonia heracleifolia, B. feasti* (some slight leaf injury—possibly from gas); *Ardisia crenulata; Tradescantia fluminensis; Zebrina pendula; Philodendron,* several species; *Scindapsus aureus;* Patience Plant; *Podocarpus neriifolia;* Flowering Tobacco (one observer reports that this died when moved to a gas-heated house); Picka-back Plant; *Lantana camara; Selaginella browni; Pandanus; Sansevieria; Maranta arundinacea;* Wax-plant; English Ivy (particularly *Hedera helix hibernica*—some of the small-leaved types are not so certain); Holly Fern; *Anthurium scherzerianum; Dracaena sanderiana, D. godseffiana; Campanula isophylla; Nephthytis afzeli;* and Rubber Plant.

Reports from others indicate that gas has no terrors for Amaryllis, Cattleya, Clivia, Gardenia, Larkspur, Marica, and Poinsettia.

Start out with a selection from these and experiment tentatively with others from the list of toughies on pages 300-1.

By the way, ripening apples give off ethylene gas which may cause yellowing or bleaching of foliage, so they should not be kept in quantity in rooms containing plants.

LIGHT

Many of the plants we grow in our homes are native to tropical forests where they became habituated to a dim light. Some of the Bromeliads, Sansevieria, Philodendron, many Ferns, Palms, and foliage plants in general can survive for long periods and sometimes even thrive in poorly lighted rooms; but most house plants need the best lighted positions available, because, as every photographer knows who takes pictures indoors, the intensity of the light there is much less than it is in the open, or even under trees.

Plants react to insufficient light by producing pale, anaemic leaves on long stalks reaching out toward sunshine, and stems which are lankier than normal. When this condition is noticed, every endeavor should be made to provide better illumination.

South, east, and west windows should be chosen for those which demand the most light—Cacti and succulents in general, and the majority of flowering plants—while "foliage" plants such as Ferns, Philodendrons, Ivy, and Peperomia can be relegated to the north windows. City dwellers especially should be careful to keep their plants as near as possible to the source of light, because so much is shut off by the pall of smoky haze which covers large cities a considerable part of the time.

Those who are really serious in their desire to grow house plants will avoid the use of heavy window drapes, using only thin curtains which let most of the light through, and disposing the extreme sun lovers between the curtains and the glass. But be careful not to overdo it. Plants whose skins have been "tenderized" by the dull days of winter may be scorched by full exposure to the sun when the days begin to lengthen. Yellowing of the entire plant, or a scalded appearance of the leaves (similar to that seen on Tomato fruits exposed by excessive pruning of the leaves) in the spring, may mean that a little shading is necessary.

Overcoming the lack of sunshine in homes by artificial light has been advocated. It is successful with some plants—African-violet, Begonia, Geranium, and others, while some—Ivy, Mother-of-thousands, Screw-pine, et cetera—do not respond.

The lists of plants for various aspects should be consulted as a guide to the selection of plants and their placement in the home.

CHAPTER XII

Rest Periods for House Plants

THERE are practically no perennial plants which go through life without a resting period, and those who grow plants in their homes must take this into consideration if they want them to remain healthy and bloom freely.

Plants are said to be "resting" when active growth ceases. In some species the resting period is not very obvious, but in others it is so conspicuous that (accompanied as it is by the complete loss of leaves; or, in some cases, by the death of the aboveground portions) it is visible even to the least observant. When either of these conditions occurs, the plant is said to be "dormant," but this often is a misnomer, for there may be significant changes going on in the cells of the seemingly inactive plant. Also, it should be remembered that even though there are no signs of life *above* ground, the roots and underground structures may be growing vigorously, as in the case of Tulips and other bulbous and tuberous plants, in the fall.

It is easy to imagine that the resting habit of plants in their natural environment was brought about, in part at least, by unfavorable growing conditions at certain seasons. It is helpful to the plantsman to know the native country of the plants he grows, and something of its climate, because this knowledge often provides a clue to the kind of treatment desirable under cultivation.

Unfavorable conditions for growth may be drought or low temperature. In the tropics and desert regions the resting period is usually associated with the dry season; in temperate climates, with the onset of winter; and some plants (such as the hardy spring-flowering bulbs) rest, or even become dormant, early in the summer, start into growth again in late summer in so far as the underground parts are concerned, and become more or less "dormant" again when the soil above or about their roots is frozen. A knowledge of the habits of these hardy bulbs is important, for they cannot successfully be forced into bloom in the home except when they are kept cool and moist during the period of root formation. Other bulbous and tuberous plants—such as *Oxalis tetraphylla,* Achimenes, Gloxinia, and Tuberous Begonias—have the habit of actively growing and flowering during the summer, presumably because conditions in their native habitats are unfavorable for growth during the period corresponding to our winter.

But while it seems reasonable to suppose that unfavorable growing conditions are largely responsible for the acquisition of the habit of resting periodically, and certainly the cold of winter by inhibiting growth brings about an enforced rest with many species, this is not the entire story. Even though conditions are apparently just right, there comes a time when active growth ceases and the plant, as it were, marks time. Thus we find with plant life generally a sort of rhythm, in which a cycle of growth is followed by a period of rest, the duration of which may be only a few weeks, but which may last for six months or longer.

The scientific theory in explanation of this—in case you are interested—is that it is caused by "the inhibition of enzyme activity due to an overaccumulation of the products of their work." In other words, an excess supply of carbohydrates in the plant tissues checks the work of the enzymes which make continuing growth possible.

Thus plants insist on their rest period even though conditions are suitable for continued growth. When I was a student gardener at Kew Gardens and knew even less than I do now, this was vividly illustrated by an occurrence which had me worried for several weeks. I had charge of a section of the large Palm house which, because of its size, accommodated a variety of tropical trees other than Palms. One of these was completely leafless—enjoying its rest period—at the time I took over. It soon came out in full leaf, but after a very few months shed them, leaving me aghast in the expectation of being fired for horticultural malpractice. But in a few weeks it again put on an entirely new suit and Montague Free once more was able to go about his chores without a sense of impending doom. The probable explanation is that the tree came from a part of the tropics which has *two* dry seasons, and so ingrained was the resting habit that when the proper time arrived it just quit, regardless of the fact that it was adequately supplied with water at the roots, and that it was high summer.

Now, it may be argued, if plants take their rest regardless of cultural practices, it is unnecessary to bother about making any changes in routine which burden the mind with something else to remember and do. But it so happens that unless the change in environment (or its equivalent), associated in nature with the rest period, is provided, then the plant may fail to grow properly when the time comes to resume activity; or it may refuse to produce flowers.

Blueberry and Trailing Arbutus are not house plants, but they are so familiar that a brief account of Dr. Coville's experiments with them may helpfully serve to illustrate the need for certain environmental changes. Blueberry plants brought into a greenhouse at the end of summer and kept there at growing temperature dropped their leaves and became dormant. Furthermore, they failed to start into growth the following spring, and some remained dormant for a full year! But Dr. Coville found that if the plants were kept at low temperatures (a few degrees above freezing was sufficiently low) for two or three months, growth would proceed normally when the plants were again given warmth. Trailing Arbutus, with several clusters of flower buds, kept in a warm greenhouse over winter, was able to open only a single flower the following spring; while a similar plant, kept outdoors all winter, bloomed profusely.

English Ivy when at home is subject to freezing temperature during winter and properly located can endure zero without much damage. It is not surprising, therefore, that it usually fails to thrive when kept in an apartment where the winter temperature ranges between 70° and 80°. Years ago I stayed at a remote little hotel in Nova Scotia which had a remarkable Ivy growing in a 12-inch pot. Its shoots were long enough to train twice around the lounge which, while not so big as that of the Waldorf-Astoria, was larger than the average living room. The room was heated by an old-fashioned stove, and my guess is that, during the night at any rate, the temperature in winter dropped nearly to the freezing point, and that this, by approximating natural conditions, was largely responsible for the exuberant growth.

Thirty or forty years ago the Norfolk Island Pine (*Araucaria excelsa*) was a favorite house plant, but it is seldom seen nowadays. The probable explanation is that, with the coming of the cussedly efficient modern heating systems, homes are kept so warm all over, even near the windows, that Araucaria just couldn't thrive as a house plant and hence its usage declined.

The finest pot-grown specimen of "Emerald-feather" (*Asparagus sprengeri*) that I have ever seen—not excluding those grown by professionals in greenhouses—was exhibited by a farmer's wife at a county fair where I was judging house plants thirty-five years ago. It was simply magnificent, and I have no doubt whatever it was grown in a home that had no central heating and consequently was exposed to chilly conditions during winter which contributed the necessary factor of rest to insure vigorous growth come spring.

Azaleas and Camellias are accustomed to cool conditions in winter and, for the most part, are not harmed by exposure to a few degrees of frost. Knowing this—and remembering Dr. Coville's experiment with Trailing Arbutus—it is easy to understand why the common practice of keeping Azaleas or Camellias in a room in which the temperature is seldom below 70° results in blasted flower buds and general ill-health.

Therefore these and other plants listed on page 303 in Chapter XX should be kept as cool as possible, but not (except for thoroughly winter-hardy plants) subjected to freezing during the winter months. Admittedly in many homes it is difficult to provide the necessary cool conditions; but often a room can be set aside, heating it only when the temperature approaches 32°; and sometimes an unheated sun porch is available. When neither of these can be provided, the next best plan is to keep the plants in a room in which the night temperature is low, trying, however, to avoid too much difference (no more than 30°) between day and night. It is probably unnecessary to say that the plants should not be exposed to a freezing blast from an open window. This may involve a daily shift, because they must be kept close to the window during the day to take full advantage of the small amount of sunlight available during the winter.

It is necessary to make a distinction between those plants—Primula, Cyclamen, Freesia, et cetera—which *grow* best at a low temperature and those which need it for resting. The former (which may be brought into the coolest, lightest part of the living room when their flowers show color) will need every possible attention in the matters of feeding and watering; the latter should not be given any fertilizer and only enough water to prevent the soil from becoming dry.

While some plants need low temperatures during part of the year, others must be kept dry. This is particularly true if flowers are expected of certain bulbous and tuberous plants; and subjects such as Wax-plant and Poinsettia.

When I was a gardener in England we found that *Iris tingitana* (a bulbous species from North Africa) in our section of the country would not produce flowers except when the bulbs were dug up, after the foliage had died down, and exposed to sunshine for several weeks to ripen them thoroughly. This was required because of the difference in the climate of England and Africa. It is not necessary to be so drastic with the bulbous and tuberous plants that we grow in our homes, but most of them should be dried off during some part of the year. Failure of Amaryllis to bloom often can be attributed to incomplete ripening of the bulbs because the soil was not kept on the dry side during fall and early winter. (It must not be thought that this is the only cause for non-flowering of Amaryllis —loss of interest in the plant as soon as the flowers have faded, resulting in lack of proper care during the time the leaves are active in manufacturing food for the bulb, is one reason for their failure.)

Calla-lilies, too, should have a rest, and under house conditions this is given by withholding water from the soil after their winter and spring season of growth. Sometimes Calla-lilies are planted in the garden to continue their growth in summer. If this is done, the plants must be dug up early in the fall and the tubers kept dry for three months or so before again starting them into growth. Calla-lilies are much more flexible than some plants in their resting habits. I remember one English garden in which they were planted outdoors under a foot of water and left there, year in, year out! This was definitely the reverse of the usual procedure, but apparently low temperatures during the winter took the place of the customary drying off. It is said that under some conditions Calla-lilies will keep on growing indefinitely.

To have it bloom freely Wax-plant (*Hoya carnosa*) must be kept on the dry side during winter, giving only enough water to prevent the leaves from shriveling; while Poinsettia may be deprived of water entirely from mid-January to mid-April.

Some of the plants commonly grown in our homes do not have a long or pronounced resting season and close observation is necessary to determine when growth ceases. Many of the so-called foliage plants—Pandanus, Dieffenbachia—belong in this group. Plants of this nature are successfully grown by those who are entirely unaware that plants require rest; so we can assume that seasonal variations in temperature (which occur even indoors) are sufficient to provide the conditions requisite for a short nap.

Many differences are exhibited in the growth cycles of various plants, and these are important to the gardener whether he grows plants indoors or out. As previously mentioned, hardy spring-flowering bulbs have two periods of active growth and two dormant. During the winter they are inactive and cease growing during the hot days of late July and in August. Sometimes flowering coincides with active shoot growth (as with Fuchsia, Impatiens, and Calla-lily); and sometimes it comes toward the end of the growing season— for example, with Tulips. On the other hand, flowering may *precede*, or go along with, the beginning of active shoot and leaf growth— some Azaleas, Amaryllis, and Meadow Saffron are typical examples.

Knowing how and when to give plants the conditions requisite to their resting stage is an essential part of a good gardener's skill. Admittedly it is a somewhat complicated business but, by following some general rules, by "doing as you are told," and by close observation of your own plants, the problem can be solved.

The first important principle to remember is that the time for resting comes *after* a period of active growth, which may be long or short according to the subject; so, when the plant is no longer putting out new shoots or leaves and flowers have faded, give it less water at the roots and a lower temperature (if cessation of growth comes at a time when it is possible to do this). Also *refrain from giving any fertilizer*. However—especially with plants grown for their foliage—avoid reducing the water supply to the extent of causing the leaves to wilt.

Those plants which have bulbs or tubers usually should be kept completely dry during part of the year—for example, Amaryllis, Nerine, Freesia, Achimenes, and Gloxinia. The "drying-off" process *should be gradual* and spread over several weeks, beginning when growth ceases and leaves begin to turn yellow. Plants (such as Clivia) which do not have a well-defined bulb should be watered carefully, giving only enough to prevent the leaves from wilting or shriveling.

The rest period of plants of temperate climates should be accompanied by cool conditions through at least part of the winter.

Potted plants brought in from outdoors in the fall usually have been growing vigorously all summer. Cool conditions in the house, which in the homes of economical families commonly precede the use of artificial heat, give them the rest they need. With the exception of subjects such as Poinsettia, which still have to complete their growth, no attempt should be made at this time to force them into growth by fertilizing or watering them heavily. This applies also to mature bedding plants that are cut back and potted, such as Begonia, Geranium, and Impatiens. On the contrary, self-sown *seedlings* of Begonia, Flowering Tobacco, Marigold, et cetera, dug up from the flower border and potted, should be kept growing by fertilizing them as soon as they have made some new roots and repotting them into larger pots when necessary. These, unlike the mature plants, are just entering upon a period of active growth, instead of just concluding such a period.

Resting House Plants

DRY OR DRYISH IN WINTER

Bromeliads—Pineapple Family: *Aechmea* spp., *Ananas comosus* vars. (Pineapples), *Neoregelia spectabilis* (Painted Fingernail), *Billbergia, Cryptanthus, Nidularium, Vriesia,* et cetera.

These should be kept fairly dry at the roots, but the foliage should be sprinkled daily. Water freely when flower spikes start to grow.

Cacti, desert forms: *Aporocactus, Cereus, Echinocereus, Ferocactus, Mammillaria, Opuntia,* et cetera.

Weekly watering usually sufficient. Keep soil moist when growth begins. Temperature 50° to 60°.

Cacti, tropical vars.: *Epiphyllum* (Orchid Cactus), *Rhipsalis* (Mistletoe C.), *Zygocactus* (Christmas C.)

Keep on dry side during November and December. Give enough water to keep leaflike stems from shriveling. Moist air desirable.

Ceropegia woodi, Hearts Entangled — Water weekly. If shoots die back, keep dry until late winter.

Clivia miniata, Kafir Lily — Give only enough water to keep leaves from wilting. Keep cool (45° to 50°).

Euphorbia pulcherrima, Poinsettia — Gradually dry off when leaves begin to fall. Cut back and water in April.

Euphorbia splendens, Crown-of-thorns — Water about every two weeks from mid-November to early January.

Fuchsia spp. and vars. — Keep cool (50°) and give only enough water to keep wood plump during October, November, December. Prune in January; water normally; temperature 65°.

Hippeastrum spp. and vars., Amaryllis — Keep dry October to January. Moisten soil when growth begins; water freely when leaves form.

Hoya carnosa, Wax-plant — Give only enough water to keep leaves from shriveling.

Sansevieria trifasciata l a u r e n t i, Snake-plant — Water at weekly intervals during winter.

Succulents: *Agave, Aloe, Bryophyllum, Crassula, Echeveria, Gasteria, Haworthia, Kalanchoe, Kleinia, Pedilanthus, Sedum,* et cetera. — Give enough water to keep leaves from shriveling. Pedilanthus may be kept completely dry in December and January. Winter-flowering species (*Kalanchoe blossfeldiana*) water until blooms fade, then keep on dry side for two months.

Tuberous plants and bulbs grown primarily for summer blooms, which are kept dry in winter include:

Achimenes spp. — Leave tubers in soil completely dry from time tops die (early fall) until March; temperature 60°.

Begonia, tuberous vars. — Store tubers in dry peatmoss until April 1.

Caladium, fancy-leaved vars. — Keep tubers dry October to January; or March, if required for summer display.

Oxalis rubra, O. tetraphylla — Dry off for three or four months. Store in cool (50°), dry place.

Sinningia speciosa, Gloxinia	Dry off in their pots; or remove tubers and keep in dry peatmoss until mid-February.

DRY IN SUMMER

Anemone coronaria vars., Poppy-flowered Anemone	Gradually dry off as foliage withers. Repot and keep soil moist in October.
Brodiaea (Triteleia) uniflora, Spring Star-flower	When leaves die down, keep dry until September.
Freesia refracta vars., Freesia	Gradually reduce water as leaves begin to turn yellow. Keep bulbs dry in their pots until fall.
Ixia spp.	Treat same as Freesia.
Lachenalia spp., Cape Cowslips	Keep dry, in their pots, from withering of leaves until August.
Nerine sarniensis, Guernsey Lily	Dry May to August. Expose bulbs in their pots to sun. Do not disturb roots.
Oxalis bowieana, cernua (Bermuda Buttercup), *hirta, lasiandra, variabilis*	Winter-flowering Oxalises should be kept dry in their pots from spring until early fall. *O. bowei*, and possibly others, if flowered in summer will not bloom the following winter unless dried off for at least two months.
Ranunculus asiaticus, Persian Ranunculus	Treat same as Anemone.
Saintpaulia ionantha, African-violet	Keep a little on dry side in summer for plentiful blooms in winter.
Sparaxis spp.	Treat same as Freesia.
Veltheimia viridifolia	Dry in summer. Start watering when new growth begins in early fall.
Zantedeschia aethiopica (Calla-lily), *elliottiana* (Golden Calla), *rehmanni* (Pink Calla)	For house culture best dried off in summer. If planted outdoors, should be dug in fall and tubers dried for three months before potting. Purchased tubers of *A. elliottiana* should be exposed a few weeks in warm room before potting.

COOL IN WINTER, 40°–50°

Araucaria excelsa, Norfolk Island Pine

Water normally.

Asparagus sprengeri, Emerald-feather

Reduce water supply.

Camellia japonica vars. Camellia
Cymbalaria muralis, Kenilworth-ivy
Cyrtomium falcatum, Holly Fern
Ficus pumila, Creeping Fig
Hedera helix vars., English Ivy
L i g u l a r i a (Farfugium) grande, Leopard-plant
Pteris cretica vars.
Pteris serrulata vars., Brake Ferns
Rhododendron indicum vars., Greenhouse Azaleas
Rhododendron obtusum vars., Kurume Azaleas

Keep soil moist. When the days are appreciably longer, these can be kept at living-room temperature. When growth begins, water freely; repot and fertilize if necessary.

CHAPTER XIII

Pinching, Pruning, Training

SOME pinching and pruning are necessary to keep shrubby plants in ship-shape condition; and training, combined with pinching and pruning, is called for by those of climbing or trailing habit.

Pinching is the term applied when the tip of a growing shoot is

PINCHING, PRUNING, DISBUDDING: *Pinching* is done to induce the formation of side shoots, resulting in a branching, bushier plant; *pruning* controls the shape of the plant, or is done to stimulate new growth from the base; disbudding has as its objective the development of larger, more perfect individual flowers as a result of limiting the number the plant will produce

removed. Usually it is done with the thumbnail (allowed to grow sufficiently long!) and finger. It promotes a compact, bushy habit of growth by checking the strong shoots and stimulating into growth shoot buds which otherwise would have remained dormant. The removal of *flower* buds to force the plant to conserve its energies until the time we desire it to bloom is another form of pinching.

Pruning is done with a sharp knife or pruning shears and consists of cutting back the branches to a greater or less degree according to the subject and the purpose in view. It may be desirable to prevent the plant from growing to unwieldy size, to promote the formation of strong flower-bearing shoots, or to improve its shape.

Training usually implies the provision of a support to which the shoots are attached by tying or otherwise, and is sometimes combined with pruning and pinching to produce the required form. Disbranching Chrysanthemums (done when the branches are no more than an inch or so long) to make them grow to a single stem, and the production of "standard" plants (those with a single straight stem of considerable height with a branching head at the top, as sometimes is done with Geranium, Heliotrope, and Tibouchina) is another form which training takes.

PRUNING AND PINCHING

Pruning cuts should be made just above a leaf which has in its axil a bud pointed in the direction we wish the bush to develop; or, when a branch is removed and not merely shortened, close to the parent branch or trunk from which it grows. The object of this is to avoid ugly-looking stubs.

Following are some of the plants, arranged alphabetically, that need, or are improved by, pruning and/or pinching:

Abutilon, Flowering Maple. Prune old plants in September by cutting back shoots of the current season about one half. Young plants and the new shoots of old plants should have tips pinched out if necessary to promote bushiness.

Camellia japonica, Camellia. Ordinarily needs little pruning beyond shortening any shoots that spoil the symmetry of the bush. This should be done immediately after flowering.

Campanula isophylla. Cut back flowering shoots to pot level when all flowers have faded. To prolong the blooming season, prevent seed formation by picking off old flowers.

Chrysanthemum frutescens, Marguerite. Old plants may be cut back one half when flowering is over; but a better plan is to raise

Pruning results in stockier, more uniformly shaped plants. Arrows indicate where wayward sprays of Flowering Maple should be cut back

young plants annually from cuttings inserted in a coldframe in June or July.

Chrysanthemum hortorum, Garden Chrysanthemum. If bushy plants are required, pinch out tips of shoots whenever they attain a length of 6 inches until mid-July. When one-, two-, or three-stemmed plants are desired, they are "disbranched" by removing all side shoots as soon as they are large enough to handle, once the required number of main shoots has been produced. Larger flowers are produced by disbudding—that is, by removing all but the strongest bud on each shoot. A modification of this procedure is to remove the weakest buds in a spray.

Dieffenbachia, Mother-in-law Plant. This sometimes becomes too tall and has too much bare stem showing, necessitating decapitation to bring it to earth. This involves air-layering, which is more akin to propagation and is treated in that chapter.

Dracaena, Corn Plant. Same treatment as *Dieffenbachia.*

Euphorbia pulcherrima, Poinsettia. Old plants should be cut

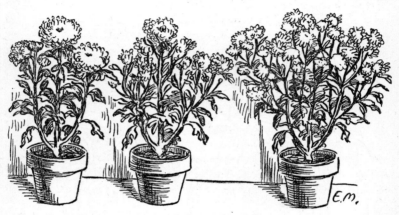

Chrysanthemums, showing progressive reduction in size of individual blooms as number of stems per plant increases

back to within 6 inches of the pot in April and repotted. If a propagating case is available (see Chapter XV), it is better to root cuttings obtained from the cut-back plants rather than to keep the old plants.

Ficus elastica, Rubber Plant. Handsomest when grown to a single stem, but sometimes people, especially Brooklynites, develop a strange affection for this plant and keep it even after it has gawky branches. Removal of the growing point from "wild" shoots will make them branch. Misplaced branches may be cut out in their entirety. This should be done outdoors in spring so that the oriental rug is not gummed up by latex dripping from the cut ends of the shoots.

Fuchsia hybrida, Fuchsia. Start old plants into growth in January or February. As soon as buds show green, cut back to the strongest and remove all dead wood. To promote bushiness of old and young plants the tips of shoots may be pinched out as soon as they have made six or eight pairs of leaves.

Gardenia veitchi, Florists' Gardenia. If plant is getting too large, prune back one third before it is set outdoors in spring. When new shoots attain a length of 6 inches, pinch out tips until August. When plants are no larger than is needed, restrict pruning to shortening any shoots which spoil symmetry.

Hedera helix, English Ivy. When a bushy plant is required, obtain the "self-branching" types, such as the variety Pittsburgh, and pinch out tips occasionally. The Irish Ivy, the one most commonly grown, does not branch freely even when pinched back. Specimens which have grown too large for their quarters should be discarded and replaced by young plants raised from cuttings; this is better than relying on pruning to get them within bounds.

Heliotropium arborescens, Common Heliotrope. Old plants dug up from the garden to serve as house plants should be cut back about two thirds. They are not very satisfactory, however, when so treated, and it is better to raise young plants from seeds or cuttings in the spring and keep all flower buds picked off until they are brought in during the fall. Shapeliness may be induced by pinching out tips of wayward shoots.

Hibiscus rosa-sinensis, Chinese Hibiscus. Cut back one third in March; or if it is still blooming then, wait until it is put outdoors in May. Thin out weak wood and prune to make bush as shapely as possible.

Hydrangea macrophylla, French Hydrangea. Cut back, leaving only two pairs of leaves on each shoot, as soon as flowers fade. Remove weak, spindling shoots entirely.

Hoya carnosa, Wax-plant. Needs little pruning. "Wild" shoots, if any, may be checked by pinching out their tips. Avoid cutting off the spurs (stubby growths) on which the flowers are produced; they will produce additional crops.

Lantana camara, Lantana. Plants which have spent a season in the flower border may be dug up, potted, and cut back three fourths, but they will be a sorry sight for many weeks. Young plants raised from cuttings or seeds in May, which have had their flower buds pinched off until September, are much more satisfactory.

Nephthytis afzeli, Nephthytis. Bareness at the base may be deferred for a while if the tips of one or two of the shoots are pinched out when they are about 8 inches tall. This will temporarily check those shoots and induce branching by stimulating lower buds into growth.

Pelargonium domesticum, Lady Washington Geranium. Cut off all weak shoots in August or September. Shorten those remaining to improve shape. If it is desired to reduce their size, they may be cut back rather severely at this time. Young plants may be made into compact specimens by pinching out tips of shoots if it seems necessary.

Pelargonium hortorum, House, Fish, or Zonal Geranium. Old plants dug up from the border should be cut back about one half,

Pinching back a young Geranium plant, and (right) more bushy growth as a result

having in mind the production of a shapely plant. It takes several months for these cutbacks to develop into presentable plants so it is best to raise new plants from cuttings in May for winter flowering. Pinch out tips of 6-inch shoots to induce bushiness, and remove all flower buds until September.

Philodendron cordatum, Heart-leaf Philodendron. Treat as recommended for *Nephthytis.*

Rhododendron indicum vars., Greenhouse Azalea. Prune for shape immediately after flowering but do not cut back any more than is absolutely necessary. Pinch out the tips of shoots which outstrip their neighbors.

Rosa chinensis minima, Fairy Rose. In January cut back resting plants one half and remove any spindling twigs.

Scindapsus aureus and *S. pictus argyraeus. See Nephthytis.*

Tibouchina (Pleroma) semidecandra, Princess Flower. Rest by keeping cool (40°) in winter. Prune in February by shortening one half all strong shoots of preceding year and removing weak twigs. Young plants should be pinched to induce the required amount of bushiness and then allowed to grow freely.

Tradescantia fluminensis, Wandering Jew. Used mainly as "droopers." If potted in good soil, growth may be so lush as to give an effect of heaviness. This can be corrected by thinning out some of the shoots, cutting them off near the pot. The cut-back stubs will produce new shoots which will take the place of older shoots that have become shabby. Even with this treatment a pot of Wandering Jew will not last in good condition indefinitely, so it is desirable from time to time to start a new pot of cuttings from terminal shoots—an easy matter.

Zebrina pendula, Wandering Jew. *See Tradescantia.*

While it is hoped that the foregoing hints will be helpful, it should be remembered that pruning and pinching are not matters of rule of thumb, but things that must be done with thoughtful consideration. Plants do not always behave according to Hoyle—environmental conditions may affect their performance. So study your plants and use common sense in conjunction with the specific instructions given above.

TRAINING

It has already been intimated that training in part is a matter of pinching and pruning. In the case of climbers and trailers it may also involve the provision of suitable supports to which the shoots are attached by ties or otherwise.

Philodendrons, Nephthytis, Scindapsus, Hoya, and others which attach themselves to their supports by aerial roots should be provided with rough material on which to climb. This may consist of unbarked length of a red cedar trunk about 2 inches in diameter; an inch-square plant stake on which narrow strips of virgin cork have been nailed; or a plant stake wrapped with Moss or Osmunda fiber held in place with thin copper wire. The supports, which are installed when the plants are potted, should extend to the bottom of the pot, and the soil must be packed firmly around them to make them rigid. Obviously supports of this kind are inclined to be top-heavy and need a weighty base to keep them from toppling. Therefore they are not satisfactory in pots of less than 6-inch size.

While these plants are able to attach themselves to supports of this nature by their air roots, it usually is desirable to give them a helping hand, in the beginning at least, by tying in the shoots with thin twine. If the situation is such that daily spraying may be practiced, the air roots will be considerably encouraged.

Morning-glories, which climb by twining, can best be accommodated by sticking three slender bamboo stakes in the soil at equal distances around the edge of the pot. About halfway up the length of the stakes install a hoop—an embroidery hoop of sufficient size will do—and fasten it with ties. Then bring the tops of the stakes together and tie them and you will have a contraption looking something like sketch at right.

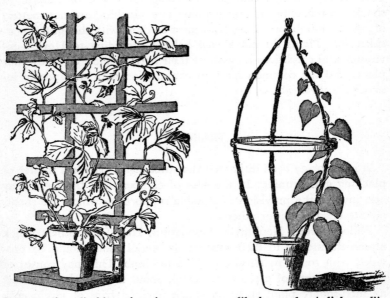

Supports for climbing vines in pots can readily be made. A light trellis, with upright slats and cross bars, secured to a block of wood on which the pot stands, is a practical arrangement. A simpler, but less substantial, support is formed by inserting three flexible pieces of wood (preferably light bamboo) in the pot itself, securing them to a small hoop at half their height, and then tying the tips together

Sometimes a simple wood trellis is the best solution to the problem of attractively supporting and displaying climbers and trailers. Usually this is handled by making a wood base to which the trellis is fastened and on which the potted plant is stood. A base of 1¼-inch material about 8 inches square will satisfactorily hold a trellis up to 30 inches in height. The uprights of 1½ × ½ inch material, planed four sides, can be attached to the base by wood screws, reinforced by angle irons. The crosspieces can be ¼" × 1" strips nailed to the uprights. The trailing shoots can be trained by tying them unobtrusively to the uprights and crosspieces, or by simply winding them back and forth behind and in front of the support. Plants which can effectively be displayed on a trellis such as this or on any other that your imagination and artistic taste may lead you to construct, include English Ivy, Kangaroo Vine, Sweet Potato, Grape-ivy, Madeira Vine, et cetera.

CHAPTER XIV

Summer Care

ON THE WHOLE, the plants which make the most successful "go" of it in our homes are those which are grown outdoors and store up enough vigor to endure a period of arduous service indoors before we get them. The hardy spring-flowering bulbs are an example of this type. Other successful plants, such as Tuberous Begonias and Gloxinias which are dormant in winter, can be grown in summer in well-ventilated rooms in which the air is not desiccated by artificial heat; and those which can be spared from their job of decorating the parlor may be given a recuperative summer vacation outdoors to keep them going through the winter.

When the weather becomes settled and warm in mid-spring, it is time to take stock of the situation and get as many plants as possible outdoors. But first dispose of those which have outlived their usefulness—which have grown too big for the niche they occupy and which cannot be reduced in size by pruning. The big Boston Fern, the Dracaena which is almost touching the ceiling, and the ungainly Rubber Plant should be deposited in the trash can or given to someone who has more room, unless there is a hole in the garden planting which they can fill until their careers are cut short by frost. If they are needed for propagation or can be brought down to usable size by air-layering (see Chapter XV), you may want to keep them a little longer.

If the loss of these and the temporary departure of others on vacation leave too many gaps in the decorative scheme indoors, you should fill the voids with such summer-blooming subjects as Achimenes, Fuchsias, and Gloxinias which, along with African-violets, are better off indoors in most sections.

While most of the plants which have served throughout the winter are benefited by a summer outdoors, it is not simply a case of putting them out and letting it go at that—there are certain preliminaries and precautions to be observed.

First look over the entire stock with an unprejudiced eye and discard any that you think are too far gone to recover and those whose ornamental quality, even when healthy, is of dubious value and which have no compensating features of interest to make it worth-while to retain them. Personally, I would place in this category Spider-plant (*Chlorophytum*), Tree Aloe, and several others whose only claim to consideration is their ability to thrive as house plants.

Then decide whether any of them need repotting in larger pots— because they *should* be kept in pots of adequate size. Do not plant them out where their roots can run freely in the garden soil. If this is done they are likely to grow with such abandon that it will be impossible to get them back into pots of reasonable size in the fall without ruthlessly chopping off the major portion of the root system, which is likely to set them back so far that they will never again be satisfactory as house plants. Poinsettias, especially, are rampant growers when planted out, and as they drop their leaves on the slightest provocation, they are likely to look like ruinous wrecks a week or less after they are brought indoors.

Perhaps this is as good a place as any to confess that I have never had any real success with Poinsettias as house plants. True, I have never gone through *all* the motions supposed to be requisite to insure blooms, but I believe the chief reason for failure is my gas-heated home. I can store them while resting, grow them well outdoors during summer, bring them in during September, and keep practically all the leaves on them *until* the heat is turned on, and then they begin to shed like a mangy dog.

Any pruning of shrubby subjects that may be necessary to promote symmetry or to achieve a reduction in size should be done before eviction proceedings are started. In some cases it is desirable to do the cutting back a few weeks ahead of the time when it becomes safe to set them outdoors. The flowering shoots of Hydrangea, for example, should be cut back to the second pair of leaves as soon as the flowers have faded so that the new shoots have time to grow and ripen before the plants are brought in during early winter; any Azalea shoots which are greatly outstripping their neighbors should be checked by pinching out their tips.

Hunt down any existing insect pests before putting the plants in their summer quarters. It is possible at this time to lay the pots on their sides and squirt water or an insecticide on the undersides of the leaves, making it much easier to get at the beasts now than after the pots are plunged in earth.

LOCATION

Sometimes it is possible to provide an outdoor bed for house plants in a location, sheltered from violent winds, which affords the variety of conditions desirable for the different kinds—shade for Palms, Ferns, and foliage plants in general; partial shade for

Summer Vacation. In putting house plants outdoors for the summer take care to provide them with congenial conditions. Cacti, for instance, like full sun, Ferns fairly dense shade, others varying degrees of shade. Also, to prevent plants from rooting over rims of pots, or through drainage holes—and also to assure good drainage—keep pot rims slightly above soil level, and surround base of each pot with clinkers. Pots should also be given an occasional half-turn

Azaleas, Christmas Cactus, and Orchid Cactus; and full sun for desert plants (Cacti and succulents), Amaryllis, and Geraniums. Such a spot often can be found in the vicinity of a high-headed tree or shrub with foliage that is not too dense, or near a building. In other gardens it may be necessary to spot the plants here and there in the flower or shrub borders, but in general it is better to group them together for convenience in caring for them. A neighbor summers her plants on the rail of a north porch by imbedding the pots in peatmoss contained in window boxes. It is desirable to provide some such anchorage as this to prevent the pots from being blown over by high winds and the peat, incidentally, helps to keep the soil moist. In a situation such as this the plants are not exposed directly to the sun but get plenty of light from skyshine.

It is necessary to remember that the light is much more intense outdoors than it is in the house, and even the sun lovers should be accustomed to it gradually by shading them for a week or so; otherwise they will sunburn just as surely as an office worker on his first visit to Coney Island. Those which are fully in the open can be shaded by throwing squares of cheesecloth over them for a week or two or by rigging up a screen made by nailing laths an inch apart on a frame of furring strips. The plants which are in the dappled shade cast by the leaves of trees or shrubs will probably need no extra attention.

To lessen the need for watering and make it possible for the owner to go on his summer vacation, the pots should be buried to their rims in soil; or, if a special bed is provided, in peatmoss or sand. The bases of the pots should rest on a 2- or 3-inch layer of clinkers or cinders to provide free drainage, to discourage roots from emerging through the drainage hole, and to repel earthworms.

House plants cannot be entirely forgotten in summer. Although they can to some extent take care of themselves when their pots are plunged to the rim in soil out-of-doors, if they are neglected the results may be disastrous, particularly if watering is not taken care of during a dry spell or insects and other pests are allowed to obtain a foothold.

Spraying plants with water from the hose is one of the best prophylactic measures against insect pests and those pesky mites commonly known to gardeners as red spiders. To be effective, however, the water must be applied in a spray with considerable force and directed particularly toward the undersides of the leaves and to the leaf axils where pests are likely to congregate. In order to kill two birds with one stone, so to speak, and to avoid giving the plants more water than is good for them, the spraying should be done when the soil is on the dry side.

Early morning is a good time to apply the spray, on the general principle that it is undesirable to wet the leaves when the temperature is falling. A thorough weekly spraying with plain water is usually all that is required, but if mealybugs gain a foothold it may be necessary to use a good contact spray such as Volck, diluted according to directions. (Do not use on plants which have been, or are to be, dusted with sulphur.) Plant lice also will succumb to this spray, or they may be killed by hitting them with a strong soap solution—2 ounces of soap flakes or powder to 1 gallon of water. If red spiders are abundant, dusting the foliage lightly with dusting sulphur, plus the weekly spraying with water, should control them adequately.

The normal summer rainfall will reduce the need for watering, and most of the house plants will come through in fairly satisfactory shape if they take potluck with the rest of the plants in the garden which ordinarily are watered with hose or sprinkler whenever a prolonged dry spell is experienced. Better results, however, may be expected if they are given a little closer attention and watered whenever they need it for, after all, their roots are confined and cannot range deeply in search of moisture as can those of plants which are unrestricted.

It may be desirable to provide additional soil fertility for actively growing plants during the vacation period. This can be done by steeping a bag of cow manure in water, diluting the liquor to the color of pale amber, and watering them with this, when the soil is moist, once every 4 or 5 weeks. Or liquid commercial fertilizer may be used as recommended in the chapter on Fertilizers.

While light shade is preferable for most of our house plants during the summer months, we must take care that it doesn't become too dense for their welfare. If shade is provided by overhanging trees or shrubs, a little judicious snipping with pruning shears may be necessary to insure that it does not become too much of a good thing.

Pruning the plants themselves during the summer is not likely to be an onerous job; all that is necessary, usually, is to keep an eye on those of a shrubby nature and pinch out the tips of shoots which are growing wildly and spoiling their symmetry. Such pinching back will make the plants more compact. Flower buds should be removed from young plants of Geranium, Heliotrope, et cetera, if they are expected to bloom during the winter.

It is particularly important to give good cultural conditions during summer to winter-flowering bulbous plants of the Amaryllis type. Unfortunately all too many gardeners lose their interest in them as soon as the flowers have faded in late winter or early spring. Forgetting, or not knowing, that the leaves which follow the flowers are responsible for building up the bulb to sufficient size and strength to produce another flower stalk the following spring, some of us dump it in an out-of-the-way corner and either neglect to water it at all or remember it only spasmodically. It is far more essential to be careful in watering, fertilizing, and providing abundant light during the time that the leaves are active than it is during the short period when the flower stalk is being produced. Therefore, those who have the welfare of their Amaryllis (or is it Amaryllises?) at heart will, when the plants are placed outdoors for the summer, remove the loose, worn-out topsoil and replace it with a mixture of ⅔ rich loam, ⅓ rotted manure, and bonemeal at the rate of a teaspoonful for each plant. Water them during droughty periods, bring them indoors in the fall, and then keep the soil almost dust dry until they start growth in late winter.

IN THEY COME!

Vacation time for house plants is over in most sections right after Labor Day. It is important to get them under cover before they are exposed to equinoctial storms, for gales can play havoc with tender foliage. (Poinsettias are particularly susceptible in this respect.) Perhaps the most potent single factor in making plants miserable in the home is the dryness of the air. Therefore, if we bring them into the house before it is necessary to use artificial heat for our own comfort, they are enabled to adapt themselves to a changed mode of living without having to endure the additional discomfort of heat without humidity.

The roots should not be injured or disturbed any more than is necessary. There will be no difficulty about this if the advice to leave the plants in their pots with a substratum of drainage material is followed, and if they are turned occasionally to remind the roots to stay in the pot where they belong.

Young plants started from cuttings will not be too difficult to handle even though they are planted in the soil rather than in pots, because their root systems will be small enough to be dug up intact. But if large plants were turned out of their pots in May and planted directly in the ground, you may have a problem on your hands. In this last case either an excessively large container must be used to accommodate all the roots or the root system must be drastically reduced with resultant injury to the top of the plant because of the inability of the roots to supply sufficient moisture to the leaves. In such situations it is better to dig up the plants in August, pot them in containers large enough to accommodate most of the roots, and reduce the top if it can be done without spoiling the shape of the plant. Then stand the pots in a shady situation outdoors for two or three weeks before bringing them into the house. During this period the tops should be sprayed with clear water two or three times a day.

If the Calla-lilies were planted out to carry on in the flower border during the summer, they should be dug up and potted. Give them a thorough soaking and then gradually reduce the supply of water until the soil is completely dry. Keep them this way for three months to give them a complete rest before starting them into growth indoors. Easter Lilies, which were kept watered after the fading of the flowers and planted out when danger of frost was over, may bloom again in the fall but will not be suitable for further growth indoors. Leave them where they are and mulch heavily with leaves; if the winter is not too severe, they may come up again the following spring.

Before bringing the plants indoors, the outsides of all pots should be cleaned by scrubbing them with a brush and water. If the plants are still actively growing the topsoil should be removed down to the roots and replaced with a mixture of ⅔ garden soil and ⅓ thoroughly rotted manure, plus bonemeal at the rate of a teaspoonful to each 6-inch pot.

It will eliminate a great deal of trouble and contribute to the welfare of the plants in the days to come if they are thoroughly cleaned of any insect pests before they are brought into the house. You can spray insecticides and slosh water around out-of-doors with a freedom which would not be tolerated in the house, where damage to furnishings is often a prime consideration. Therefore, better look your plants over carefully, and if there are any signs of lice (aphids), mealybugs, or spider mites, get after them right away. (See Chapter XVI.)

Be unkind to weak sisters: It is a good plan to become hard-boiled at moving time and consign to the compost pile all those plants which because of ill-health are no longer decorative. If they did not recover during their vacation outdoors, they are not likely to improve when brought inside. Those which are retained should be given locations near windows, sunny or shady according to their preferences, and be accorded routine daily care.

CHAPTER XV

Propagation

GOOD gardening, both indoors and out, always involves keeping an eye on the future, which explains why it is an excellent idea to look over the house plants critically from time to time to decide whether anything needs to be done to make them more presentable and useful. Perhaps the Rubber Plant has lost its symmetry or has grown too large for its quarters. The Dracaena may be hitting the ceiling (or almost), and the Dieffenbachia looking as leggy as a young colt. These faults can be corrected by air-layering.

The strong-growing climbing members of the Jack-in-the-pulpit Family (Nephthytis, Philodendron, Monstera) after a season of growth in the home will be bare below and reaching up into the air above the supports; the Geraniums and Patience Plants may be getting far too large; so, remembering that juvenility rather than senility is an asset so far as house plants are concerned, we make preparations to start new plants by means of cuttings.

Emerald-feather (*Asparagus sprengeri*) is a useful house plant, but it is also a voracious feeder and, after a while, unless potted annually into larger and larger pots, its "leaves" become yellowish and unattractive. Young plants of this, in common with many other house plants, can be more effectively raised from seeds than from cutting or layers. All these operations involve some form of plant propagation.

Now, plant propagation at home not only affords us an opportunity to correct the faults of many of our plants, it also gives us a chance to increase our stock of special favorites, to raise new plants in an environment to which they are already accustomed, and is an operation of absorbing interest.

Equipment: Fortunately very little is needed in the way of equipment. In the home it may consist of nothing more than sand, flowerpots, and glass tumblers or preserving jars of sufficient size to be set on the pots to cover the cuttings within. If the terrarium is not working, it can be pressed into service as a propagating case; or one can be made easily at home as described on page 23. If there is no room in the house for your propagation experiments, they can be carried on outdoors at a suitable season in a coldframe; or cuttings can be inserted in sandy soil in a shaded spot and covered with battery jars and preserving jars; or such subjects as Geraniums, Christmas and Orchid Cacti can be rooted without any covering.

For air-layering you will require Sphagnum Moss, twine, some impervious covering material such as wax paper, and a sharp knife. Sphagnum Moss is the kind used for stuffing the frames on which funeral wreaths are built. Your florist probably will gladly give you some or you can raid the dump pile in your local cemetery, where you are likely to find it in abundance.

Nothing much is needed in the way of equipment for seed sowing, division, and ground-layering which is not already included in the regular supplies of anyone at all interested in plants.

Air-layering: Air-layering, Chinese layering, or, if you want a five-dollar name, *marcottage,* are terms applied to the method whereby roots are produced on shoots while they are still attached to the parent plant. When this is done, a rooted plant of considerable size and vigor can be produced in a comparatively short time without the loss of leaves that would ensue if the shoot were treated as a cutting. While air-layering can be done at any time, roots seem to be emitted more freely in the spring. In any case it is preferable to carry out the operation when the plants are indoors because there is less likelihood that the Moss in which the roots are produced will be allowed to become dry.

The operation is a simple one, consisting merely of cutting a notch extending one third of the way into the stem at the point where it is desired to have the roots form. In the case of a Rubber Plant this would be from 9 to 15 inches below the growing tip; in Dracaena and Dieffenbachia, just below the lowermost leaf; and the same goes for Monstera and strong-growing Philodendrons, except that, because there is a limit to the size of the portion that can be successfully layered, the cut should not be more than 2 feet from the tip. The wound should be wrapped with a large double handful of wet Moss tied firmly in place. The Moss must be kept constantly moist, so it is desirable to cover it with cellophane, wax paper, or oilcloth to prevent undue loss of water by evaporation. An opening must be left at the top so that additional water can be applied to the Moss as needed.

Rubber Plant, Dracaena, and Dieffenbachia are readily propagated by air-layering. A small notch is cut in the stem and surrounded by wet moss covered with cellophane or wax paper. New roots form inside the moss

In about eight weeks (sometimes longer) the Moss should be filled with roots, at which time the layer may be cut off and potted up in the usual way without, however, disturbing the Moss which surrounds the roots. The old plants are then thrown away; or, in the cases of Dieffenbachia and Dracaena, the stub which is left behind can be used for propagating purposes, if additional plants are needed, by cutting it into lengths of 2 to 3 inches. These pieces should be partly buried, horizontally, in a flat or box of moist sand or sand and peatmoss and kept, if possible, in a temperature between 70° and 80°. The propagating case or glass-covered box (page 124) for leaf cuttings of Begonia will provide even better growing con-

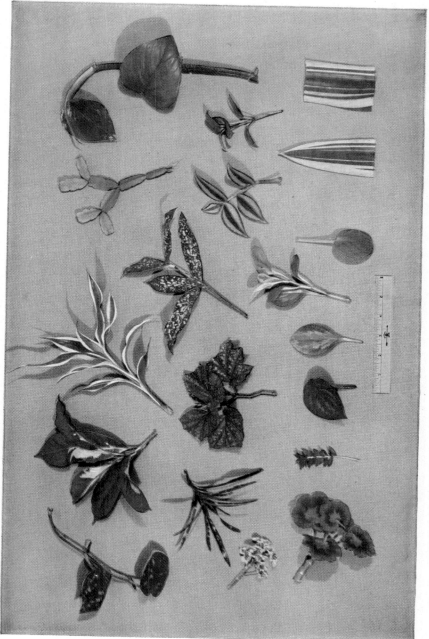

Stem and leaf cuttings of various house plants prepared for propagating frame

*Homemade propagating frame, with cuttings inserted in rooting medium.
Removable glass top conserves moisture and thus prevents wilting*

ditions. In the course of time a young plant will be produced. The thick fleshy stems of Chinese Evergreen and Monstera can be similarly treated. The essential point is to make sure that a growth bud is included in each specimen. This can be done by making sure that each piece contains a leaf scar.

Cuttings: Cuttings of most plants can be rooted with greater assurance of success if the air around them is saturated with moisture. This limits loss of water from the leaves by transpiration

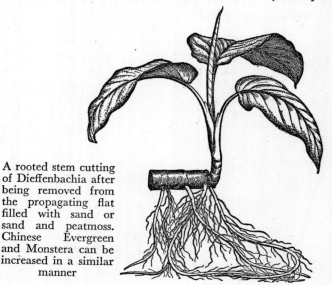

A rooted stem cutting of Dieffenbachia after being removed from the propagating flat filled with sand or sand and peatmoss. Chinese Evergreen and Monstera can be increased in a similar manner

and enables them to carry on until enough roots are formed to supply their needs. The saturated atmosphere is provided by putting the cuttings in a tight propagating case (page 23); in a terrarium or a converted aquarium if holes are drilled in the bottom for drainage; or by covering them with glass tumblers or something similar. Any of these will retain the moisture evaporated from the leaves and the wet rooting medium instead of allowing it to become dispersed in the surrounding air.

Rooting media: The cuttings may be inserted in soil suited to the species, with a layer of sand on top (as described later); in sharp, gritty sand; or in a 50-50 mixture of peatmoss and sand. The last, perhaps, is most generally useful.

Whatever the medium used, it should be packed firmly in the container because it is most important to bring the bases of the cuttings in close contact with it. Stem cuttings are inserted by making a hole (1, 2, or 3 inches deep, depending on the size of the cutting) with a dibber (small stick or pencil) the blunted point of which should be at least equal in size to the base of the cutting.

A pot of cuttings covered with a battery jar to provide the right amount of air humidity and prevent wilting

When inserting the cutting, make sure the base touches the bottom of the hole and then pack the sand or soil closely around it with the dibber. After all the cuttings have been set give a thorough soaking with water to help settle the sand around them.

Future care: Very little watering will be needed because not much moisture is lost to the outside air, but keep an eye on the rooting medium anyway and add water if it begins to approach dryness.

While the cuttings of some plants can get along satisfactorily without any ventilation, it is a good plan to remove the covering for about ten minutes every morning and wipe away the condensed moisture on the glass to prevent supersaturation. If any evidence of mildew or decay shows up, remove affected leaves and ventilate more freely. Any dead or fallen leaves should be promptly removed.

Except when they are set in soil the cuttings should be removed as soon as they have roots 1 or 2 inches long and potted up in a soil mixture suited to them but containing a little more sand than usual. (See Chapter VI.) This is to avoid their becoming stunted from lack of nutrients. Such lack may retard their growth even if they are planted in fertile soil as soon as the condition is noticed. While it is important to pot up the cuttings as soon as they have roots 1 or 2 inches long, you should not dig them up every day to see if they have reached this stage. When you think the time has arrived when they should have roots, give one or two of the cuttings a gentle tug—if they do not come up, they probably have roots, which can be determined by carefully digging them up with a stout-bladed kitchen knife. If they have no roots or if the roots are not long enough, put them back immediately, not forgetting to make the sand firm around them. The time needed for rooting varies greatly according to the subject. Coleus and Wandering Jew may be sufficiently rooted in two or three weeks; shrubby plants ordinarily take much longer.

The best time to make and insert the cuttings varies somewhat with the subject; in general they are most likely to be successful between March and September, provided young but not sappy shoots are available. Consult the table beginning on page 256 for special cases.

When potting up the cuttings, use flowerpots large enough to contain the roots without crowding them but *no larger*. Use the soil mixture recommended for cuttings in the chapter on Soils, and the potting technique described for cuttings in the chapter on Potting. Water them thoroughly and keep somewhat shaded until they begin to form new roots, which will be in about two weeks, then give them the aspect suited to their needs. Spraying them daily with clear water during the time they are getting settled in their new pots helps them to recover from the shock of transplanting.

Many plants readily form roots from cuttings placed in jars of water. These include English Ivy, Wandering Jew, Chinese Evergreen, Oleander, and Pandanus. Special care must be taken to avoid bunching the roots of plants treated in this way when potting them in soil.

One of the commonest complaints regarding Pandanus as a house plant is that if it grows, it quickly gets too large for the window space. If your plant is approaching this stage, make ready to discard the old plant by rooting one or more of the suckers or offsets which grow at its base. These should be removed when their leaves

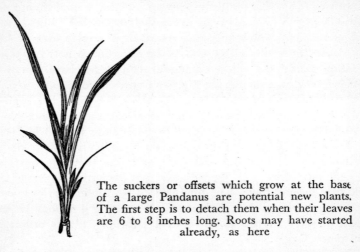

The suckers or offsets which grow at the base of a large Pandanus are potential new plants. The first step is to detach them when their leaves are 6 to 8 inches long. Roots may have started already, as here

are 6 to 8 inches long. Hold the shoot near its attachment with thumb and finger and press down. It usually comes free quite easily, and you may find that one or two roots have already started. If it does not readily part from its parent, help matters along by pushing a sharp knife or wood chisel between its base and the trunk.

After the leaves of the Pandanus sucker have been cut back to about 4 inches, the base is set in sandy soil and covered with a glass tumbler or jelly jar to prevent undue evaporation

The next step is to draw the leaves together in one hand and cut the tips off with a sharp knife or scissors about 4 inches from the base. The main object of this is to make it possible to cover the

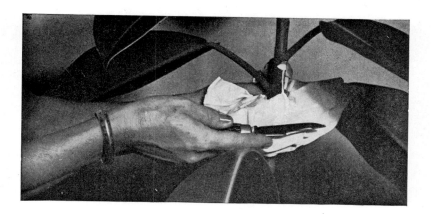

Air or "Chinese" layering, employed in making new plants of some
species that grow too tall for house comfort. A Rubber Plant is notched
(*above*), and the milky "sap" caught on a paper towel

(*Above*) Next, a ball of moist Sphagnum Moss is tied about the
wound. (*Below*) The Sphagnum ball encased in a cellophane or
waxed-paper wrapper to help keep it moist until roots form

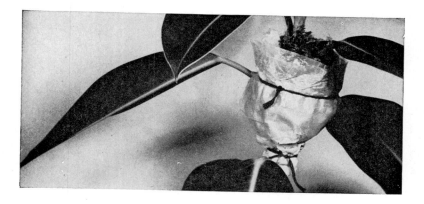

A homemade propagating case.
(1) A deep, strong flat is provided with drainage holes, over which crocks are placed

(2) Four panes of glass, cut to fit, are inserted around the sides, held at the corners with adhesive tape; a fifth pane forms cover

(3) Box is filled with the rooting medium, (sand or other material) which is pressed down to a half-inch or so below edge of flat

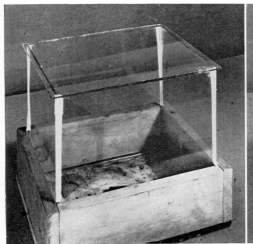

(4) After cuttings have been firmly inserted, water is applied through a fine rose, until rooting medium is thoroughly moist; cover is then put in place. If moisture collects in drops on cover, it is raised slightly to provide ventilation

(5) Leaf propagation: A Rex Begonia leaf, with cuts made across main ribs, is placed flat on rooting medium, with stem inserted to hold it in position

6) Flat may be covered with glass to retain moisture. In several weeks new plantlets will have formed where the ribs of the leaf were severed

Heat and mistreatment won't bother the Snake-plant (*Sansevieria zeylanica*) shown in bloom at the left

Another "toughie" that can take its share of neglect—the Fiddle-leaved Rubber Plant (*Ficus lyrata* [*pandurata*])

entire cutting with a glass tumbler or jelly jar after the base has been inserted 1 inch deep in sandy soil in a 4-inch pot. If a larger glass vessel is available, such as a battery jar or small fish globe, or if you have a propagating case which will contain the leaves entire, it is not necessary to cut them back. If you don't want to go to all this trouble just put the base of the cutting in a jar of water.

Among the easiest of house plants to root are Coleus, Wandering Jew, Impatiens, Ivy, Philodendron, and Geranium. These can be

Wandering Jew is one of the easiest if you use tip cuttings 3 or 4 inches long and set them firmly in damp sand

handled by inserting them in sand, but they are so amiable that some of the steps can be eliminated and the cuttings rooted in the pots in which they are to grow by the following procedure: a flower-pot should be prepared by putting in a ½-inch layer of clinkers or flowerpot chips for drainage. Then fill it to within ½ inch of the rim with a mixture of 2 parts each of sifted soil and leafmold and 1 part sand. Press down with the fingers, make the surface level, and cover with ¼ inch of clean sand. When the cuttings are dibbled in, a small amount of sand falls to the bottom of the hole and provides a well-aerated cushion on which the base of the cutting rests—air is necessary for root formation. Preferably the tips of the shoots should be used, 3 to 4 inches long in the case of Impatiens and Wandering Jew and 8 to 10 inches long for Ivy and Philodendron. The basal cut should be made with a sharp knife or razor blade, about ¼ inch below the junction of leaf and stem, and the lowermost leaf or leaves removed. Make a hole in the soil with an unpointed pencil or something similar, insert the cutting so that its base is pressed on the bottom of the hole, and pack the soil firmly. After all the cuttings are in (nine will be sufficient in a 6-inch pot) give the soil a thorough soaking, cover with a battery jar, and put in a shaded but light spot until rooted, when the glass can be removed and, after

Impatiens cutting ready for insertion. Some propagators believe better results are obtained if flowers are removed

a few days, the plants placed on display in light sufficiently intense for their needs. If small covers are used, put fewer cuttings in small containers to correspond. Geraniums do not need any cover other than something such as cheesecloth or newspaper to shade them from bright sunshine. Avoid sappy shoots, using none but those with firm wood. Cuttings of Nephthytis, strong-growing Philodendrons, and Monstera may be up to a foot in length. Obviously these cannot be accommodated under a tumbler or even under a battery jar—they need the room afforded by a propagating case. As a matter of fact, if you are planning to raise any considerable number of plants from cuttings, it is far more convenient to do so in a propagating case than it is to bother with numerous individual containers.

Leaf cuttings: Some plants root with great facility from leaf cuttings; for example, Picka-back Plant, Peperomia, African-violet, Gloxinia, Snake-plant, and Rex Begonia. In the case of the Pickaback Plant, cut off mature leaves with about 2 inches of leaf stalk and insert in the rooting medium so that the blade of the leaf is touching the surface. This will also quickly root if the leaf stalk is placed in a small jar of water with the blade barely touching the surface. With Peperomia, Gloxinia, and African-violet the pro-

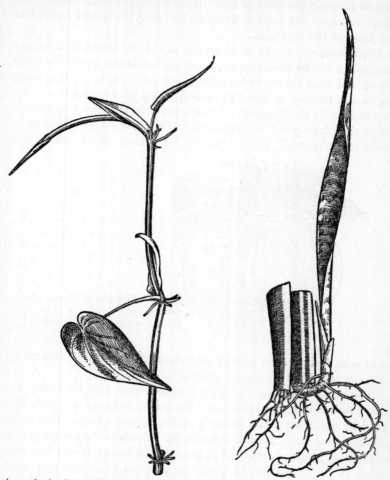

(LEFT) A tip cutting of *Philodendron micans*. Roots are starting at the joints even before it is placed in the sand. (RIGHT) Piece-leaf cuttings of Snake-plant are made about 4 inches long and inserted half their length in the rooting medium

cedure is much the same except that it is not necessary for the leaf blade to touch the surface, because the new plants are formed at the base of the leaf stalk.

With Snake-plant the usual way is to cut the leaves into lengths of about 4 inches and, keeping them right side up, insert them for about half their length in the rooting medium. An interesting thing about this method is that the striped leaves of the parent are not reproduced in the progeny. If you want to retain the longitudinal stripe the plants must be propagated by division of the rhizome or main root "crown." Except for the Picka-back Plant, which will

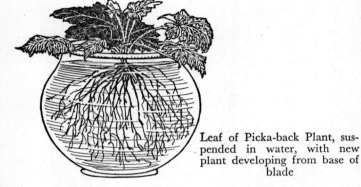

Leaf of Picka-back Plant, suspended in water, with new plant developing from base of blade

root with facility even though uncovered, it is desirable to treat all these as described for stem cuttings.

There are two ways in which Rex Begonias may be handled—one involves using an entire leaf; the other, pieces of the leaf. Proceed by obtaining a box about 9 inches square and 5 inches deep. Make two or three ½-inch holes in the bottom for drainage, put in a layer of peatmoss, then fill it to within 2 inches of the top with sand. A 50-50 mixture of peatmoss and sand is sometimes used. (This suffices also for stem cuttings of Dieffenbachia, et cetera.) If you have a propagating case or terrarium not fully occupied, it can be used instead.

In the spring choose a mature but not a fading leaf and cut it off with about 1 inch of leaf stalk attached. Turn it upside down on the table and with a sharp knife cut through all the main veins just below the place where they divide. Turn it right side up, make a hole in the sand to receive the stalk, and then place the leaf so

Here is a bulb pan of Daffodils after the rooting period at a low temperature, and ready to start growth indoors. Under the right conditions roots like those shown below should have developed before top growth is encouraged

Leaf cutting of Rex Begonia
The main ribs on bottom of leaf are severed and the leaf is placed, bottom side down, on moist sand in cutting box. New plantlets form at the cuts. Triangular pieces of the leaves can also be used, as shown in top left corner of box below—four inserted, and one lying on surface

that it is lying flat on the sand. Cover the box with a pane of glass and wait until plantlets grow from the leaf. The plantlets, if dug up and potted, will grow along to make nice specimens for next winter. The other method of dealing with Rex Begonia is to cut the leaf into triangular pieces, 2 to 3 inches high, each containing a good-sized vein. The end nearer the vein should be inserted to a depth of ½ inch in a tumbler-covered pot, a propagating case, or a box similar to that just described.

A leaf of Rex Begonia which, lying on damp sand, is producing young plants where its veins were severed

Several Ferns (*Asplenium bulbiferum* as an example) develop plantlets on their fronds. These may be detached and potted when they have two or three leaves; or the frond may be laid on moist sand and the plantlets allowed to grow there for a while by the method described for entire leaves of *Begonia Rex*.

ROOTING CUTTINGS OUTDOORS

If you are cramped for room, it is good to know that cuttings of many varieties of house plants can be successfully rooted outdoors. A shaded coldframe is excellent for the purpose. The cuttings may be inserted in a suitable medium contained in pots or flats or directly in the soil of the coldframe if it is sufficiently porous. A coldframe is very useful for handling those cuttings which are too large to be accommodated in the indoor propagating case.

If your garden does not boast of a coldframe (by the way, a very useful adjunct for many gardening operations), the cuttings can be inserted in a shaded spot in soil made porous, if necessary, by mixing sand with it. The cuttings can be covered with preserving jars or something similar; or, in the case of Geraniums and Cacti, merely shaded from sunshine.

Rooting may be accelerated by using one of the root-inducing chemicals, and you may be interested in experimenting with them.

They are obtainable in several brands from garden supply firms with directions for use. It must be remembered, however, that these chemicals are not a substitute for good gardening, and the requirements of suitable cutting material, care in making the cuts proper environment, et cetera, must be fully met.

GROUND-LAYERING

Some plants produce runners very much like those of the Strawberry which, when properly treated, will make excellent vigorous youngsters to carry on the family line. Examples of runner-forming house plants are Strawberry-geranium, or Mother-of-thousands (*Saxifraga sarmentosa*), Boston Ferns, and that plant with striped leaves known to many as Spider-plant (*Chlorophytum*) which increases by means of plantlets produced on the ends of its flower stalks. This, however, is one of those linsey-woolsey things that is not worth the trouble of increasing it. (Forgive me if I seem to have a "down" on *Chlorophytum*. It is one of those complexes, and I can't help it!)

One way of handling these runner makers is to fill a 3- or 4-inch flowerpot with a mixture of half loam and half leafmold with a little sand if the loam is sticky, and then pin the runner with a hairpin in the center of the pot of soil. As soon as roots have formed the runner can be severed from the parent plant to lead an independent existence.

Another method, excellent in the case of Boston Ferns, is to plant the pot outdoors in the spring, dig up the soil around it, and mix in a 3-inch layer of sifted leafmold and sand in which the runners will root. The runners, by the way, are those fuzzy, string-like growths which originate in profusion around the base of the Boston Fern. (Many amateurs seem to get hot and bothered about them, not knowing whether they should be cut off or left to grow. If they seem to you to make the plant look untidy, they can be cut off unless they are needed for propagation.) When the runners have made two or three leaves they should be dug up, potted in 3-inch pots, and kept in a shaded spot (preferably in a coldframe) and well watered until they are established. You will find, in all probability, that these young plants are more satisfactory for your purpose;

and, if the old plant is scale-ridden, they afford an excellent means of by-passing this pest.

DIVISION

The habit of growth of some plants is such that division constitutes the proper method of propagating them. The best time to do this is when new growth is just beginning—usually during late winter. Saintpaulia, Aspidistra, and Pteris are good examples to illustrate the methods of division.

If you carefully examine a Saintpaulia which has been growing in the house all winter you will see, in all probability, that it has split up into several crowns each producing a tuft of foliage. If at this time flowering is on the wane it is a good plan to turn the plant out of its pot, gently loosen the soil ball, pull the crowns apart without any more root injury than is absolutely necessary, and pot them up in individual pots. These separated plants are likely to develop into far better flowering plants than the old plant potted on without division. Saintpaulia is one of those plants which grows better in a rather loose soil so don't press it down too firmly.

Aspidistra, or Cast-iron Plant, is one of those which will remain in good health year after year if progressively repotted into a pot of larger size. This is all very well, but after a time it becomes a veritable white elephant capable of being moved by no one but the strong man from the circus. Therefore, lest it become unwieldy, the Aspidistra should be divided every three or four years at a time when the new leaves can be seen as tiny pointed spears at the base of the plant. Turn the plant out of its pot (I should have a record made of this phrase!) and slam it on the bench to loosen the soil. With a knife cut through the rhizomes (horizontal stems) at the points selected for division and pull off sections containing from three to nine leaves, according to the size of plant you wish to retain. Some ruthless gardeners merely chop the plant into sections of the required size with a spade, but considerable wreckage is likely to result unless the job is skillfully done. If the operation is purely propagational the smaller sizes are preferred; but if one or two larger plants of immediate good appearance is the objective, then use the nine-leaf divisions. Repot these in pots large enough to contain the roots without crowding and make the soil quite firm. The old leaves will tend to point every which way as a result of rhizome displacement. This can be corrected when potting by manipulation of the rhizomes—wedging them with soil so that the leaves are vertical; or by temporarily holding them upright with thin plant stakes.

The roots of Pteris, Adiantums, and other Ferns grow into such dense, fibrous masses completely filling the pot that usually the best plan is to slice off first about 2 inches from the bottom of the root ball with a stout knife or a hatchet, and then with vertical cuts separate the remainder into pieces of the desired size. While this method destroys many roots it is perhaps less harmful than to attempt to tease out the matted roots with the fingers. This, however, is done commercially when a large increase is sought and the stock plant is separated into individual crowns.

In all cases when division involving much root disturbance is practiced, care must be taken to avoid overwatering during the period preceding the formation of new roots. Shade from bright sunshine must be given for a few weeks, and, if possible, a daily overhead spraying with clear water.

PROPAGATION BY SEEDS

So far only "vegetative" methods of propagation have been discussed—that is, securing new plants by using some part of an existing plant other than seeds. Some house plants, such as *Asparagus sprengeri, Cordyline (Dracaena) indivisa, Kalanchoe blossfeldiana,* and certain Cacti produce better plants or can be handled more conveniently if seeds are used.

Earthenware seed pans, small flowerpots, or bulb pans can be used to hold the soil in which the seeds are sown. They must be drained by putting in the bottom a half inch or so of broken flowerpots, clinkers, or coarse cinders as described in Chapter IX.

The soil should be porous enough to allow water to pass through it freely and at the same time retentive enough to eliminate the need of frequent watering. A mixture of equal parts by bulk of loam, leafmold, and sand fills these specifications.

The gardener is likely to be plagued by pre-emergence or post-emergence damping-off caused by various fungous organisms, especially when seedlings are raised indoors. If you have experienced trouble in the past, if your seeds failed to germinate, or if the seed-lings decayed and toppled over at the ground line, it would be well to sterilize or partially sterilize the soil before planting.

For partial sterilization watering the soil with boiling water is usually effective. The soil mixture is passed through a ¼-inch or ½-inch sieve and the pots filled with it and prepared for sowing. They are then watered twice (to do a good job) with boiling water applied by means of a watering can with a fine rose (sprinkler) attached to the spout to avoid disturbing the surface. When the soil has cooled, the seeds may be scattered on the surface, pressed in with a tamper, and covered with dry sand.

The soil can be sterilized with chemicals applied in dust or liquid form. Formaldehyde dust containing 15 per cent commercial forma-lin which can be obtained under a trade name from firms dealing in garden supplies is thoroughly mixed with prepared soil at the rate of 8 ounces to a bushel and the seeds planted immediately. It is safer to wait twenty-four hours before sowing seeds of some plants, such as Anchusa, Campanula, and Petunia, which are subject to injury if sown before some of the fumes are dissipated.

I have had good success by using liquid formaldehyde as follows: add 2½ tablespoonfuls of commercial formalin to 12 tablespoonfuls of water, sprinkle over 1 bushel of prepared soil, and mix thoroughly. Then put the treated soil in a box and cover with something—oil-cloth, wax paper, board—to keep the fumes in for twenty-four hours, after which the pots can be filled with the treated soil, the seeds sown, and *watered thoroughly.*

Other means of circumventing the damping-off organisms are to sow the seeds in Sphagnum Moss (the Superintendent of Docu-ments at Washington, D.C., will be delighted to send you a copy of a bulletin telling you all about it—if you send him five cents) or in sharp sand which must be watered with nutrient solution. Use one of the formulas in the section on soilless culture (page 60) diluted 1 part to 5 parts water until seedlings have made the first true leaf, then increase the concentration to 50-50; and, after a week or two, use at full strength.

Filling the pots: The pots should be "crocked" (page 71) and the drainage covered with ¼ inch of Moss or the rough material re-jected by the sieve when screening the soil. Then fill the pots more than full of soil and strike off even with a piece of lath. If very fine seeds are to be sown—Begonia, Gloxinia—the top inch of soil should be passed through an ⅛-inch sieve. With a circular tamper (made from a ½-inch section of a branch about 2 inches in diameter screwed to a 3-inch length of broom handle), or a flat-bottomed tumbler, press the soil down so that it is about ½ inch from the pot rim. Put the labels in place close to the pot edge and sow the seeds thinly. Try to allow at least ⅛ inch between small seeds and ¼ inch between those of fair size. If this is done, there is less danger of

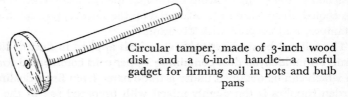

Circular tamper, made of 3-inch wood disk and a 6-inch handle—a useful gadget for firming soil in pots and bulb pans

damping-off. Gently press the seeds into the soil with a tamper.

After the seeds are sown, stand the pots in a baking or roasting pan containing about 2 inches of water and allow them to stay there until moisture shows on the surface. Very small seeds will need no soil covering, but the pots should be covered with a pane of glass or wax paper until the seeds begin to germinate, when it should immediately be removed or tilted to admit air. Larger seeds should be covered with sand to a depth equal to twice their diameter. This can conveniently be accomplished by putting sand in the flour sifter and turning the handle to dispense a sufficient amount of sand. (Be careful to remove all grit from the sifter before making a pie.) Needless to say, all this work should be done in a place where there is no danger of spilled sand, soil, and water spoiling rugs or waxed floors.

The pots may be stood on a layer of pebbles in an empty terrarium or aquarium; or they may be put in a flat or shallow box with moist peatmoss between them. Spray gently with water to settle the sand and shade with newspaper.

Keep close watch on the pots and water them whenever the soil shows signs of becoming dry. This can be done by partially immersing them in a pan of water or by overhead spraying which must be done carefully to avoid disturbing the surface. As soon as the seeds germinate, move them to a light and more airy location but shade with newspaper or cheesecloth from bright sunshine for a few days, gradually reducing the amount of shade until they are fully exposed. When the seedlings make their first true leaf (as distinguished from the initial or cotyledonary leaves) they should be pricked off (transplanted) 2 inches apart in flats or into small pots, thus giving them room in which to grow.

Here are some of the house plants which can easily be raised from seeds:

Asparagus sprengeri, Emerald-feather; *A. plumosus,* Asparagus-fern (use the variety *nanus*—it is better adapted to house culture). The seeds of Citrus fruits, especially Grapefruit, are useful for providing a pan of greenery if the seeds are planted about an inch apart. Don't raise Oranges, Grapefruit, et cetera, from seeds if your objective is flowering or fruiting plants—they are too long-winded.

Cordyline indivisa, Blue Dracaena, is best raised from seeds, and the seedlings are useful for providing variety in Fern dishes. Seeds of all of the above should be soaked overnight in lukewarm water just before sowing them: Cacti in great variety can be sown if you are interested in them. Almost every seedsman offers packets of mixed seeds, but if you want named kinds, you will probably have to go to a specialist. The soil mixture should be made very porous, which can be done by adding to the standard mixture ¼ part of old mortar or flowerpot chips broken up to pass through a ¼-inch sieve.

Better plants of *Kalanchoe blossfeldiana* and Black-eyed Susan Vine are produced by raising them annually from seeds; and annuals such as Marigold, and Sweet Alyssum must, of course, be raised from seeds.

RAISING FERNS FROM SPORES

Prepare a seed pan as for sowing seeds. Then break up a new flowerpot so it will pass through an ⅛-inch sieve and cover surface with the chips to a depth of ⅛ inch. Water thoroughly with boiling water; when the soil has cooled, the spores may be sown.

Spores are produced in cases in lines or dots, usually on the under side of the frond. Sometimes they are formed along the margins of the frond, which seems to roll over. It is important to collect the spores at the right time, which is when the spore cases are beginning to split open; examination with a magnifying glass may be necessary in some cases to determine this.

Two methods may be followed in sowing the spores: (1) Cut the spore-bearing frond into ½-inch pieces and lay them, spore side down, on the surface of the prepared soil in the seed pan. The spores will drift out and sow themselves. When the spores have been dis-

Types of spore cases on Ferns. They are sometimes mistaken for scales or disease. A—Pteris; B—Polypodium; C—Adiantum

charged, remove the portions of frond. (2) Gather fronds bearing ripe spore cases and place them in paper bags or wrap in paper and keep in a warm, dry place. In a few days the dustlike spores will be shed and they can be scattered thinly on the surface of the soil.

Immediately after the spores have been sown, cover the seed pan with a pane of glass and stand it in a saucer which must be kept constantly filled with water. Never attempt overhead watering until leaves are visible.

When the spores germinate they first form a flat, delicate plate of green tissue (the prothallium) on the underside of which the reproductive organs are formed. After fertilization is effected, the young plantlets begin to grow, and when this happens, the glass covering may be removed and the seed pan watered from overhead if more convenient.

Once you get started on plant propagation you will find it so interesting that you will raise many more plants than you can accommodate—or have pots for. Usually there is no difficulty in disposing of the surplus if they are good specimens. They can be given to friends, used as party favors or bridge prizes, or sold at charity fairs.

CHAPTER XVI

House-plant Enemies

For a good many years I told my classes in house-plant culture, with tongue in cheek, that there was no excuse for the presence of pests on house plants. Actually there is a good deal of truth in the assertion. If plants are properly grown and not subjected to the hot, dry air that provides favorable conditions for an epidemic of spider mites; if they are given prophylactic treatment by thoroughly spraying them at weekly intervals with plain water; if vigilance is exercised to avoid bringing infected plants in contact with healthy ones; and if a close watch is kept and measures taken to control disease and insects before they make much headway—then little trouble need be experienced.

Usually house plants are not much bothered by fungous diseases, presumably because the hot, dry air is more inimical to pathogens than it is to higher plants. When leaf spots which seem to be of fungous origin are noticed, pick off the affected leaves immediately and destroy them by burning. If this does not stop the disease, or should the entire plant be affected, the best plan is to discard the plant and start afresh. Of course you can spray with a fungicide, hoping to prevent the spread of the disease. Bordeaux mixture is standard and easily obtainable but leaves a disfiguring residue and you may prefer to use ammoniacal copper carbonate, or a proprietary remedy such as Fungtrogen, either of which is less objectionable in this respect.

Mildew, which looks like a grayish-white powder on the leaves, can be checked by covering the plant with a thin film of dusting sulphur.

Wilts and root rots usually are controlled by discarding affected plants; by modifying cultural practices to provide free ventilation; by thoroughly aerating the soil by making it porous; and by the avoidance of overwatering. (See the list at the end of this chapter.)

Yellowing of the foliage may be caused by insufficient nitrogen in the soil, to be rectified by repotting or feeding with a nitrogenous fertilizer; by over- or under-watering; by getting cold water on the leaves (in the case of African-violet) ; by too much sun; or, in the case of Gardenia, by alkaline soil which can be remedied by incorporating acid peatmoss in the potting mixture or by watering occasionally with iron-sulphate solution. (See list.)

Unusual pallor of the leaves, especially when associated with abnormal lengthening of the stems, may be due to insufficient light. The remedy is obvious—a better-lighted position.

INSECT PESTS

I am a great believer in the Saturday morning bath as a means of keeping those plants which can stand it free from red spiders (spider mites) and insect pests. But plants with fuzzy foliage (African-violets, Gloxinias, and some succulents) are catlike in objecting to water on their fur; some Begonias, fine-leaved Ferns, and any fragile plants are likely to suffer mechanical injury if sprayed with water forcibly enough to dislodge insects.

Usually the best way to spray house plants with water is to put them on their sides in the bathtub, remove the stopper, and then, with the bathroom sprayer, squirt water on *both* sides of the leaves and particularly in the angles formed by the leaf and stem, with the purpose of washing the insects down the drain.

In addition to the use of plain water, insects can be fought with insecticides of various kinds. House plants ordinarily are not bothered by leaf-eating insects, and if they do put in an appearance they are usually few in number so that they can be picked off by hand. If the plants are attacked by too many leaf-eaters for manual control, the foliage can be sprayed with lead arsenate, 2 tablespoonfuls to 1 gallon of water. This is a deadly poison.

Sucking insects are attacked with contact insecticides (sprays or dusts) which must be applied so as to hit the insects. A handy, nonpoisonous one which is effective against plant lice is soap and water —1 to 2 ounces of flakes or powder to a gallon. Try the weaker solution first.

A more effective spray is made by adding a teaspoonful of 40 per cent nicotine sulphate (poison) to a gallon of soapy water. Rotenone or proprietary contact sprays, if you have them on hand, can be used in accordance with directions on the package. Household sprays used against flies and mosquitoes may be altogether too strong for use on plants.

Fumigation is effective against certain insects, especially white flies, but there is an element of danger in its use in the home so I do not recommend it.

Methods of control: Nicotine and rotenone insecticides are available in dust form. Perhaps housekeeping considerations would prohibit their use in the living room, but you might be able to put the affected plants in a large carton in the cellar (or outdoors if the weather is warm enough), close it, insert the nozzle of a dust gun through a hole in the side, and puff until you think the insects are sufficiently covered.

Liquid insecticides can be used as sprays or dips. The latter method is often the most convenient and effective when the plants are not too large. Place the insecticide in a fairly large shallow container such as a roasting pan. (Be sure to wash it before cooking the Thanksgiving turkey.) Then make a wad of newspaper and with it cover the soil of the pot to prevent it from spilling into the mix-

A roasting pan makes a good bathtub for dipping plants in soapy water. Soil is held in place by covering surface of pot with newspaper

ture, hold it in place with one hand, invert the plant, and gently swish it through the insecticide, making sure all parts are covered. Lay the plant on its side to drain for a few hours out of the sun.

When the plants are too large to be dipped, the insects can be sprayed with a hand sprayer. Remember that most of the insects that concern us must be hit with the insecticide, so direct the spray to the locations where they usually congregate—the tips of the shoots, underside of leaves, and junction of leaf and stem.

Always it is desirable to spray the plants thoroughly with clear water a few hours, or a day, after they have been treated.

Among the important insects affecting house plants are the following:

Mealybugs: There are several species of these ubiquitous pests, but it is not important to be able to distinguish between them. They are oval, varying in size from ⅙ to ¼ inch long, covered with a mealy, waxy material which sheds insecticides. They fall into two groups—long- and short-tailed. Those in the first group have four extra-long filaments at their rear ends; the others have bodies margined with leglike filaments of equal length. The short-tailed species lay eggs (300 to 600 of them!) in a cottony sack; the others give birth to living young. They attack almost every kind of plant, being especially partial to African-violets, Fuchsias, and Gardenias. The weekly spraying with water, properly done, is usually sufficient to keep them down. Prompt action as soon as they are discovered is essential. When they are few in numbers the egg masses can be removed with thumb and finger and the adults touched with a camel's-hair brush or cotton swab on a toothpick which has been dipped in alcohol. This last is probably the best method of dealing with them when they attack African-violets or when they shelter behind the spines of Cacti.

Scale insects: These are related to mealybugs but differ considerably in appearance. They may be flattened or hemispherical; round, oval, or scurflike; one species looks like a short, thin line made with a pen dipped in India ink. (Sometimes the spore cases on the fronds of certain Ferns are mistaken for scale insects.) When mature they are immobile, and are covered with scale-like armor which usually resists insecticides at strengths not injurious to plants. They are vulnerable when they are young and running around, either to a water spray which knocks them off the plants, or to contact insecticides. But mature insects usually are best removed manually, using a softish brush, a rag, or a sponge wet with soapy water. Be careful in the use of these methods, for the cuticle of some plants is easily marred by harsh treatment.

White flies: These are tiny white flies that look like miniature moths. The nymphs congregate on the undersides of leaves. Fuchsia, Lantana, and Nicotiana are especially subject to attack. This is a particularly difficult pest to control because the adults fly off as soon as they are disturbed by spraying. The best remedy is fumigation, but as that is out for use in the house, the next best is to spray the underside of the foliage with nicotine-soap solution every four or five days until the infestation is cleaned up.

Plant lice: Known also as green-flies, black-flies, and aphids; winged, or wingless according to the stage of development. These, in common with some scale insects, secrete a syrupy substance known as honeydew which gives the leaves a varnished appearance and on which a black mold may grow, to the detriment of the appearance of the foliage. They are soft-bodied insects and usually succumb readily to contact insecticides; but it is very desirable to get rid of them when they first appear before they have a chance to cause much damage. Often their feeding causes the leaves to curl and wrinkle, making it much more difficult to reach them with a spray.

Spider mites: Commonly called red spiders, these are not true insects. They are minute—barely visible without the aid of a magnifying glass—and often the first observed indication of their presence is injury manifested by a speckled yellowing, browning, or graying of the leaves or stems (in the case of Cacti). Examination of infested leaves with a hand lens is likely to disclose a silken web, crawling with eight-legged mites, up to $\frac{1}{60}$ of an inch long, red, green, yellow, or black in color. Hot, dry air favors their development; therefore every effort should be made to humidify the air and keep the temperature at reasonable levels—below 70°. A thorough spraying with water once a week is helpful. Once they have obtained a foothold other measures must be taken. Badly infested plants, unless very valuable, should be discarded. If the leaves are large enough to admit of washing them with a sponge wet with soapy water many of them can be removed by this means. Dusting the plants with dusting sulphur helps to keep them down; and certain proprietary sprays, such as Loro, Rotecide, et cetera, are effective.

Miscellaneous insects: Tiny black flies often may be seen hovering around the plants. They are harmless to plants and only mildly annoying to humans. They come from maggots in the organic matter in the soil. Watering the soil with nicotine, a teaspoonful to a gallon (no soap), will most likely kill the maggots; and spraying the adults with a contact spray will probably put them out of business. I have never tried it, never having been sufficiently bothered by them.

Often complaints are made concerning small white jumping insects, which appear either on the surface of the soil or in the water contained in the plant saucer. These are springtails, which are innocuous, living as they do on decaying organic matter. If they give you a creepy, crawly feeling try the measure suggested above for the black flies.

Earthworms: There are some who advocate the introduction of earthworms to flowerpots for their alleged beneficial effects on the soil. Personally, while I recognize their value as tillers of the soil in field and garden (they can be decidedly obnoxious when infesting a fine lawn, though), I have always regarded them as a minor nuisance when operating within the confines of a pot where they may disturb the plant roots and indirectly cause waterlogging by depositing their "casts" in the drainage. Far be it from me to suggest the *wanton* destruction of any living creature, but if your plants are not thriving as they should and there are worms in the pots, I would advise ejecting them by watering the soil with lime water; or, if acid-soil plants are concerned, with mustard water made by mixing a teaspoonful of powdered mustard in a quart of water. T. A. Weston, well known as a good cultivator of potted plants, advocated the use of ½ teaspoonful of potassium permanganate to a quart of water to eject worms and to oxygenate the soil.

I am indebted to Cynthia Westcott, the Plant Doctor, for permission to use the following list which appeared originally in the *Home Garden* magazine. In it you will find other pests and other remedies than those described and suggested above.

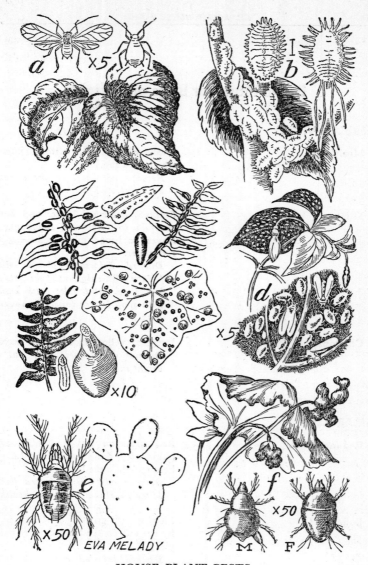

EVA MELADY

HOUSE–PLANT PESTS

The most commonly encountered insect pests of house plants are: (a) Plant Lice or Aphids—both the wingless and winged forms are shown; (b) Mealybug; (c) Scale insects of various types—the Hemispherical, Long, Fern, and Red scales (on Ivy leaf) are shown; (d) White Fly, in adult and nymph stages; (e) Red Spider; and (f) Cyclamen Mite

Battle Plans for Bugs and Blights

AFRICAN-VIOLET

Mealybugs

Oval, white, soft, cottony insects which suck sap.
Remove with soft brush; discard badly infested plants.

Mites

Stunted, deformed leaves and flowers due to Cyclamen mite; glassy leaves, to broad mite; yellowing to red spider.
Discard deformed plants; dust foliage with sulphur; space pots so leaves do not touch; wash hands with soap before touching healthy plants.

Chlorosis

Irregular yellow mottling on leaves.
Do not wet leaves; keep out of bright sun.

AMARYLLIS

Red fire disease

Red spots on leaves, flowers, and bulb scales; flower stalks and foliage bent and deformed.
Remove and burn infected parts. Make sure new bulbs are healthy.

Bulb flies

Maggots of greater or lesser bulb fly eat out centers and destroy basal plate.
Discard infested bulbs; or treat with hot water at 110–111.5° F. for four hours.

Mealybugs

May infest bulb scales and leaf bases.
Scrub off with nicotine sulphate and soap solution.

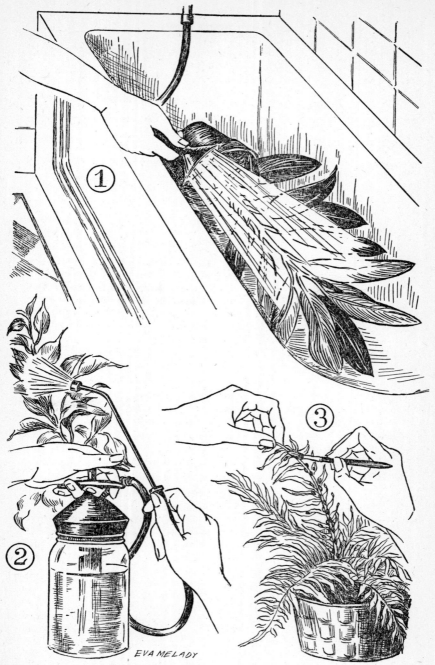

EVA MELADY

Controlling Plant Pests: (1) forceful spraying with clear water; (2) hand sprayer for applying insecticides; (3) method of applying insecticides to scales

ASPIDISTRA

Leaf spots

White spots, brown margins on leaf blades, stalks; pale spots on leaves.
Remove and burn infected leaves.

Chlorosis

Yellow leaves, possibly due to too strong light.
Try location out of direct sunshine.

Fern scale

White male, brown female scales.
See Fern.

AZALEA

Red Spider

Leaves yellow, webby, mealy on underside.
Grow at low temperature, high humidity; syringe foliage.

Lace bugs

Leaves stippled whitish; brown spots underneath.
Spray with nicotine sulphate and soap.

Chlorosis

Yellowing from too alkaline soil; iron unavailable.
Use plenty of acid peat in potting soil.

BEGONIA

Mealybugs

White, dusty bugs in axils of leaves and branches.
Spray with nicotine-soap before blooming or syringe with pure water, or remove with toothpick swab.

Aphids

Serious injury from Melon aphids and others if numerous.
Syringe with water, or spray with nicotine-soap solution; during blooming use rotenone or pyrethrum.

Leaf nematodes

Discolored russet areas in leaves, which curl up and drop.
Keep plants well separated; avoid handling or wetting foliage; dip leaves in hot water (115–118° F.) for three minutes.

Mites

See African-violet.

Blight

Grayish mold on leaves and flowers.
Avoid syringing; remove infected parts.

Leaf drop

Foliage loss from too heavy, wet soil, hot, dry air, or drafts.
Use porous soil, cool room, high humidity.

CALLA-LILY

Root rot

Leaves streaked, flowers malformed and brown.
Destroy infected plants and soil.

Soft rot

Base of stem and corms decayed.
Discard infected corms.

Aphids

Occasionally numerous on leaves.
Spray with nicotine-soap solution.

CACTI

Mealybugs

White, fuzzy insects at base of spines causing yellowing.
Remove with pointed brush; try mist spray, nicotine sulphate, or pure water (plant on side); as last resort use Volck 1-50; wash off later with water.

Root mealybugs

Live in soil on outer roots; may kill plant.
Remove from pot, wash off soil and insects; repot in clean soil.

Scale

Grayish, circular, hard-shelled insects.
Scrape off with soft brush or rag.

Red spider

Mealy cobwebs over yellowish surface.
Spray of water with plant on side.

Rot

Decay starting around wounds or depressed areas.
Do not water from above or overwater; cut out infected parts.

COLEUS

Mealybugs

White cottony insects at leaf and branch axils.
Spray with nicotine sulphate and soap, Volck or Lemon Oil, wash off with water, or remove with cotton swab on toothpick dipped in alcohol.

Black leg

Stalks black, water-soaked at base, plant wilts, may die.
Destroy infected plants; use fresh soil for new cuttings.

CRASSULA

Mealybugs

Neglected plants often covered with bits of white fluff.
See Coleus.

Mites

Leaves rusty brown, rough, finally die.
See Cyclamen.

CYCLAMEN

Mites

Leaves deformed, curled; blooms distorted; plant stunted due to mites too small to see with naked eye.
Spray with nicotine-soap solution or rotenone, or dust with sulphur; space so that leaves do not touch; immerse in nicotine solution or hot water at 110° F. for fifteen minutes; try a small ball of paradichlorobenzene in pot.

EVA MELADY

Some House Plant Troubles: (1) ring spot on Peperomia, with resulting stunted growth (normal plant at right); (2) Chlorosis of African-violet foliage; (3) Powdery Mildew on Kalanchoe; (4) leaf spot on Aspidistra; (5) leggy growth due to insufficient light; (6) gas injury to Begonia (normal plant at left)

Rot

Soft, slimy rot at crown; plant wilts.
Water from below; do not wet crown.

Yellowing

Yellowing and drooping after plant leaves florist.
Keep in cool sunroom (not over 60° F.) and place pot in saucer with an inch of water.

DIEFFENBACHIA

Leaf spots

Orange spots with bacterial ooze, or reddish-brown spots with decidedly darker borders; the first infection often entering through open wounds
Avoid syringing plants; space far apart; control mealybugs and avoid wounds.

DRACAENA

Red spider

Minute eight-legged mites which cause yellowing of leaves and general debility of infested plant.
Sponge foliage weekly.

Leaf spots

Brown areas, yellow margins, black dots in center, or tip blight.
Cut off and burn infected parts; try copper carbonate as spray.

FERNS

Scales
   Soft brown
   Fern

Low, convex, reddish-brown scale.
Males white, conspicuous, females ocher-brown.

Florida wax

Convex, oval scales.

Hemispherical

Large, convex, brown scales on fronds and stem.
Dip fronds in nicotine sulphate-soap solution or spray with Lemon Oil or Volck (with the exception of the Maidenhair); rinse thoroughly with water three to four hours after treatment; keep plant out of sun temporarily. Controlling ants will help.

Mealybugs	Long-tailed type sometimes on fronds. *See Scales.*
Nematodes	Reddish to black bands from midrib to border of fronds caused by microscopic eelworms. *Remove and burn infested leaves or plants; can immerse Bird's Nest Fern in hot water, 110° F., for ten minutes.*
Florida Fern caterpillar	Fronds stripped at night by green or black, white-striped caterpillars. *Spray or dust with rotenone or pyrethrum.*
Anthracnose	Tips of Boston Fern turn brown and shrivel. *Keep foliage dry; remove infected leaves.*
Tip blight	Loss of color; ash-gray spots with purple margins. *Spray with dilute (1-1-50) Bordeaux mixture.*
Sooty mold	Dark fungus growing in honeydew secreted by scales and mealybugs. *Control insects.*

FUCHSIA

White flies	Plants turn yellow, wilt, and are covered with minute white four-winged flies, pale-green oval nymphs. *Spray frequently with nicotine-soap solution, or pyrethrum or thiocyanate spray; hit underside of foliage.*
Mealybugs	White, cottony insects often present in leaf axils which suck sap, causing yellowing and general debility of plant. *Control as for white fly. See also Coleus.*
Sooty mold	Growing in white-fly honeydew. *See Ferns.* *Control insects.*

GARDENIA

Chlorosis

Yellow leaves due to soil too alkaline, iron unavailable, too wet or too dry, too low humidity.

Keep pH of soil around 5.6; temperature 62° F.; pot in sandy loam with ⅓ peatmoss; if yellowing persists, water with ferrous sulphate (1 ounce to 4 gallons water).

Bud drop

Buds yellow and drop off just before opening; due to high temperature plus lack of sun.

Cooler temperature in winter.

Mealybugs

Wipe off with cotton dipped in alcohol. See also Coleus.

White flies

See Fuchsia.

Sooty mold

See Ferns.

GERANIUM (*Pelargonium*)

White flies

Leaves turn yellow, drop, often covered with sooty mold.

Spray with warm nicotine solution using excess of soap and rinsing off next day. See Fuchsia.

Mites

Young leaves curled, spotted, look scorched.

See Cyclamen.

Black leg stem rot

Cuttings rot at base, stems of older plants turn black.

Take cuttings only from healthy plants; use fresh or sterilized sand for rooting.

Blight

Gray mold over water-soaked areas in leaves and blossoms.

Avoid overwatering; keep tops dry.

Oedema

Water-soaked spots, turning corky—physiological disease.

Do not overwater in cloudy weather when transpiration is reduced.

IVY

Red spider
Leaves yellowish, cobwebby, and sticky.
Prevent by weekly bath in cool water; if established, dip foliage in nicotine-sulphate solution or immerse for thirty seconds in water at 120° F.; grow at cooler temperature.

Aphids
Black lice clustering on new growth; leaves drop.
See Red Spider

Scale
Oleander scale (males white, females buff) or soft brown scale.
Scrub off with soapy water or spray with nicotine-soap, Lethane, Loro, or Volck.

Mealybugs
More common on Grape Ivy.
See Scale, above, and Coleus.

Leaf spots
Greenish, water-soaked spots turning brownish.
Avoid high temperatures and keeping the foliage too wet.

JERUSALEM-CHERRY

Gray mold
Grayish yellowing of leaves and fruit, which shrivels.
Provide better aeration; avoid syringing.

KALANCHOE

Stem-rot wilt
Blackened stems, rotting flower stalks, wilting.
Use porous soil; avoid nitrogenous fertilizer; do not plant too deep or overwater.

Powdery mildew
Gray-white mealy growth on leaves and stem.
Dust with sulphur.

NARCISSUS (Paper-white)

Blind buds

Buds do not develop, or blast, due to starting too early, growing at too high temperature, insufficient water.
Start after October 15, root in dark then bring to light in cool room; keep roots covered with water.

Rot

Bulbs decay.
Do not let water cover top of bulb.

PALM

Scales

Many species on leaves.
Keep leaves sponged off with soapy water. See Ferns.

Leaf spots

Gray or brown spots.
Cut out infected parts.

PEPEROMIA

Ring spot

Foliage disfigured with concentric zonal markings, probably caused by a virus.
Discard infected plants; keep free from insects.

PHILODENDRON

Dying leaves

Possibly due to root injury or too dry air.
Grow in water with piece of charcoal or in soil watered regularly.

PICKA-BACK (Tolmiea)

Mealybugs

See Coleus.
Grow in cool room.

POINSETTIA

Mealybugs

Common on underside of leaves and in axils.
Remove with toothpick; wash with water. See Coleus.

Root aphids

Yellow-green cottony lice infest roots.
Loosen earth ball and immerse in nicotine-soap solution at 110° F.

Leaf drop

Leaves yellow and drop.
Keep Christmas plants in warm, light, humid room; do not place by cold windows at night.

PRIMROSE

Blight

Gray mold on leaves and flowers.
Keep foliage dry; remove infected parts.

RUBBER PLANT

Anthracnose

Tip burn and scorching of foliage.
Pick off and burn infected leaves. Do not let water stand on foliage.

Scales

Several species on leaves.
Keep leaves wiped off, or spray. See Ferns.

Mealybugs

At base of leaves and undersides, with sooty mold growing in honey-dew.
Wipe off or spray. See Coleus.

SANSEVIERIA

Leaf spot

Sunken reddish-brown spot, yellow borders.
Destroy diseased leaves; avoid syringing.

CHAPTER XVII

Flowering Plants

THE successful cultivation of flowering plants provides a thrill of accomplishment that one does not get in so large a measure from foliage plants. Except for the few constantly in bloom, they provide a change in the decorative scheme and add a note of gaiety to the ensemble. The annual show put on by the exquisitely beautiful though evanescent flowers of the Apostle Plant (*Marica*), and the gorgeous blooms of Hippeastrum and Orchid Cactus, give us something to look forward to. Some flowers, while not especially ornamental—for example, those of Hearts Entangled (*Ceropegia*)—intrigue us with their interesting structure; and some, such as the Fragrant Olive (*Osmanthus*), please us with their scent.

With the exception of African-violet, which will bloom in a north window, and a few others, such as Hepatica and Lily-of-the-Valley, which are transients so far as house culture is concerned, flowering plants demand the light afforded by east, south, or west windows, though sometimes it is necessary to shield them from undiluted sunshine.

For convenience in dealing with cultural details, it is desirable to group them to some extent as follows: (1) those which may be kept year after year; (2) annuals, and those which, though perennial, are best renewed annually; (3) bulbs, corms, and tubers; (4) Cacti and succulents; (5) Orchids; (6) those which are definitely shrubby in habit; (7) those grown primarily for their fruits; (8) vines and trailers; (9) "gift plants," many of which are not adapted to permanent culture in a home; and (10) house plants throughout the year, with timetable.

PERENNIALS

Anthuriums: Surely the record for "long-lastingest" must be held
by the inflorescence of *Anthurium scherzerianum*. I received a plant
in a 3-inch pot at the end of September with a bloom which did not
fade until a new one started at the end of December! This species
is comparatively small—about a foot tall—with a deep red spathe
and a coral-colored, curly spadix decorated with tiny circles of
white pollen. It is not commonly offered by dealers, but its ease of
culture and tolerance of house conditions make it worthy of the
effort of shopping around. It needs a well-drained pot and a soil
mixture of Orchid peat (Osmunda fiber), Sphagnum Moss, charcoal, and sand, with plenty of moisture.

Other Anthuriums—those spectacular kinds known under the
generic title of Flamingo Flowers, whose showy spathes look as
though they had been varnished—are not easy to grow but are
worthy of a trial by those who have warm, *moist* air in their homes
at all times. These grow much larger than *A. scherzerianum*—up to
3 feet high and as much across.

Beloperone (Shrimp Plant): The Shrimp Plant, *Beloperone guttata,* is a comparatively new introduction to the house-plant scene.
About 18 inches tall, its leaves are ordinary, but its inflorescence is
showy. The flowers are white, spotted with purple. The chief effect,
however, is made by the long-lasting reddish-brown bracts beneath
which the flowers originate. (Bracts are leafy or membranous organs,
often brightly colored, usually associated with inflorescence. The
conspicuous parts of the inflorescences of Dogwood and Poinsettia
are bracts.) The chief defect of the Shrimp Plant is its tendency toward gawkiness and bare legs. This can be overcome to some extent
by raising new plants annually from cuttings and pinching out tips
of shoots in the early stages to promote bushiness. It needs sunshine, a well-drained pot, general potting mixture, and plenty of
water at the roots.

Begonia—various species and varieties: In more ways than
one Begonia heads the list of house plants which may be looked on
as permanent and annual bloomers. The genus is a large one with
the estimated number of species ranging between 500 and 1,300;

and the number of varieties produced by crossing and otherwise runs into the thousands. It is a group which offers splendid opportunities for the collector provided he has the right growing conditions—moist air free from deleterious gas, 60°–65° temperature, abundant light, but no undiluted sun during the summer months. The fact that country dwellers succeed in growing Begonias to perfection while urbanites fail miserably with most varieties is an indication of the importance of clean, moist air. Without devoting a book entirely to them (which already has been done by Bessie Buxton and others) it is impossible to do more than sketch in the highlights; therefore many desirable species and varieties must go unmentioned.

Angel Wing Begonia (*Begonia coccinea*), often sold under the name *B. rubra,* has tall, cane-like stems, oblique leaves about 5 inches long, and coral-red flowers in clusters. It has many excellent named varieties such as Dielytra, Lady Lou, and Shasta; and is one of the parents of several hybrids—President Carnot, Lucerna, Marjorie Dow, and many others, some of which have leaves marked with silvery spots.

The semi-tuberous group could be represented by **B. dregei,** which has annual freely branching succulent stems rising to a height up to 3 feet with conspicuous swellings on the older portions. The white flowers are produced profusely in winter. This species should be rested by keeping the soil definitely on the dry side after growth and flowering are completed.

Beefsteak (what a name!) **Begonia** (*B. feasti*) is one of the very common house plants in country districts. It has thick, almost round leaves, green above and red beneath, with white whiskers on the margins. The flowers are pink, carried effectively above the foliage in winter. According to one catalogue this is "the finest pot Begonia for house culture. Grown as easily as a Geranium." This is probably true, but with me the flower stalks blast when they are about 6 inches tall. I advance my usual alibi—impure air—to account for this. (*Begonia heracleifolia,* which we shall come to in a couple of paragraphs, seems to be unaffected.) There is a variety of *B. feasti,* known as *bunchi,* which has the edges of the leaves crested and ruffled, and one in which the lobes are spiraled like a snail's shell.

Begonia haageana. (*See B. scharffi.*)

The specific name of **B. heracleifolia,** Star Begonia, means "having leaves like the Cow-parsnip," which is good enough so far as it goes because in general outline they do resemble that coarse perennial herb. But you should imagine a much refined Cow-parsnip, with smaller leaves marked with silver, red, or black-green in some of the varieties; and white or rose-colored flowers on stalks which may be from 2 to 4 feet long and produced from February to April. This is one of the toughest of the Begonias and I have before me a plant in a 4½-inch pot with leaves 8 inches in diameter and two flower stalks which look as though they will attain 2 feet in spite of the cramped quarters occupied by the roots.

A spring-blooming kind, **B. manicata,** is remarkable for the striking fleshy red hairs arranged in collars around the leafstalks. The pink flowers are displayed in airy, elegant panicles on foot-long stalks and are very effective. There is a variety, *aureo-maculata,* the leaves of which are blotched with white and yellow; and *crispa,* whose leaves have crested and ruffled edges.

Begonia metallica is a handsome plant about 4 feet high when well grown. Its leaves are glossy olive-green above with metallic purple veins and red beneath. The flowers, borne in clusters, are large and light pink in color. It has long been known as an excellent house plant.

I am looking at a nurseryman's catalogue which lists over fifty named varieties of *Begonia rex,* the **Painted Leaf Begonia.** This does not by any means represent all the forms there are of this extraordinarily variable species which includes a series in which the leaf lobes are spiraled like the end of a snail's shell. The flowers of the Rex Begonias are nothing much in comparison with the leaves, which are among the most decorative of any in the plant kingdom. They often have a metallic sheen, and exhibit an array of colors, arranged in broad, irregular zones, impossible to describe accurately. Among the varieties commonly grown are Beauty of Pembroke, Lord Palmerston, Louise Closson, Magnifica, Perle de Paris, and Rajah.

These Begonias are not for those who have nothing but hot, dry rooms in which to grow them unless they are kept within the confines of a Wardian case to give them the moist air they need. But those who live in regions where an excessive amount of artificial heat is unnecessary, and can supply them with plenty of light without direct sun, should by all means give them a trial.

Begonia ricinifolia is a hybrid, very vigorous, with large leaves arising from a prostrate rootstock which, less deeply lobed than *B. heracleifolia* (one of its parents), are bronzy green and resemble those of *Ricinus,* the Castor-oil plant. The rose-pink flowers are displayed in panicles a foot or more across on stems up to 4 feet tall, in winter and early spring.

If you are looking for a plant to display in a large hanging container consider **B. scandens.** This has drooping stems (they may be trained on a support if preferred) clothed with comparatively small, shiny, light green leaves and abundant white flowers. When well grown, it needs plenty of room, for the stems may attain a length of 6 feet.

One of the most beautiful Begonias is **B. scharffi,** which has large rose-pink flowers in hanging clusters and is almost never out of bloom, though most floriferous in summer. An upright grower with hairy olive-green leaves, red on the undersides, it is often listed under the name *haageana.* Another source of confusion is one named *B. scharffiana,* an entirely different plant with white flowers, reputed to be difficult to grow.

The best known of all is the **Wax Begonia** (*B. semperflorens*) used largely as a bedding plant outdoors in summer. The method of handling it from seeds for use as a house plant is described on page 130; but it should be remembered that the Wax Begonia is a perennial and may live five years or longer. It is a tremendously variable species with many named varieties and a number of hybrids. The varieties may be grouped as tall, medium, and dwarf. Recommended varieties are: Tall—Christmas Cheer, deep crimson; Masterpiece, large flowers, pink; Pink Radio, rose; Silver Wings, large flowers, white. Medium—Carmen, bronze leaves, rose-pink flowers; Darling, light pink; Indian Maid, bronze leaves, scarlet flowers; King of the Reds; Scandinavia White. Dwarf—Adeline, bright pink; Ball Red; Ball White; Luminosa Compacta, scarlet red. A rare but beautiful variety, difficult to grow, is Westport Beauty, with small rose-like double flowers.

The **Calla-lily Begonia** belongs in the *semperflorens* group. New England housewives seem to have better success with this variety than professional growers farther south, even though the latter have the asset of a greenhouse. This seems to indicate that summer coolness is a factor in its successful culture. Overwatering is to be avoided. This is the Begonia whose youngest leaves are white and have a remote resemblance in form to a Calla-lily. There is considerable variation in the color of the flowers and the habit of the plant; and there is a variety with double flowers known as Calla Ruby Jewel.

The spectacular and floriferous hybrids of the **Gloire de Lorraine** group, resulting from a cross between *B. socotrana* and *B. dregei,* sold in immense numbers in florists' stores around Christmas, are not adapted for house culture.

The leaves of **B. templini,** which has clustered pink flowers from January to March, are blotched with white, yellow, and red, and have ruffled margins. This is reputed to be a sport of *B. phyllomaniaca,* a species characterized by an amazing production of tiny plantlets on the leaves and stems.

Begonias will grow in a variety of soils provided only that they are porous. One very successful grower in California recommends 2 parts rather coarse leafmold, 1 part cow manure, 1 part sandy loam, with a sprinkling of commercial fertilizer and fine charcoal. Another, in New York, suggests a rather heavier soil for kinds such as *feasti, heracleifolia, manicata, ricinifolia,* et cetera, namely: equal parts loam, leafmold, sand with ⅛ part by bulk of dried cow manure and a pint of bonemeal to each bushel. Or you could use the mixture for Begonias suggested on page 51.

While the soil must be made sufficiently firm to hold the plants upright, it should be left looser than for the general run of pot plants. The pots *must be well drained*—put a concave piece of broken pot over the hole in the bottom, and on that a layer, ½ to 1 inch deep, depending on the size of the pot, of crocks broken into pieces of about ½-inch size. This will help to prevent fatal waterlogging. Except for tuberous and semi-tuberous varieties (which should be kept dry, or nearly so, during their resting periods), the soil should be watered thoroughly whenever it is beginning to get dry.

Shade Begonias from bright sunshine except in the depth of winter; avoid exposing them to drafts and violent fluctuations of temperature. If they are placed outdoors in summer, it should be in a situation sheltered from strong winds.

The popular summer-flowering garden race of Tuberous Begonias, to which the name *B. tuberhybrida* has been applied, is discussed in Section 4, p. 193.

The Begonias form a fascinating group, exceedingly diverse, and yet all exhibiting definite characters which enable one at once to say "This is a Begonia." Window gardeners are fortunate that so many of them are amenable to house culture because they are free-flowering, long-blooming, and most of them have decorative foliage.

Bromeliads, Air-pines: For more than twenty-five years I have been a voice in the wilderness advocating without much effect the use of Bromeliads as house plants. During the past few years, however, there has been considerable interest shown in them and at least two commercial growers—one in Florida and one in California —are featuring them. These relatives of the Pineapple are extraordinarily interesting and infinitely varied, ranging from the soft, slender droopiness of the Spanish Moss to the harsh uprightness of some of the Hohenbergias. Some grow in soil; others perch themselves on rocks, trees, or even telegraph wires. Practically all have decorative foliage and the inflorescences of some exhibit color combinations unique in the vegetable kingdom. Here, for example, are some flower descriptions culled at random from a catalogue before me: "flower head, maroon, green, and yellow" (*Aechmea fosteriana*); "pink bracts, green petals edged with blue" (*Billbergia nutans*); (I might add that this species has conspicuous golden anthers providing another note in color contrasts); "spectacular flower head of yellow, gray, and purple" (*Tillandsia capitata*).

In general, they belong to the group known to botanists as xerophytes. That is, they are especially adapted to survive periods of drought. They seem to be able to withstand dim light and all kinds of neglect (though this is not advocated in their culture!). I have seen offsets of several species of *Cryptanthus* inadvertently knocked off the plants, kicked around on the greenhouse floor, finally to come to rest in the gravel under the benches where they rooted and throve. Practically all that I have tried under house conditions have done well, though doubtless there are some, Spanish Moss, for example, which will refuse to thrive. I have a specimen of *Neoregelia carolinae* which I kept for a time in an unheated, poorly lighted basement room; then it was placed in a sunny window and given the reasonably good conditions of the plant room; then it took a long trip in a cold auto to be photographed in a decorative window arrangement. Now it is in the dry living room (the humidifier on the furnace is not working!), beginning to develop a brilliant crimson coloration on the central leaves which is, I hope, preliminary to the production of its lavender flowers.

This is a large family of about a thousand species and many hybrids; obviously only a few can be mentioned here: *Aechmea marmorata,* **Grecian Vase,** has stiff, recurving, mottled leaves in vase-like form. Originating from the center, the pendulous inflorescence carries pale pink bracts and blue-petaled flowers. *A. fulgens* has pale green spreading leaves from a basal rosette and numerous blue-tipped flowers with red calyxes arranged on a stiff panicle which remains ornamental over an extended period. Many other Aechmeas are equally worthy of cultivation.

Some of the Billbergias have their leaves arranged to give an almost tubular effect; in common with many Bromeliads the clasping bases are constructed to hold water. **Billbergia nutans,** the parent of many hybrids, has already been mentioned. A hybrid of *B. saundersi,* which I am trying to induce to bloom, has green leaves, suffused with reddish tones, mottled pale green and white, with faint gray bars on the undersides. They are abruptly recurved at the tip. The flowers will be likely to have green petals tipped with blue attended by brilliant red bracts. The Billbergias are among the most free-blooming of the Bromeliads.

As might be guessed from the name, Cryptanthus, this genus is not noteworthy for its floral display, but some species make up for it by their bizarre foliage. Mention has already been made of their toughness. In recent years several species have been noticed appearing rather frequently in commercial made-up dish gardens.

Cryptanthus bivittatus, a practically stemless kind, has leaves with undulating spiny margins striped with brownish green and pinkish cream. They seem to do equally well in a sunny window and in rather dense shade. *Cryptanthus zonatus* ought to be called Zebra Plant (maybe it is!) from the crinkly leaves marked with transverse bands of white, green, and brown. These have a tendency to extend themselves horizontally and recurve as though trying to clasp the pot in which they are growing. A very striking plant.

Guzmannia zahni, which I have never seen in bloom, has curving leaves up to 2 feet long, gracefully arranged in a rosette. They are almost translucent and have longitudinal pencilings of bronze and red, which gives a delightful effect when the leaves are seen against strong light. In my experience this is not so amenable to house culture as some of the other Bromeliads and probably needs more atmospheric moisture than I am able to supply.

Neoregelia carolinae (also sold as *Aregelia* and *Nidularium*) I have already spoken of. Other noteworthy species are *N. marmorata,* with leaves almost a foot long, marbled with red-brown patches. It's head of pale violet flowers is produced down in the center of the rosette. Painted Fingernail (*Neoregelia spectabilis*) looks as though someone had dipped his thumb in red ink and pressed it on the tip of each leaf. This makes a rosette of foot-long curving leaves slightly undulated along the margins and barred on the reverse with narrow bands of silvery scurflike hairs. This is another species which has been pushed around from pillar to post in my house without any apparent ill effects.

Nidularium innocenti has leaves tinted with reddish brown; the central leaves become bright red prior to the production of the white flowers well down in the center of the rosette. *N. striatum* has broad lorate (strap-shaped) leaves conspicuously striped with white. The plant is vase-like in form and, if desired, cut flowers can be placed in the water-holding bases of the leaves.

Spanish Moss (*Tillandsia* or *Dendropogon usneoides*) has several relatives with long 1½-foot slender, tapering leaves gracefully arranged in rosettes. I have not myself tried these in the house, but some years ago I gave one, *T. fasciculata,* to a friend who, to the best of my recollection, reported excellent results. Neither have I tried *T. lindeniana* with tapering green leaves and a spectacular inflorescence. The carmine bracts are closely imbricated (overlapping) to form a flattened structure which reminds one of a cock's comb. The large purple flowers emerge in succession from the bracts, alternately from side to side over a long period.

Vriesia carinata has an inflorescence somewhat similar to the above, but more loosely constructed, and the bracts are scarlet at the base and yellowish at the tip; the flowers are pale yellow; the leaves are thin and pale green. *V. hieroglyphica* is grown chiefly for its foliage strongly marked with dark hieroglyphs.

Many Bromeliads hold water in considerable quantities in their leaf bases which makes them worthy of consideration as humidifiers and enables them to be used as living vases. Care should be taken when inserting cut flowers to avoid injury to the leaves of the "vase."

I have had best success with those Bromeliads which grow on

trees and rocks by growing them in pots filled ⅓ with broken flower-pot (they resent stagnant water around their roots, which must have access to air) ; and using Orchid peat (Osmunda fiber) mixed with a few lumps of charcoal as a potting medium. Osmunda fiber sometimes is difficult for amateurs to obtain unless they have access to a swamp in which Osmunda Ferns are growing, so that they can dig their own. Possible substitutes are flaky leafmold or peatmoss, mixed with equal parts coarse sand and charcoal broken into ¼-inch pieces.

During winter they should be kept on the dry side at the roots, but the leaf bases of those equipped to hold water should be kept filled. Occasional overhead spraying is good. It is believed that certain cells in the leaf bases are capable of absorbing nutrients contained in the water they hold. Don't, however, try to help them along by adding commercial fertilizer to the water. This was once done to a collection under my charge (without first consulting me) with disastrous results. In many species the old rosette is useless after flowering and should be discarded, and the young plants developing around it potted up separately to carry on.

The terrestrial species *Ananas* (Pineapple), *Bromelia, Dyckia, Hechtia,* et cetera, should be potted in sandy soil with about ⅓ leafmold and ⅙ rotted cow manure. Avoid overwatering them during winter. These, with a few exceptions, are less appealing than the epiphytic kinds. *Bromelia* is too spiny to be handled comfortably. The Dyckias, though their flowers are interesting, have stiff and rather forbidding leaves. *Hechtia argentea,* however, even though spiny, is so spectacular with its dense rosette of silvery, recurving leaves, 1 inch wide and up to 2 feet long, that it is worth a trial if it can be obtained. I have never grown it in the house and it is reputed to be difficult of culture even in a greenhouse. *Ananas comosus,* the Pineapple of commerce, has several varieties in which the leaves are variously striped with white or yellow, some with reddish tones. These are well worth growing and under very favorable conditions might even produce fruit.

Impatiens—Patience Plant: The names Patience Plant and Patient Lucy are interesting examples of how the original meaning of a plant name can be reversed. The vernacular names are derived from the botanical name *Impatiens,* coming from the Latin meaning "impatient," referring to the sudden bursting of the seed pods.

Patience Plant has for many years been favored as a house plant because of its long-blooming habits, ease of culture, and tolerance. The Patience Plants originally grown as house plants were *Impatiens sultani* (known also as Zanzibar Balsam) ; then a very similar species, *I. holsti,* also a good house plant, was introduced to cultivation; hybrids between the two were produced so that the nomenclatorial situation today is in pretty much of a mix-up. Some of the plants going under the name of Patience are *I. sultani;* some are *I. holsti;* and some are hybrids.

There are many house-plant enthusiasts who try to collect all the different forms, of which there are many, with flowers ranging in color from white through pink to scarlet and purplish; and there are varieties with variegated or bronze-colored leaves. Under favorable conditions *I. sultani* may make a compact, bushy plant 2 feet high; *I. holsti* may get a little larger. If they become too large for their quarters, they may be cut back in the spring; but if small plants are preferred, a better way to handle them is to start new plants from seeds annually in May or June; or from cuttings in midsummer. A package of seeds is likely to produce several forms; the best can be propagated by cuttings and the remainder discarded. Use general-purpose mixture for potting with the addition of a cupful or so of pulverized limestone to each bushel of soil if it is on the acid side. Avoid overpotting—large plants can be produced in small pots. Give a sunny situation during the winter months; in summer half-shade is desirable.

Marica—Apostle Plant: The Apostle Plant, or Twelve Apostles, is so called because the individual fans or tufts commonly contain twelve leaves. These are sword-shaped, about 2 feet long, light green, and very decorative. It is a much more effective plant when only one "fan" is allowed to develop in each pot. The species most commonly grown, and the best, is *Marica northiana.* Very few commercial growers offer it for sale—perhaps because it is so easily obtained from friends by those who wish to grow it. The exquisite but ephemeral iris-like flowers are 3 to 4 inches across and pure white, with the inner segments marked with violet. The other species sometimes grown in the house is *M. gracilis,* smaller in all its parts. Its white flowers are marked with yellow, brown, and blue. Old plants of either species may be divided after flowering; or the plantlets which sometimes develop on the flowering stems may be used for propagation. Seldom attacked by insects, *Marica* needs nothing more than routine care and general-purpose mixture for potting.

Pelargonium—Geranium: The semi-shrubby plants commonly known as Geraniums, but more correctly as Pelargoniums, fall into four groups, any one of which contains enough varieties to make it worthy of the consideration of the "collector." These are (1) Show Pelargonium (*Pelargonium domesticum*), also known as Lady Washington Geraniums and Pansy-flowered Geraniums; (2) House Geraniums (*P. hortorum*), also known as Bedding, Horseshoe, Fish, and Zonal Geraniums; (3) Ivy-leaved Geraniums (*P. peltatum*); (4) Scented-leaved Geraniums, represented by many species.

The Lady Washington types are *not* perpetual bloomers. The showy flowers, often conspicuously marked with black or dark-colored blotches, are produced around Easter at the tips of the shoots rather than several inches back, as is the habit of the next group. There are many varieties ranging in color from apple-blossom pink (Gardener's Joy) to amaranth red (Easter Greeting). Other good varieties are Mme. Layal, pink, white, purple, and black; and Schwaben Maid, black-blotched, reddish carmine.

Cuttings may be taken after flowering and grown outdoors until September, when they should be brought indoors and kept in a sunny window. During the early stages of growth, judicious pinching of the tips of shoots should be practiced to promote bushiness and a shapely plant. Do not carry on with this beyond February lest you destroy potential flowering shoots. Keep cool during the winter (50°) and be careful to avoid overwatering. In February and March, when they begin to grow, a sprinkling of commercial fertilizer (teaspoon to 6-inch pot) on the surface will be helpful. After flowering, the plants may be placed outdoors and rested by keeping them on the dry side. In August or early September prune them into shape and cut out weak shoots. Repot them in general-purpose mixture; if the pot becomes crowded with roots, shift into a larger size pot in January.

There is a bewildering number of varieties in the Zonal Geraniums, with single or double flowers; some with handsomely colored foliage. Good varieties are: Alphonse Ricard, scarlet, semi-double; Beaute Poitevine, salmon; Mme. Buchner, white; Paul Crampel, scarlet; Peach Blossom, pink and white; Pink Beauty, rose-pink; Radio Red, scarlet; S. A. Nutt, semi-double, dark crimson. Varieties with colored foliage are: Happy Thought, green and cream, with dark zone—flowers scarlet; Mme. Salleroi, a dwarf, compact sort with white-edged leaves; Mrs. Pollack, leaves bronzy-red, crimson, and yellow; Wm. Langgreth, leaves edged white; scarlet double flowers.

Although one often sees ancient plants of this group completely filling the window space of country cottages, usually it is a better practice to raise new plants from cuttings (see Chapter XV) annually in May and keep them growing along, but removing all flower buds until October so that they will be vigorous producers of winter blooms.

The Zonal Geraniums are easily raised from seeds sown in pots indoors in spring, but the progeny is likely to be inferior to named varieties. However, it is a cheap way of obtaining Geraniums, and if you should happen to get a superior form, it is easy to perpetuate it by cuttings. Sometimes plants which have served a season planted out in the flower beds are dug up in the fall, cut back, potted up and brought in the house. These are seldom, if ever, satisfactory for winter bloom under the arduous conditions they encounter in the average home. They are not so good-looking as cut-back plants, and it takes them months to grow out of their stumpy awkwardness.

For potting, use general-purpose mixture; make it quite firm in the pot; avoid overpotting, but when roots become crowded, shift into a larger size—preferably not over 6 inches, however. When they have filled the ultimate pots with roots, fertilize with commercial fertilizer every four to five weeks. Keep in sunny window in a cool (45–50° at night) room, and water only when soil is beginning to get dry, then give a thorough soaking.

The Ivy-leaved Geraniums are characterized by the trailing habit and glossy leaves. They are not so easy to grow as the other types and on the whole not so free-flowering, but under favorable conditions they may have blooms from late winter until fall. They are more likely to succeed where the air is not so dry and in regions where the summers are cool. In England they are favored plants to trail over the edges of large outdoor vases in summer. There are many varieties of Ivy-type Geraniums—a commercial grower's list that I have before me has over a score of them. The following are reputed to be free bloomers: Charles Monselet, red; Charles Turner, rose-pink; Comtesse Degrey, salmon pink; Giant Lavender, lavender with red markings; Jeanne d'Arc, lavender with dark stripes;

(*Above*) Among the less usual Geraniums is this scented-leaved type (*Pelargonium graveolens*, var. Filbert)

(*Right*) Another choice Geranium form is the Pansy or Lady Washington (*P. domesticum*)

Begonia feasti, the Beefsteak Begonia, which does well in considerable shade, has decorative foliage and most attractive pink blooms; an old and well worth-while favorite

Rex Begonia, with its large leaves, often spiraled, is valued for its interesting design and coloring; the flowers are inconspicuous

Scarlet Beauty. L'Elegante has variegated leaves and pink flowers. These plants may be displayed in hanging pots or baskets or trained on a trellis in a sunny window.

The scented-leaved Pelargoniums are a varied group in leaf size and structure, in flowers and in fragrance. As a rule their flowers are not so large nor so showy as those in the preceding groups. They are grown partly for their foliage but chiefly for their fragrance— the Rose Geranium, one of the oldest of house plants, is (or was) used to adulterate attar-of-Roses. Sprigs of the small-leaved kinds are in demand to place in fingerbowls, and single leaves of the large varieties are used for the same purpose.

More than fifty species and varieties of scented Pelargoniums are obtainable from specialists dealing in them. A selection of outstanding kinds follows: *P. capitatum,* Rose-scented, large leaves on trailing stems; flowers Rose-purple. *P. crispum,* Lemon-scented, small leaves on compact little bushes; several varieties available, including Prince Rupert with foliage variegated green and white. *P. denticulatum,* large, finely cut leaves prompting the appellation "Skeleton Leaf," which is Pine-scented, with Lilac-colored flowers. *P. graveolens,* one of the old-time Rose Geraniums, with large, deeply lobed and toothed leaves; flowers pink or pale purple. There are several forms of this, distinguished in part by their odor such as balsamic, camphor, and Rose-mint combination. *P. limoneum* is the Lemon Geranium, with larger leaves than *crispum* and showy purplish flowers. *P. odoratissimum,* the Nutmeg Geranium, has rounded leaves about 1½ inches across and small white flowers. There is a form with variegated leaves and one with Apple fragrance. *P. tomentosum* has long-stalked, Peppermint-scented leaves, so clothed with hairs on both sides that they are velvety to the touch. The flowers are small and white.

Pelargoniums in general need what the professional gardener calls a buoyant atmosphere, promoted under greenhouse conditions by free ventilation and the use of artificial heat with ventilators open on dark and muggy days in winter. Go easy on spraying and avoid wetting the leaves when the air is very humid as this favors the fungous diseases which sometimes attack them.

Saintpaulia—African-violet: The African-violet, *Saintpaulia ionantha,* which is not a Violet at all but is related to the Gloxinia, gives the lie to a statement made almost a hundred years ago in a book on window gardening, "that plants with soft, woolly leaves are utterly unfitted for house culture." The rapidity with which African-violets have risen in the esteem of the house-plant public is remarkable. Twenty years ago they were scarcely known outside botanic gardens and the larger private greenhouses. Now almost everyone who grows any house plants at all has at least one specimen; and there are many who make a hobby of collecting the several varieties which have been placed on the market during the past few years.

Its free-flowering habit, ease of culture and propagation, ability to stand the high temperature common in living rooms, and the fact that it thrives even in a north window, have contributed to its popularity. The species has Violet-colored flowers, but the most popular varieties today are Blue Boy, with flowers up to $1\frac{1}{2}$ inches across, and Blue Boy Improved, with still larger flowers. Blue Girl is distinguished by the scalloped edges of its leaves, and White Lady, as the name implies, has white flowers. The names Pink Beauty and Orchid Beauty are descriptions of their flower coloration.

Saintpaulias will grow almost anywhere in the home provided the temperature does not fall below 60°, but they bloom very sparingly in a north window during the winter and give up entirely if they are exposed to the slightest trace of artificial gas. Mine stopped blooming just as soon as the gas furnace was put in operation, and while healthy looking, I do not anticipate flowers, even though they are growing in a sunny window, until the weather allows freer ventilation and less artificial heat.

While they will grow and bloom in a north window, east or west aspects are preferable. They may be grown in a south window provided they are protected from hot sun by thin curtains. Use the humusy soil mixture recommended for these plants (see Chapter VI) and add enough ground limestone, if necessary, to make its reaction pH 6 to 6.5. When potting or repotting, avoid making the soil too firm. They may be divided or repotted into larger pots in the spring—usually the former is preferred. Because of their low stature, they are more effective and there is a better balance between pot and plant when they are kept in pots or bulb pans 4 to 5 inches in diameter. If they are repotted annually, there is little need for additional fertilizer, but when the pots are filled with roots, a 5-10-5 fertilizer could be applied to the surface soil and scratched in every four or five weeks, using at the rate of $\frac{1}{2}$ teaspoon to a 5-inch pot.

African-violets should be kept constantly moist at the roots; they are well adapted to wick-watering. Doubtless you have read or have been told that water should never be allowed to touch the leaves of African-violets, but this is an exploded notion. They are not harmed by overhead watering *provided* the water temperature is not lower than that of the air. I have seen them growing in a greenhouse where they were almost constantly wet with spray from a fountain. While I don't make a practice of spraying mine, they do occasionally get spattered when the other plants get their shower bath, but this has not caused "ring spot," which comes only when water of lower temperature than the air gets on the leaves.

They are not immune to pests, so keep a close watch, especially for mealybugs, and scotch them before they have a chance to get around to laying their eggs. Mite-infested plants—manifested by curling leaves—had better be discarded. (See Chapter XVI.)

New plants may be raised from seeds sown in the spring (flowering is prolonged if seed formation is prevented by snipping off faded flowers; so if plenty of flowers is the objective, let someone else attend to seed production); by leaf cuttings, which root easily in moist sand or in water, and by division. (See Chapter XV.)

The African-violet is one of the few house plants which is not benefited by being placed outdoors in summer, and it does not seem to require a resting period.

ANNUALS, AND OTHERS TREATED AS ANNUALS

We now come to those plants which usually give better results if they are renewed annually. Some of these are true annuals—that is, they die when they have performed their function of seed production; but others (some of them shrubs) are perennial in nature.

Personally I must confess I have not been any too successful in deliberately raising annuals for house use. This can be attributed to lack of interest (a reprehensible idiosyncrasy, no doubt) and to procrastination, which resulted in starting the seeds when the days were approaching their shortest. However, even at that, Sweet Alyssum and Garden Balsam grew and bloomed freely, even though they were not transplanted from the 3-inch pots in which they were sown.

My best success with annuals has been with seedlings dug up from the flower border early in the fall, notably with Flowering Tobacco. Those who have a garden in which such plants as Wax Begonia (not an annual), Sweet Alyssum, Marigold, Nicotiana, and Torenia are grown will find it profitable to hunt around and in between the plants with a view to picking up seedlings originating from self-sown seeds. Of course if you are meticulous in the use of the hoe you may not find any, but if you are like me, always biting off more than one can chew, and in consequence having only time to hit the more conspicuous spots with the hoe, you are likely to find plenty from which to choose.

Medium-sized plants are preferred because they can be dug up with the root system nearly intact, resulting in almost no check to growth when the plants are potted up. Nicotianas about 6 inches in diameter; Begonias, Sweet Alyssum, Marigolds, and Torenia of 3 to 4 inches in size will be about right. Pot them in well-drained pots large enough to receive the root ball, water thoroughly, and stand them in a shady place for a week or so before bringing them indoors. Then give them a sunny window indoors and pot them in larger pots when the roots become crowded.

You can, if you wish, make a seedbed outdoors and sow the seeds of these, and others mentioned below, in May (for Begonias), June July, or early August, but you will have the trouble of caring for them and will miss the pleasure that comes from getting something for practically nothing.

You may be tempted to dig up small **Snapdragons**, *Antirrhinum majus* varieties from the border, but these are not likely to be so successful as the strains developed primarily for winter blooming. Seeds of these may be sown in July; or you may find it more convenient to get a few plants from your local florist in the fall. These should be grown as cool as possible—50° at night is sufficient.

Browallia speciosa is a semi-trailing plant, usually about a foot tall though it may get larger, with freely produced violet-blue flowers in the variety *major* up to 2 inches across. The seeds of these may be started any time from June to August. This Browallia, with its color forms—white, pale lilac, and blue—is, for some obscure reason, seldom offered in the seed catalogues; but *B. viscosa*, var. Sapphire, not nearly so attractive, appears in almost every list—perhaps because it produces seeds more freely. This is an upright grower with small flowers but worth growing if you can't get *speciosa major*.

There are two types of **Forget-me-not** commonly grown—the True Forget-me-not, *Myosotis scorpioides*, a Eurasian perennial with partly prostrate stems, which grows wild on the banks of streams and in wet ground; and *M. sylvatica*, the Wood Forget-me-not, which is an erect species with many varieties, usually a foot or more high when in bloom, commonly grown as a biennial. Both species have small blue flowers with a yellow eye.

The seeds of the True Forget-me-not may be sown in May or June and the flowers kept picked off until they are brought indoors in the fall, if the plants are desired for winter flowering. The soil should be kept quite wet at all times. The seeds of *M. sylvatica* (*oblongata*), Ball Early, for winter bloom; and Bluebird to carry on in March, should be sown in August. Normal watering is sufficient for these.

While you may want to try self-sown seedlings of bedding **Marigolds** (*Tagetes patula*), better results are likely to be obtained if seeds of winter-flowering varieties such as Australian Tree, Lieb's Brown and Gold, and Winter Harmony are sown in August.

All of these annuals and near annuals should be grown in the general-purpose mixture and shifted into larger pots as their roots become crowded. All need a sunny window and, except for Nicotiana, which does not mind 70°, should be given a temperature as near as possible to 50°.

Other annuals grown by florists for cut flowers in winter—Candytuft, Calendula, and Stock, et cetera—are of sufficient merit to tempt the adventurous to experiment with them if favorable growing conditions (coolness, ample light, and air uncontaminated with gas) are available. I took a chance on Stock, but so far, at the time of writing, all it has done is to writhe snakily about, producing plenty of good foliage but no flowers.

For trailing and climbing annuals, you are referred to page 246.

HERBACEOUS PERENNIALS AND WOODY PLANTS RAISED ANNUALLY

Garden and greenhouse Chrysanthemums (*Chrysanthemum hortorum* varieties), when intended for display in the house, are handled to best advantage by letting them spend most of their time outdoors or in a coldframe.

The so-called "hardy" varieties may be grown in the garden in the usual way by digging up old plants as soon as the ground is workable in the spring and pulling off strong-rooted shoots and planting them 1 foot to 18 inches apart in rich soil. When the flower buds begin to show, those plants destined for indoor decoration should be thoroughly watered a day in advance of digging them up with a good ball of soil about their roots. Plant them in pots just large enough to hold the root ball, soak thoroughly, and keep shaded for a few days. Then bring them into an enclosed but unheated

Suckers of Chrysanthemum, with roots attached, can be broken off and potted up to provide new plants

porch to open their flowers. This procedure affords us a chance to enjoy late-blooming varieties which would be cut by severe frost if left outdoors. When the flowers have faded, the plants should be cut back and, in their pots, plunged in sand or peatmoss in a cold-frame if they are wanted for propagation purposes.

If you are ambitious to produce enormous flowers 6 or more inches in diameter, it is better to grow the plants in pots almost from the start. First it is necessary to choose varieties which are capable of producing large blooms if properly grown and disbudded. Among these are Mrs. H. E. Kidder, yellow; Smith's Early White; Bronze Lode, Indianola, light bronze; and Lustre, pink. These bloom about mid-October. Varieties which bloom in late October and early

November are Yellow Ambassador, Golden Ball; Ambassador, white; Mrs. David Roy, red; Cambria, bronze; Lady Knox, pink.

A convenient way to get a start is to buy rooted cuttings in the spring and pot them in 3-inch pots in the mixture recommended for cuttings. In about a month they will be ready for a shift to larger pots, this time using the general-purpose potting mixture. They must have abundant light and free ventilation. If this cannot be provided by growing them in a sun porch, it is better to keep them in a sunny coldframe, putting an extra covering of mats on the glass if frost is anticipated. The sash may be removed entirely as soon as danger of frost is past.

The plants must be shifted to larger pots whenever the roots become crowded, until they receive their final potting (make soil very firm) in pots 6 to 10 inches in diameter about the beginning of June. During the time they are outdoors the pots should be plunged in sand, peatmoss, or coal ashes to reduce the need for watering, which must be carefully attended to. When the pots are plunged after the final potting, put an inch or two of clinkers beneath the pot for drainage and turn the pot every week or so to discourage roots from emerging through the drainage hole. When the plants become potbound, they may be fed at weekly intervals with half-strength liquid fertilizer (see page 56), never applying it, however, when the soil is dry. As soon as the flower buds show color, feeding must stop. Bring them indoors when frost threatens and keep them in a cool (45°), sunny room.

Training and disbudding: So far you have had only part of the story. To get large flowers, the plants must be restricted to one, two, or at most three shoots; and no more than one flower bud should be allowed to develop on each. If two stems are allowed to develop, the flowers will be smaller than if the plants are restricted to one, and still smaller if they carry three stems. If plants with more than one stem are required, the tip of the shoot is pinched out when the plant is potted and two or three of the strongest shoots are allowed to develop. All side growths on these are rubbed off as soon as they are visible. If single-stem plants are needed, obviously only one shoot is allowed to develop. Some growers pinch out the tip of the main shoot or shoots every time the plant is potted up until the first of June, in order to reduce the height of the tall varieties. Continue removing side branches from the main stem or stems. A flower bud ("first-crown" bud) may make its appearance in June or July. This will not develop into a good flower and it must be removed by pinching, together with *all but one* of the side branches developing around it. The shoot that is left will produce the "second-crown" bud. If this appears in mid-August or later, retain it for flower production, removing all the remaining flower buds and auxiliary shoots. This is a simplified procedure designed to eliminate the necessity for keeping a chart (as is done by many professional gardeners) telling the exact date for taking and the

Disbudding. Side buds removed from Chrysanthemum, to induce remaining bud to develop into a larger flower

kind of bud—first crown, second crown, or terminal—desirable for each variety.

Not many have the facilities for raising large-flowered Chrysanthemums. This much abbreviated account of their culture is included for the few who may wish to try them and as a matter of academic interest to others.

Cyclamens: We may as well face the music and recognize that Cyclamens (sometimes given the misnomer "Persian Violet" and sometimes unromantically called "Sow Bread") are not easy to grow. If your rooms are kept at a temperature of 70° in the winter you had better just cross them off your list and forget about them. They are gloriously beautiful, and it is well worth while to try to provide their rather exacting requirements. It is encouraging to know that there are some house-plant enthusiasts who are able to grow them either from seeds or as tuberous perennials persisting year after year.

First, as to its care when you receive a Cyclamen as a flowering plant from the florist. Remember it was grown in a humid greenhouse in which the night temperature was maintained around 50°

Three popular gift plants—
Cineraria, Cyclamen, and Azalea—in the order shown

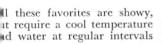

ll these favorites are showy,
ut require a cool temperature
d water at regular intervals

Hot, dry rooms are not at all
to their liking; under such conditions they quickly pass out

Dish gardens, or living pl
arrangements, make an
triguing hobby for the de
rator. Material may be gro
for the purpose, obtained fr
the florist, or gathered fr
woods and fields

with a rise of 10° during the day. Try to give approximately these conditions in your home. You will not be able to match them exactly, but perhaps you have a cool room with an east window in which the plant may be stood; or a slightly heated enclosed porch with plenty of light but with shade from bright sunshine except

No house plant is lovelier than a fine Cyclamen in full bloom—especially if you've grown it!

early in the morning. Never allow the soil to become dry during the time the plant is in bloom.

A *Home Garden* reader boasts of a 6-year-old plant which produces as many as 30 blooms at a time. Her method is as follows:

Gradually reduce the water supply after growth wanes toward April. Then the pot is stored in a cool room until the weather warms up outside, when it is placed under a Grape arbor. During all this ripening time the soil is lightly moistened about once in two weeks.

Early in August the corm is lifted and the soil replaced by a fresh mixture—old hotbed soil, 2 parts; sand, 2 parts; and Oak leafmold, 1 part. Then the corm is reset, high in the *same* pot, if possible, and the plant watered and placed under the Grape arbor again where little headway is made until cool weather sets in near the end of the month. Early in September the Cyclamen is brought in to a window with morning sun where 3½- to 4-inch leaves soon develop.

Here the plant stands on a thick block of wood in a deep bowl always filled with water which is replaced daily with more *at boiling temperature*. This often rises to cover the pot base for 1 inch with no harm to the plant from the heat, if it is in need of moisture. The humidifying effect is marvelous, of course. Subsequently all the moisture needed reaches the roots via the wooden block. Weak liquid manure is given monthly. Leaves reach a fine size and do not discolor. Flowers first open soon after the turn of the year and many buds continue to appear.

There is considerable deviation in the living-room temperature —a variation from 45° at night to 65° during the day. Still my Cyclamen lives and blooms for some three months each winter and continues to do so *year after year*.

Notice particularly the temperatures 45° at night to 65° in the day. Notice, too, how the watering is done. While I am dubious about the necessity of using *boiling* water, the method otherwise is admirable.

September is considered the best month for sowing when raising them from seeds, and you must figure on a wait of fifteen to eighteen months before you get blooms. The seeds should be sown in a well-drained bulb pan in the mixture advocated for seed sowing (page 128). Moisten by standing the pan in a vessel of water until the surface soil seems moist, then cover with a piece of glass shaded with paper. Remove covering when the seeds germinate; keep in a well-lighted place but shade from direct sun during the hottest part of the day. When the seedlings have two leaves, transplant them an inch apart in a flat of soil—loam, 1 part; sand, 1 part; leafmold, 2 parts.

Transplant again to give them more room when the leaves begin to touch. Throughout the winter try to keep the temperature within the 50° to 55° range. In April pot them in small individual pots and shift into progressively larger pots whenever the roots become crowded. For the second and subsequent pottings use the general-purpose mixture. Always be sure that the pots are well drained and raise the corm so that it is half in, half out of the soil. Five- or 6-inch pots will be large enough for the final potting, but when these become filled with roots and the first flower buds are to be seen, an occasional watering every three or four weeks with liquid fertilizer is beneficial, though be careful not to allow it to touch the crown of the plant. One way of avoiding this is to apply it by subirrigation as described above—actually it is a good plan to water by this means all the time the plants are indoors.

From mid-spring until fall the plants should be kept in a cool,

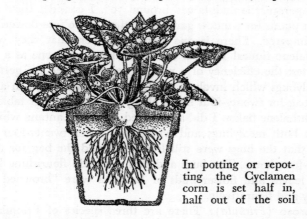

In potting or repotting the Cyclamen corm is set half in, half out of the soil

well-lighted spot outdoors, shaded from bright sunshine during the hottest part of the day. When they are brought indoors give them, if possible, an east window and stand them on pebble-filled trays containing water to increase the humidity. Ventilate as much as you can without drafts and without reducing the temperature to less than 45°.

Heliotrope (*Heliotropium arborescens*): If you happen to have a plant of Heliotrope that is really fragrant and want it to bloom in the house in early winter, you should insert cuttings in a shaded coldframe in June or July, pot them in general-purpose mixture when rooted, and keep the flowers pinched off until September. (Heliotrope can also be raised from seeds, but the plants so often lack the fragrance that is the chief reason for growing them.) When brought indoors early in September give them a sunny window and keep the night temperature down to 50°. Spray the foliage on sunny days. When they stop blooming, rest them by giving less water at the root. Plant outdoors as soon as danger of frost is past and start the circle over again with cuttings in June. The old plant will bloom all summer, but it will suffer greatly if dug up, potted, and brought indoors in the fall and will not be nearly so satisfactory for winter bloom as young plants handled as described above.

Lantana (*Lantana camara* vars.): These shrubs, related to Verbena, with showy, flat-topped, varicolored flower heads 2 inches or more in diameter, are handled in much the same way as Heliotrope. They are, however, much easier to grow, and thrive even though the temperature is maintained around 70°. I consider them among the best plants for window gardening; they are so free-flowering and good-tempered. There is one thing, however, that they resent— naphthalene fumes! I found this out when I used one as a guinea pig to test the efficiency of a method recommended for getting rid of mealybugs which involved placing the infested plant in a closed paper bag for twenty-four hours along with a couple of tablespoons of naphthalene flakes. I did as directed, using a Lantana which was host to both mealybugs and white flies. After twenty-four hours, seeing that the bugs were still lively, I closed the bag for another twenty-four hours. The bugs and flies were still flourishing but the young leaves and flower buds of Lantana were "browned off"— literally and figuratively.

Primrose (*Primula*): There are three species of Primula, each with many varieties, which can be used as house plants provided the necessary cool conditions, 50° to 55°, can be given them during the winter. These are Chinese Primrose, Fairy Primrose, Poison Primrose, *P. sinensis, P. malacoides,* and *P. obconica,* respectively. A hybrid between *P. floribunda* (Buttercup Primrose) and *P. verticillata* (Arabian Primrose), known as *P. kewensis,* is another possibility requiring the same culture as those mentioned above. The English Primrose (*P. vulgaris*), a winter-hardy variety, appeals especially to people of English descent. If its flowers are wanted in advance of the normal blooming season outdoors, strong plants may be dug up early in September, potted up, plunged in a shaded cold-frame, protected from very severe weather by mats on the sash, and brought indoors in late February or early March.

The Fairy Primrose gives a graceful, airy effect with myriads of flowers arranged in tiers on slender stalks. Colors range from white through rose to red. The Poison Primrose, so called because the leaves irritate the skin of sensitive persons, has large leaves and large flowers in umbels, white to red and purple. The Chinese Primrose has lobed leaves, flowers of many colors, which in the variety *stellata* are arranged in superimposed umbels. Under suitable conditions all these Primroses remain in bloom for many weeks.

For winter bloom the seeds are sown from January to March in a temperature of 60° to 65°. The seedlings are transplanted to flats, adding ½ part rotted manure to the seed-sowing mixture. They are subsequently potted up, using the humusy mixture recommended for Begonias but without charcoal. During the summer they should be kept in a coldframe shaded by a double thickness of cheesecloth supported well above the frame so that they get plenty of air. Bring them indoors before frost and give a temperature as near as possible to 50°; 45° will not harm them. Plenty of light is needed, but shade lightly from bright sunshine except in the depth of winter.

All are perennials, but better results are obtained by raising them annually.

Senecio cruentus (Florists' Cineraria): Among the showiest of florists' plants, with flowers up to 4 or 5 inches across in some of the exhibition strains, Cinerarias demand growing conditions which are beyond the facilities of the average household. They must be grown cool; and they are subject to attacks by plant lice which can most effectively be controlled by fumigation.

Cinerarias fall into two main groups: the dwarf, large-flowered kinds and the *stellata* type which has smaller flowers, a more open habit of growth, and greater stature—up to 3 feet. To me it seems that these run to a preponderance of distressing, muddy purple tones in their flowers, without the clear purity of color found in the dwarf large-flowered types, which have a color range extending from white and blue to deep crimson. Often two colors are arranged on the flowers in well-defined zones.

For autumn and winter flowering the seeds are sown in May; for spring bloom, in August and September. They must be kept as cool as possible at all times. We used to grow ours during summer in a coldframe set on the north side of a building where they got no direct sun (but plenty of sky-shine) except in early morning and evening. Brought indoors before frost, and given a light, airy situation, during the winter they were provided with a night temperature of 45°, rising to 55° during the day. This just about outlines the kind of environment they need. Use general-purpose potting mixture and avoid allowing them to become potbound, until they are in their flowering-size pots, which may be from 5 to 7 inches according to size of plant. Feed with liquid manure when pots are full of roots.

BULBS, CORMS, TUBERS, AND HARDY PLANTS FOR FORCING

In this very general and heterogeneous grouping we have some of the most showy of all house plants. For convenience in handling cultural details they are segregated as follows: (1) hardy spring-flowering bulbs; (2) hardy spring-flowering non-bulbous plants; (3) tender spring-flowering bulbs; (4) summer-flowering bulbs—the name "bulbs" in every case being stretched to include corms, tubers, pips, et cetera.

(1) Hardy spring-flowering bulbs

It is a big advantage when we can use as house plants those which have been grown outdoors and are kept in the house only for a comparatively short time to enable them to bloom a little in advance of their outdoor season. The hardy spring-flowering bulbs possess this feature beyond all others because normally they are produced under ideal conditions in regions especially suited to their culture. Stored within the confines of the bulbs are all the makings for the successful production of roots, leaves, and flowers, and they will do this provided they are given a reasonable chance. Usually they are inexpensive, so that we don't feel too badly about discarding them when their blooms have faded. If putting them on the compost pile is too great a shock to your notions of thrift you can continue to water them until the leaves wither naturally; or until it is warm enough to plant them outdoors in the perennial border or other appropriate place. Treated thus they probably will bloom the following spring—almost certainly in two years, but only if they are left outdoors; bulbs forced one year are not satisfactory for forcing the following season. Always purchase best-quality bulbs for house culture—you start off with two strikes against you if you use inferior bulbs.

The kinds most favored for house culture, in order of their importance, are: Narcissus, Tulip, Hyacinth, Crocus, Grape-hyacinth, and Scilla. There is a host of "lesser bulbs" including Snowdrop, Winter Aconite, Fritillary, et cetera, with which the adventurous and those who like variety will experiment.

A list of varieties suitable for house culture, of the three principal kinds, is given below. It can be augmented, if necessary, by using the forcing varieties recommended by dealers in their catalogues. Those Narcissi which will not survive severe freezing are included among the "tender" bulbs.

DAFFODILS

February Gold	Aerolite	Silver Star
Spring Glory	Croesus	Queen of the North
King Alfred	Diana Kasner	Cheerfulness

TULIPS

(F=Fragrant)

Single Early	Grenadier	William Copeland (F)
De Wet (F)	Inglescombe Pink	The Sultan
Fred Moore (F)	Inglescombe Yellow	William Pitt
Prince of Austria (F)	Mrs. Moon (F)	Zwanenburg
La Rève (Hobbema)	Dido (F)	*Breeder*
White Hawk	Marvel (F)	Bronze Queen
Triumph	Yellow Rose, double (F)	Cardinal Manning
Flora	*Darwin*	Dom Pedro (F)
Lord Carnarvon	Bartigon	*Double*
Cottage	Bona Est	Couronne d'Or
Avis Kennicott	Clara Butt	Murillo
Ellen Willmott (F)	Farncombe Sanders	Peach Blossom

HYACINTHS

L'Innocence (white)	Etna (red)	King of the Blues (dark)
Queen of the Whites	Schotel (light blue)	Buff Beauty (yellow)
Lady Derby (rose pink)	Queen of the Blues	City of Haarlem (yellow)

Roman Hyacinths, which produce several smaller spikes with fewer flowers from each bulb, are preferred for early bloom. By potting them in late August or early September and bringing them into warmth at three-week intervals they may be had in bloom from November to spring. Should not be exposed to severe freezing.

Containers: Commercial growers who force these hardy bulbs into bloom to obtain flowers for cutting commonly plant the bulbs thickly in shallow boxes (flats), but this method is not likely to appeal to the average householder who would do better to stick to ordinary clay flowerpots and bulb pans. The pots and their contents may be subjected to freezing during the preliminary treatment, so you will not want to expose fancy, expensive containers to the hazards of breakage and to possible injury to the finish from contact with the soil. If the appearance of the ordinary flowerpots offends your artistic eye they can be slipped inside jardinieres or dressed in a valance of waterproof paper or something similar during the time they are in bloom and on display.

It is well to adapt the container to the bulbs. For tall, strong-growing Daffodils and Darwin Tulips use 6-inch standard pots which will take about three Narcissus bulbs or five or six Tulips. For Hyacinths use 4½- or 5-inch pots for single bulbs; or plant three in a 6-inch ¾ pot which in height is between the standard pot and the bulb pan. For smaller bulbs—Crocus, Scilla, Grape-hyacinth, and Netted Iris—the regulation bulb pans in 6- to 8-inch sizes are satisfactory. These can also be used for Tulips and Daffodils, but to my mind the proportions between plants and container are not so good. As a general rule a space of 1 to 1½ inches should be allowed between the bulbs.

Soil: The fact that many bulbs can be brought into bloom by growing them in water, pebbles and water, Moss, and fiber—all of which are deficient in nutrients—is an indication that the quality of the soil, provided it is porous, is less important with these hardy forcing bulbs than it is with most plants. Nothing you can do between the time of planting the bulbs and their blooming will increase the number of flowers they will produce. Good soil and good growing conditions, however, will improve the size and quality of the flowers; so, if possible, use the soil mixture suggested on page 51. This, perhaps, is a good place to point out that improper handling (sometimes, but rarely, before you get the bulbs) may result in the blasting and non-development of the flowers.

Planting: This can be done any time in the fall up until December, but usually the earlier the bulbs are in the soil the better it is for them. Hardy Narcissi and Winter Aconites especially are likely to be harmed if left out of the ground too long.

SPRING BULBS FOR WINTER BLOOM
Bulbs are placed close together in crocked bulb pan, thoroughly watered

Bulb pans are then buried in trench, covered with peatmoss and soil, for rooting before being brought in

Or a bed may be prepared against north side of a wall or fence, and pots covered with straw or litter

Hyacinth bulbs placed in a glass bowl for forcing, with root growth showing through glass

A bulb pan of Daffodils grown in soil and brought into flower after new roots have formed

Don't mix varieties requiring differing periods for development in the same pot, because the appearance of the late ones will be marred by the presence of fading leaves of the early ones and the pot as a whole will never be at its best.

The pots and pans should be scrubbed with water and a stiff brush and allowed to dry before using. New pots should be soaked in water for a few hours or they will take too much moisture out of the soil.

Put a piece of broken pot over the hole in the bottom of the pot, cover this with a handful or two of the coarser parts from your soil pile, and then put in enough soil, pressed down *lightly,* so that when the bulbs are placed in position their noses are about ½ inch below the rim of the pot. Gently press the bulb into the soil, but *not* with a screwing motion—such treatment may rub off developing rootlets. When bulbs are in place fill the pot with soil and press down *firmly* so that the surface is at least ½ inch below the rim. If the soil beneath the bulbs is packed too hard, and that above too loose, the growth of the roots may force the bulbs out of the pot. After the bulbs are planted give the soil a thorough watering, either by repeated sprinklings or by standing the pots in a tub or pan containing a few inches of water, leaving them there until moisture shows on the surface.

Rooting: The treatment from now on has a most important bearing on the success or failure of the bulbs. An old rule says: provide a temperature of 40° for rooting (a period of six weeks or longer); 50° for three weeks or so for growth of stem and leaves, and 60° for flower production. These ideals are usually impossible of attainment under home conditions, but you should approximate them as closely as you can. There are several ways of arriving at the same destination.

(a) *The plunge pit:* A well-drained location is selected in the coolest part of the garden—perhaps in the shade of a building. A trench or pit is dug a foot deep, large enough to accommodate the bulbs. Three inches of cinders or clinkers are placed in the bottom to provide drainage and to discourage worms from entering the pots. Sprinkle a thin layer of sand (or peatmoss) on the surface of the soil in the pots; this will make it easier to separate covering material cleanly from the pot soil when the bulbs are brought in. Stand the pots on the drainage layer and fill in between and over them with the soil removed in making the pit, forming it into a mound. Leave it this way until the surface freezes ½ inch deep and then put on a layer of straw, hay, or something similar in sufficient thickness to prevent the soil around the bulbs from freezing solid. Not that this would harm them, but it might make it impossible to get them out of the pit without much labor and breakage of pots when the time comes to bring them indoors. A variation of this method is to use peatmoss or leafmold in place of soil for covering.

(b) A method which I am coming to think is the best for the average house-plant enthusiast is to stand the pots on a 2-inch layer of cinders in a box about the size of a bushel apple box. Leave a space

Pots of bulbs packed in moist peatmoss may be kept in an apple box during the rooting period

of 2 inches between the pots and the side of the box and fill this with moist peatmoss, which should also be packed between and over the pots, filling the box. Place the box (or several stacked closely together) out doors in a cool place; and, when severe weather threatens, cover top and sides of the boxes with a thick layer of straw or its equivalent. Even if the peatmoss does become frozen it is a comparatively easy matter to bring the entire box indoors to thaw out so that the pots of bulbs can be removed without breakage. In boxes, it is easy to protect the bulbs from rodents by covering all possible entrances with ¼-inch mesh hardware cloth.

If you are lucky enough to have a cellar entry on the north side of the house (as I have—though it is not too spacious!), the box of bulbs may be placed there and covered with burlap bags if the weather becomes so cold that they are likely to freeze.

(c) An unheated house cellar or a root cellar where the temperature hovers between 35° and 45° is a good place to store bulbs during the rooting period.

Labeling and arrangement: If a variety of bulbs is planted it is necessary to label them so that you will know what you are bringing in; and unless you have so few pots that all are brought in at the same time, you will want also to arrange them in the plunge pit so that it will not be necessary to open it up in its entirety to find the kinds you need.

One method of labeling is to write the names on wired wooden tree labels (obtainable from seed stores) and affix them to the top of 15- to 18-inch plant stakes. These are pushed into the pots when the bulbs are potted (take care not to spear any of the bulbs) and will project above the plunge-pit covering so that you know where to dig to get what you want. If the bulbs are placed in a storage cellar ordinary 4-inch wooden pot labels can be placed directly in the pot; or you can write an abbreviation of the name with grease crayon on the rim of the pot. There is no chance for Junior to transpose the labels when your back is turned if this last method is adopted; but if the same pots are to be used the following season, be sure that the name is erased if a different variety is planted.

Arrange the bulbs in the plunge pit in the order in what they are to come out so that you can open one end and remove as many pots as are needed without disturbing the remainder. If you follow the plan of putting them in boxes, the selection of kinds in each box can be a forcing unit. The regulation 1⅛-bushel apple box will hold two 5-inch pots and four 4½-inch; or three 6-inch and two 4-inch, which is as many pots as most of us want to bring in at one time.

Bringing in the sheaves: When the pots are filled with roots, which will be in five to eight weeks, depending on kind, the bulbs are ready to be brought indoors to make their top growth. Remember the nearer it is to the natural flowering season the easier it is to achieve success; and it will do no harm to leave the bulbs in the plunge pit (in northern climates) until January or February. But if you want early flowers, take a chance in November or December. If the roots are making their way through the drainage hole in the bottom of the pot, they are sufficiently advanced. When no roots are outwardly visible, their condition can be determined by turning the bulbs out of the pot. This is done by placing the left hand (if you are a right-handed person) with fingers spread on the surface of the soil and, inverting the pot, tapping its rim on the edge of bench or table. The roots should look like those shown facing page 124. Do not spend too much time admiring them—return them gently to the pot as soon as you have satisfied yourself as to their condition.

When they are brought indoors follow the pattern set by Nature —increase the temperature gradually. Keep them in a temperature of 45° to 50° for ten days to three weeks before exposing them to greater warmth—if you can possibly manage it. During this period the light should not be too intense. When they have made a few inches of top growth they can be placed in a sunny window, preferably in a temperature of 60° and certainly not over 70°. When the flowers are opening, and until they fade, you will, of course, want to keep them on view in living-room temperature during the daytime. It is quite all right to do this, but you will find that the flowers will last longer if, every night, you put them in a cool place (40° to 50°) just before going to bed.

From the time the bulbs are potted until the foliage withers (if you are planning to plant out the bulbs), the soil must be kept constantly moist; and during the time the tops are in active growth and until the flowers fade it is important that ample supplies of water are provided.

These methods are applicable to hardy spring-flowering bulbs in general. It remains to say that Crocus, Snowdrop, and Winter Aconite will not tolerate severe forcing, and it is better to bring these along to the flowering stage in a temperature not in excess of 50°.

Water culture: At one time it was a common practice to force hardy bulbs, especially Hyacinths, in water. Hyacinth glasses, obtained from seed stores, were used, enough water put in them barely to touch the base of the bulb set on a constriction near the top of the vase, and then kept in a cool, dark, airy place until roots reached the bottom of the vase. See also Paper-white Narcissi, page 186.

Few plants are capable of supplying so much color and beauty in the home with so little effort as the hardy spring-flowering bulbs; and, although they are only transients, they are nonetheless welcome.

(2) Non-bulbous spring flowers

It is possible to get a preview of spring by hurrying along certain plants which normally bloom very early in the spring. Among them are: Astilbe, Claytonia, Convallaria, Dicentra, Hepatica, Sanguinaria, Shortia, Tiarella, and Trillium. (See Timetable for Flowering House Plants.) Those who are interested in native plants and have access to wild areas in which they can dig without violating conservation laws or property rights doubtless will enjoy trying other kinds such as Anemonella, Columbine, Early Saxifrage, et cetera.

General care: The general practice to follow is to dig up the plants in the fall, taking care not to injure the root systems more than is necessary. Pot them in soil similar to that in which they are growing, water thoroughly, and plunge them in a coldframe. When several hard frosts have been experienced, mulch them with salt hay, Pine needles, or something similar, and forget about them until near the end of February. Then bring them indoors and keep in a well-lighted position in a temperature of 50° until their flower buds show, when they can be brought into the living room.

Deviations: Roots of *Astilbe japonica,* called Spirea by florists, can be purchased in fall. The root mass should be soaked in a pail of water, potted in general-purpose mixture, watered thoroughly, and stored as cold as possible for six to eight weeks. Then bring indoors in a well-lighted window (60° temperature) and keep soil *wet*—stand pot in a saucer constantly filled with water.

Ordinarily, retarded "pips" of Lily-of-the-valley (*Convallaria*) specially grown and prepared for forcing (use no other) are available from dealers. These can be potted in sand or almost any material that will hold moisture (one grower who forced them by the million used sawdust) after the tips of the roots have been trimmed with a sharp knife. Space them 1 to 2 inches apart with the pips (buds) just above the surface. Water thoroughly, keep in a dark moist place (a closed ventilated box will do) for ten days at 70°, and then gradually expose them to light. You should have blooms within three weeks after planting if all goes well.

Two species, at least, of *Dicentra* have been used for forcing— Dutchman's Breeches (*D. cucullaria*)—which does not really belong here because it has tubers—and Bleeding Heart (*D. spectabilis*). Doubtless others, such as Fringed Bleeding Heart (*D. eximia*), could also be used. The Bleeding Heart will not stand for hurry-up tactics. As an example, one plant, dug up and potted September 25, was left outdoors until the end of January when it was brought into a cold room. A month later it was transferred to the living room, where it proceeded to grow apace, the pastel coloring of the young shoots and the gray-green ferny foliage giving much pleasure. But the flowers blasted—never a one getting beyond pinhead stage. Of course I could advance my usual alibi—gas in the home—but I'm inclined to believe it was too much heat too soon.

Hepaticas (and possibly others) do not demand a long rest period. The plant used in the small plant arrangement (facing page 48) was dug up on November 17 and three weeks later bloomed in a Greenwich Village apartment!

If you have no coldframe, or don't want to be bothered with the care of hardy plants in fall and winter, it is possible to hunt around in the fields and woods for early-blooming plants, to be dug up and potted as soon as new growth is visible, and brought indoors to get a few days' jump on the season. Marsh Marigold and Bluets respond well to this treatment.

The plants in this section can be planted outdoors as soon as their attractiveness wanes, with the exception of Lily-of-the-valley which, as it makes no new roots when forced, is of no further use.

(3) Tender spring-flowering bulbs

These are mostly plants which cannot endure freezing. Generally they are not forced to bloom out of their natural season; therefore, when grown in good soil in a greenhouse, they may be rested and used another year. In the home, however, it is seldom that good enough conditions can be provided so that, with the exceptions noted below, it usually is better to buy new bulbs annually—bulbs which have been grown outdoors in a favored climate.

Narcissi of the Paper-white type, such as Grand Soleil d'Or and the so-called Chinese Sacred Lily, are included in this section because they cannot endure severe freezing. Usually these bulbs are grown in fiber obtained from seed stores or in water with pebbles in the bowl to keep them stable. The method is to plant them so that about $\frac{5}{6}$ of the bulb is above the rooting medium. Don't attempt to start them before the middle of October, then place them in a cool, dark place for two or three weeks, or until growth starts, when they should be brought into a sunny window and a temperature of 60° to 65°. Keep fiber constantly moist; and, if grown in pebbles, maintain the water at a level which is just below the base of the bulb. Although the Paper-white Narcissus is almost foolproof, lanky leaf growth and blasting or non-development of the flowers are likely to occur if they are started too early and kept all the time in temperatures above 70°. Buy the bulbs from a reputable source to be sure of getting good ones. They should be discarded after flowering.

Here are some of the most important tender bulbs to be grown in soil recommended for bulbs on page 51, except where otherwise indicated. If acid, add enough ground limestone to bring it up to the neutral point.

The ever-popular, sweet-smelling **Freesia** is native to South Africa and is grown in quantity in California to provide bulbs for culture in greenhouses and homes. Today Freesias are obtainable in many color forms in tones of white, yellow, pink, and violet. They should be potted in the fall, six bulbs to a 5-inch pot, at intervals of three or four weeks if a succession of blooms is required. Cool culture and plenty of sunshine are essential, so it is a good plan to give them a start in a sunny coldframe, bringing them indoors when frost threatens. Go easy on the watering until top growth is visible, then soak them whenever the surface appears to be dry. In the house give them a sunny window and a temperature as near 50° as possible. They will need some support which can be given by placing three or four 1-foot slender stakes or stout wires around the edge of the pot and connecting them with thin twine.

The plant commonly known as **Amaryllis,** but more correctly as *Hippeastrum,* provides almost the largest flowers it is possible to grow in the home. The old-time *Hippeastrum,* itself a hybrid, shown in color, facing page 241, has been superseded by improved varieties in a great range of colors. Dormant bulbs may be purchased from dealers between October and April. When received they should be potted singly, with ⅔ of the bulb above the surface. Do not use pots whose diameter is more than 3 inches greater than that of the bulb. Keep them in a temperature between 60° and 70° and do not water until the flower bud is visible, and then only sparingly until the leaves start to develop, after which they should be watered freely. The treatment accorded after flowering will determine whether or not flowers will be produced the following year.

There are two schools of thought as to the best means of handling them, both of which insist on outdoor culture during the summer with special attention to feeding and watering. Where they differ is

In potting Amaryllis a pot or bulb pan only slightly larger than the bulb is used; and only the bottom part of the bulb (about one third) is covered with soil

in whether the plants should be kept in their pots or planted out in the open ground. If you have more than one bulb, try both methods to determine which is better in your location. After flowering is past, the bulbs should be kept in a sunny window, watered regularly, and given a dose of weak liquid manure every two or three weeks. When danger of frost is past, put them outdoors, either planted out or plunged in their pots. In the fall, when the weather begins

Amaryllis, long a favorite with indoor gardeners, is one of the most easily grown, as well as one of the most colorful of all bulbs

(*Above*) An excellent bulb is Ixia, with slender stalks bearing unusually attractive flowers; (*Right*) Oxalis has long been a popular bulb for the house, ideal for a hanging pot or basket

Two that flower quickly from bulbs; above, Paper-white* Narcissus (*N. tazetta variety*)

Muscari, the always popular little Grape-hyacinth, ordinarily used for naturalizing outdoors

to cool, bring them indoors (potting those which were planted out) and gradually reduce the supply of water at the roots, giving only enough to prevent the leaves from wilting. Some varieties will go completely dormant, losing all their leaves; others may retain some of theirs. These last must be kept in a light situation and watered occasionally. It is not necessary to repot annually if the bulbs are not planted out in summer, unless they are becoming crowded in their pots. Merely remove, when new leaf growth is beginning, as much of the topsoil as you can without disturbing the roots and replace with a 50-50 mixture of loam and thoroughly rotted manure, with a teaspoonful of bonemeal to each 5-inch pot.

The **Cape Cowslips** are botanically known as *Lachenalia*. The ones commonly used, varieties of *L. pendula superba*, grow from 6 to 10 inches high with spikes of pendent flowers (somewhat after the manner of the English Bluebell) which usually are coral-red tipped with green or purple. The bulbs may be potted just below the surface, about 1½ inches apart, in 6-inch bulb pans. They must be grown under cool conditions, and could well be kept in a cold-frame until frost threatens to penetrate it, when they should be brought into an unheated, frost-free, sunny room. My own experience with them has been disappointing because of poor bulbs supplied by the dealer; they grew well enough, but the bulbs contained no flower spikes and therefore blossoms did not materialize.

Other "Cape bulbs"—*Babiana, Ixia, Sparaxis,* et cetera—are available for those who want to experiment with this class of plants. My best success has been with *Ixia* treated as one would *Freesia*.

The **Easter Lily** (*Lilium longiflorum* varieties) is not reliably winter hardy in northern climates. The bulbs should be potted singly in 5- or 6-inch pots with one to two inches of soil under them (they are "stem-rooters," hence the deep planting) in September or October. If the weather continues mild, keep them in a shaded coldframe for a month and then bring indoors and give a 60° temperature. Keep soil moist, give all the light available, and watch out for aphids.

In **Oxalis,** the group to which the Bermuda Buttercup belongs, we have several species and varieties with a more or less floppy habit suitable for hanging containers. All the commonly grown kinds have three-parted Clover-like leaves. The Bermuda Buttercup (*O. cernua*) has yellow flowers; *O. bowieana* is pink with lush foliage;

Grand Duchess is lavender; and *O. hirta* has violet or purple flowers. These bulbs start into growth with fragile shoots whether or not they are planted, so it is desirable to obtain and pot them as early as possible in the fall to avoid damage. They may be set 1 inch deep, singly in 3-inch pots; or six in a 5- or 6-inch pot which must be well drained. Add enough limestone to the soil to make it slightly alkaline. Water sparingly until growth shows above the soil, and then water normally, but don't keep the soil sopping wet all the time. A sunny window is essential and a temperature around 60° is desirable.

The **Calla-lily,** formerly known as *Richardia africana,* has had a fast one pulled on it by the botanists and is now *Zantedeschia aethiopica.* For small homes either the Godfrey Calla, a free-flowering kind, or the Baby Calla, both smaller than the type, should be used. The Yellow Calla (*Z. elliottiana*) is not so robust as *aethiopica* and has yellow spathes ("flowers") and white-spotted leaves. The Pink Calla (*Z. rehmanni*), about a foot tall, has rose-

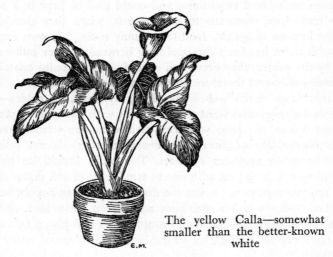

The yellow Calla—somewhat smaller than the better-known white

colored spathes. Tubers of all these kinds are obtainable in the fall when they should be potted in general-purpose mixture. Apply weak liquid manure every three weeks when potbound. Some growers recommend keeping the tubers of the Yellow Calla in a warm, dry place for a few weeks prior to potting them. The tubers may be started in 4- or 5-inch pots and given larger sizes when they become potbound. Water sparingly at first but when growth is well above the surface keep them constantly wet. Grow them in a sunny window and give a 70° temperature. When the weather becomes settled and warm, turn them out of their pots and plant them in the flower border to be dug up in the fall, dried off for a month or two, and used to start the cycle over again.

Occasionally one sees **Devil's Tongue** advertised, or recommended, for house culture. This is the plant variously known as Sacred Lily-of-India (though it is not a Lily and is native to Cochin-China), Snake Palm (not a snake and not a Palm), Umbrella Arum, and botanically as *Amorphophallus rivieri* (or nowadays *Hydrosme rivieri*). Granted that this plant of many aliases can be grown in the house, and admitting that its large purplish-maroon and spotted inflorescence (up to 6 feet in height) is arresting in its appearance; and that its enormous, single leaf, 4 feet in diameter, is definitely ornamental—I submit that it should never be brought into the house during the time its flowers are discharging their offensive carrion odor, which at its height is sufficiently strong to gag a maggot.

Kept at room temperature the dormant tubers ordinarily throw up their inflorescences in March. If it were possible to keep them at a low temperature (say around 45° to 50°), it is likely that their flowering could be delayed until the advent of warm weather, which would enable us to place them outdoors where they could be seen and not smelled. This ought to be feasible, for in spite of their tropical origin I have known them to survive a New York winter when planted outdoors and mulched with about 6 inches of leaves.

If dormancy is prolonged by low temperature, Amorphophallus then becomes a house plant only in the sense that its tubers are stored indoors during the winter, for its real growth is made when planted in rich soil in a sheltered location outdoors as soon as the ground has warmed up in spring and there is no longer any danger of frost.

Monarch of the East, or **Lizard Arum** (*Sauromatum guttatum*), is similarly foul-smelling but has a tailed, "greenery-yallery" spathe with black-purple spots. Its smaller size makes it a better bet as a house plant. It is also hardier when planted outdoors, and may be expected to withstand freezing temperatures if the tubers are planted 6 inches deep and mulched.

Both species are capable of producing their inflorescences without benefit of soil or moisture provided their tubers are of flowering size —4 inches or more in diameter for *Amorphophallus;* 3 inches for *Sauromatum.* Immediately after flowering, however, the tubers should be planted out, or, if the weather is not sufficiently warm, put in large flowerpots with rich soil.

(4) Summer-flowering bulbs

With outdoor activities in full swing there is, perhaps, less incentive to work hard to insure a supply of flowering house plants for the summer months. However, oftentimes something is needed to take the place of the plants which are recuperating outdoors; and some of these "bulbs" are so gorgeous that anyone interested in plants can hardly forego the pleasure of growing them.

Achimenes: The plants known as Achimenes have flowers somewhat reminiscent of those of Gloxinia (to which they are related) produced on slender stems, 1 to 2 feet tall, clothed with opposite leaves. Of velvety texture, their flowers range from mauve to violet and crimson. They tend toward floppiness in growth habits and may be supported by twiggy shoots stuck in the soil around them; or allowed to droop over the edge of a hanging container. They are mostly derived from such species as *Achimenes grandiflora, A. longiflora,* and *A. patens,* but so far I have found them offered commercially only in an unnamed mixture.

The scaly rhizomes, or tubers, look like catkins or miniature Pine cones, and these are planted ½ inch deep in shallow boxes of moist sand and leafmold from January to March. When the shoots are from one to two inches tall they are carefully dug up and potted in bulb pans, in Begonia soil, using six plants to a 6-inch container. Keep the soil moist and shade from bright sunshine, but give them plenty of light. When the pots are filled with roots, water them occasionally with weak liquid manure. As soon as they are through flowering gradually reduce the supply of water; and when the foliage has withered keep them entirely dry. Before winter the tubers should be removed from their pots and stored in dry sand in a temperature of 50° until it is time to start them again.

Begonias—tuberous-rooted kinds: The Tuberous Begonias are among the showiest of all plants, with flowers varying in size from 3 to 8 inches in diameter—and their culture is not difficult, especially in those regions favored with a cool summer climate. There are various types available with colors ranging from white through pink to rose, scarlet, and crimson; and from pale yellow to salmon, orange, and apricot. They may be single or double. The singles may have

Tuberous Begonias, though usually grown out of doors, do well as summer bloomers in a north or west window or on a shady porch

plain petals, or be frilled and ruffled, or decorated with a crest on the center of each petal ("Cristata"). The double types may exhibit the exquisite form of the Camellia-flowered varieties, look like a rosebud, or have the congested, frilled, and serrated petals of the "Carnation" type which I do not like. Then there are those with trailing stems (suitable for the front edge of window boxes or hanging containers) such as *Begonia lloydi*. Usually these Begonias are sold under types and colors, but some named varieties are available such as Red Sensation, single; Rose Dawn, Camellia-flowered; and Autumn Glow, a Cristata type with copper and apricot coloring.

Their culture is much the same as that of Achimenes. The tubers may be started in March or April in peatmoss and sand, or leafmold and sand. When growth begins, lift them carefully and pot them singly in 3- or 4-inch pots to be transferred later to larger sizes (use soil recommended for Begonias, page 51), or they may be put directly into the containers in which they are to bloom—6- or 8-inch bulb pans. As with all Begonias, drainage is important, so don't fail to put an inch or so of flowerpot chips in the bottom of each pot. Shade them from bright sunshine, keep soil constantly moist, and spray foliage daily with clear water. When they show signs of going to rest gradually withhold water; and, when they have completely died down, remove the tubers and store at 50° to 60° in dry sand or peatmoss. While the usual practice is to purchase tubers, the adventurous can raise Tuberous Begonias from seeds and may get blooms the same year if they are sown in February; but it is a ticklish proposition for the amateur.

Caladium bicolor varieties—Fancy-leaved Caladiums: I suppose Caladiums do not really belong here for their flowers are insignificant; but the fancy-leaved kinds have much the same color effect as flowers so here they are. There are hundreds of varieties of *Caladium bicolor,* a native of Tropical America with long-stalked, arrowhead leaves, which in some varieties are almost transparent. Their coloration is immensely varied, as may be deduced from the few varieties described below. The plants range in height from 1 to 2½ feet. A popular variety is Candidum, which has white leaves edged with green and green veins. This is one of the best for an early display—it can be had in full leaf in January. Lord Derby is translucent rose, with green veins and edges; John Peed is bright red and green; Sorocaba, pink and white with greenish veins; Mme. Truall, a dwarf variety, is red and bronze, and Cleo has pink, white, and yellow veins, crimson ribs, on a ground of green blotched with pink.

Preferably the tubers should be started in March or April in a high temperature (80° to 85°) in shallow boxes of leafmold and sand, covering them about ½ inch deep. When the roots begin to grow, pot them in 3-inch pots in 3 parts leafmold, 1 part loam, 1 part sand. As soon as these pots are filled with roots shift them to 5- or 6-inch sizes and use 2 parts loam, 2 parts leafmold, 1 part decayed manure, 1 part sand. Shade from bright sunshine and water freely. When the leaves begin to fade, gradually reduce water until soil is dry. Store in the soil of their pots or in dry sand or peatmoss in a temperature not less than 60°.

Sinningia speciosa—**Gloxinia:** There are not many flowers that can beat the Gloxinia (*Sinningia speciosa*) in size and variety of coloring. The flowers are broadly tubular, with flaring petals which may extend their diameter to 5 inches. Some are dark-spotted on a light ground; some have white throats with the remainder of the flower pink, blue, purple, or red; and some have their petals margined with a broad band of contrasting color. Although most commonly sold in mixture, named varieties are available such as Bavaria, dark blue with white throat; Brunhilde, pure white; Etoile de Feu, bright red; Monterey Rose, deep pink; and Sky Blue, a pale blue-purple. The method of growing them is practically that of Tuberous Begonias except that it is wise to avoid getting water on the

Gloxinias, though usually grown in greenhouses, make good plants for summer bloom indoors or on a porch

fuzzy velvety leaves. During the winter they may be stored as suggested for Begonias or kept dry in their pots. If this last is done, it is possible to get by without repotting them for a year or two at any rate if some of the surface soil is scraped off and replaced by a 50-50 mixture of soil and rotted manure, with a teaspoonful of bonemeal.

Four or five years ago I gave an old lady in the country a small plant of Gloxinia which was proudly displayed for my admiration when I called on her last summer. And she had a right to be proud, for that year the plant, in a 6-inch pot, had produced thirty-five blooms, it was 26 inches in diameter, and many of the leaf blades were 9 inches long. It was kept in a south window shaded by curtains and, from the west, by a porch.

Gloxinias can be propagated from seeds in spring (flowers in about seven months) or by inserting leaf cuttings. A propagating case is desirable but not absolutely necessary. Last year, being in an experimental mood, I put one leaf in a glass of water in the house and another in a pot of soil in the shade of a building outdoors. Both produced tubers—that started in soil being the larger.

Other summer-flowering bulbous plants available for pot culture include *Gloriosa, Hymenocallis, Lycoris,* and *Zephyranthes.*

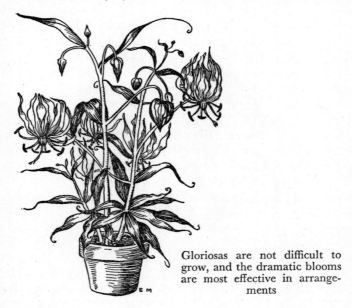

Gloriosas are not difficult to grow, and the dramatic blooms are most effective in arrangements

CACTI AND SUCCULENTS

The plants included under the above very general terms include some of the most useful and popular of all for house culture. Most of them are specially adapted in nature to survive under conditions of extreme drought and atmospheric dryness, a characteristic which makes them particularly suitable for culture in sunny windows of hot, dry rooms. No other group offers so many inducements to the collector. Many of the Cacti remain small even when mature so that a large number of species and varieties can be accommodated in a limited space; and the same is true of certain genera included in the succulents. But before going any further it would be well to define what is meant by Cacti and succulents.

Cacti are plants belonging in the Cactus Family, their position being determined by their floral characteristics. With very few exceptions all Cacti are succulents but not all succulents are Cacti. "Succulent" is the term applied to plants which have thick fleshy stems or leaves; and they are to be found in a large number of different plant families, including the Fig-marigold, Stonecrop, Euphorbia, Milkweed, Thistle, and many others. Purslane, that pernicious weed of the vegetable patch, is a succulent, and so is the Snake-plant, although neither is to be considered in this chapter.

Contrary to popular belief not all spiny succulent plants are Cacti though some—certain Euphorbias, for example—look more like Cacti, until you come to examine their flowers, than do some true Cactuses, such as Pereskia, which is a spiny, scrambling, climbing shrub with rather everyday leaves and is nothing at all like the usual conception of a Cactus. Yet its relationship is clear to the initiated, not alone on account of its flower structure, but because it can be used as an understock on which other Cacti are grafted. It is interesting that similar environmental conditions in different parts of the world should have brought about drought-resisting adaptations, resulting in superficially similar appearances in widely separated (botanically) plant families. But this is a book on house plants, and I must not get involved in abstruse discussions.

While the structure of Cacti and succulents is such that they are adapted to endure drought, not all of them are desert plants. Some, such as the Orchid Cacti and the Mistletoe Cactus, grow wild perched on the trees in tropical forests; hence they require more atmospheric moisture and different cultural conditions than most Cacti. I have seen huge masses of Mistletoe Cactus growing wild on trees in Trinidad in a Turkish-bath atmosphere.

Cacti

This is an extremely diverse group. Some, such as the Giant Cactus or Sahuaro, may reach a height of 60 feet and weigh many tons; others, such as certain Lobivias, may never be more than one or two inches high. There are some which hug the ground; others climb trees and clamber over walls if any are near by. The flowers may be a foot long and almost as much across in some of those to which the name Night-blooming Cereus is given, or no more than ¼ inch in diameter as in some of the Mistletoe Cacti. Many of the smaller types bear flowers which are larger than the plant from which they spring. In general, Cacti have no true leaves, their functions being carried on by the globular, cylindrical, triangular, quadrangular, or flattened stems.

There are some house-plant enthusiasts to whom Cacti appeal because of the adaptability of most of them to culture in hot, dry rooms; others consider them ideal plants to put in small plain or fancy pots to stand on a window shelf; while to some the gorgeous blooms of the Orchid Cacti and Christmas Cacti are more alluring. Still others are content to do without flowers while admiring the bizarre shapes and interesting spine patterns offered by many species. Those who are interested in plants as a means of "doing something" will turn to Cacti because of the ease with which they can be grafted or the possibilities they offer for the construction of desert scenes in dish gardens.

The Cactus Family is a large one, with more than 1,300 species divided among about 200 genera. Their nomenclature is a nightmare. The genus Cereus has been split up into dozens of genera, and those who learned about Cacti under the old dispensation have difficulty in finding their way around among the new names— which doubtless are all to the good in the long run. Often the descriptions in the commercial catalogues do not tally with those given in botanical reference works.

The selection of species and varieties which follow consists for the most part of those especially recommended by experts for house culture. It is less than a tithe of those offered in one commercial catalogue alone, so those who feel that the eighty species and varieties described here limit their capabilities will find no difficulty in adding to the list.

The plants below are grouped in three sections: (1) Those of small size especially suitable for culture in small pots to be displayed on window shelves. (2) Those of greater stature, including climbing and scrambling forms. (3) The Orchid Cacti and similar kinds requiring a moist atmosphere.

While all Cacti can be grown in small pots when they are babies, it is better, when the objective is the cultivation of an extensive collection, to restrict oneself to those which never become large. Most of the plants included in this section may be expected to bloom—some of them when they are no more than 2 inches in diameter.

Astrophytum—Sand Dollar, Bishop's Cap, Star Cactus: The Sand Dollar (*Astrophytum asterias*) has a flattened, spineless body, 1 inch high, 3 inches across, pale green divided by the ribs into about seven sections shaped like pieces of pie. The flowers are 1 inch long, yellow in color. Bishop's Cap or Bishop's Hood (*A. myriostigma*) is more or less globose, about 2 inches high, with five prominent ribs or ridges and no spines. A striking species, especially when the large yellow flowers are seen against the white body. There are several varieties of this. Star Cactus (*A. ornatum*) may grow to a foot in height, but it blooms when small. It has clusters of inch-long spines on the ridges; the body is flecked with white dots. The flowers are lemon-yellow and up to 3 inches broad. This, too, has many varieties.

Chamaecereus silvestri—Peanut Cactus: This species quickly forms clumps made up of peanutlike joints about 2 inches long covered with soft white spines. It must be handled gently for the joints snap off very easily; any that are knocked off can be planted to start a new colony. This is an intriguing little plant with orange-scarlet flowers 3 inches long. The variety *johnsoni* is reputed to be a hybrid with heavier stems and orange-yellow flowers. If these Cacti are required for display in 2- or 3-inch pots, it is wise to keep a supply of young stock coming along to take the place of the pots whose occupants have overflowed the container.

Echinocereus—Hedgehog Cereus: These, in general, are characterized by large flowers on a comparatively small plant, but *Echinocereus delaeti* may make a cluster up to 8 inches tall covered with white curly hair. The flowers are pink. A lone wolf, *E. fitchi*, makes a solitary body up to 4 inches tall with large pink flowers. *E. luteus* has cylindrical stems up to 10 inches tall and yellow, fragrant 3-inch flowers with conspicuous contrasting stigmas. One listed as *E. melanocentras* blooms when 2 inches in diameter with rosy flowers larger than the plant. *E. perbellus* may have single or clustered stems up to 4 inches tall and purple flowers. *E. pulchellus* forms an upside-down cone, blue-green or gray-green in color and pink flowers. The Lace Cactus is *E. reichenbachi*, which has light purple, fragrant flowers on a stem which may get up to 8 inches tall. The Rainbow Cactus, *E. rigidissimus*, can hardly be seen for its interlocking spines.

It has purplish flowers with white centers and is reputed to be less easily grown than some.

Echinopsis—Sea Urchin Cactus, Easter Lily Cactus: These have for the most part globular bodies and white flowers sometimes tinted with pink, purple, or green. *E. eyriesi,* which will flower from seed in about two or three years, has large white flowers. The variety *grandiflora* has dark pink flowers. Trade names include *E. hamatacantha,* a small, flattened globe with white flowers which may be tinged with rose, much taller than the plant. It is advisable to shade it from very bright light and give moisture at all times. Easter Lily Cactus, *E. hybrida,* makes a deeply ridged globe with abundant white flowers. *E. multiplex,* with pink flowers 6 to 8 inches long, may grow to 6 inches or more tall.

Espostoa lanata—Snowball Cactus: Although this species may grow up to 15 feet tall, it is included here because even young plants are covered with white cottony hair which gives them a unique appearance, something like that of the Old Man Cactus.

Gymnocalycium—Chin Cacti: These are generally small globular Cacti with large flowers. *Gymnocalycium damsi* may get to be 2 inches in diameter with pink flowers more than an inch across. It is said to be able to get along even in the shade. The Striped Chin Cactus, also a midget, makes a flattened, ridged globe with a rippled effect along the ridges. The flowers may be white, pink, or yellowish. Its botanical moniker is *G. mihanovichi.* Then there is *Gymnocalycium schikendantzi* (how's that for a name!), which may attain a diameter of 4 inches and has white or pinkish blossoms 2 inches long. The name Chin Cactus comes from a chinlike protuberance below each cluster of spines.

Hamatocactus setispinus—Strawberry Cactus: So called, presumably, because of its red fruits which to me look more like Cranberries. It has yellow flowers with a conspicuous red throat, produced when the plant is no larger than a ball 2 inches in diameter. Old specimens may get to be 6 inches high.

Lobivia—Cob Cactus: The name Lobivia is an anagram of Bolivia where many of this genus grow wild, though they are also found in Argentina and Peru. *L. aurea* has large lemon-yellow flowers on globular or cylindrical stems up to 4 inches tall. *L. cinnabarina* has scarlet flowers nearly 2 inches across on a plant broader than it is high. Hertrich's Cob Cactus (*L. hertrichiana*) is a flattened globe which may reach 4 inches across but is seldom more than 2 inches under cultivation. It has scarlet flowers almost 3 inches across, produced in great profusion.

Lophophora williamsi—Peyote, Sacred Mushroom: This plant with dull, bluish-green, flattened globes up to 3 inches in diameter is not much to look at even when displaying its white or pink 1-inch blooms, but it is an interesting plant to grow because of its former association with the religious ceremonies of the Indians of the Southwest. It has a thick taproot and should be grown in a deep pot.

Mammillaria—Pincushion Cactus: This genus contains some of the most delightful Cacti for growing in small pots, though many of them, when given room, may make large clumps. The Powder Puff Cactus (*Mammillaria bocasana*) has globes 1½ inches across. The slender green tubercles are set on a pink body and topped with tufts of silky hairs and hooked brown spines which, however, are not in the least bit vicious. The Bird's Nest Cactus (*M. campotricha*) ultimately makes clumps of globes 2 inches in diameter with large tubercles surmounted by four to eight conspicuous, flexible spines. The flowers are small, white, and greenish on the outside. *M. carnea,* which blooms all summer with pink flowers up to 1 inch, has cylindrical stems up to 3½ inches high and quadrangular tubercles. There are several varieties of the Golden Lace Cactus (*M. elongata*), sometimes called Golden Stars from the harmless yellow spines which radiate from the tubercles. This is a fast grower with small white flowers, quickly making clumps of 4-inch long cylindrical stems. Thimble Cactus (*M. fragilis*) makes a short cylindrical stem with clustered globes at the top which readily break off to start new plants. Each tubercle has twelve to fourteen white spines radiating from it. The flowers are small, white, and pinkish on the outside.

The Old Lady Cactus (why not Old Woman, since *Cephalocereus senilis* is called Old Man?) is *M. hahniana.* It has a globular stem up to 4 inches high covered with white hair when old. It has rose-carmine flowers. *M. kewensis,* one of the larger, quick-growing Mammillarias—it may reach a foot in height—is recommended for its free-flowering habits. It has crimson or reddish-purple flowers and pink berry-like fruits. *M. microhelia* is a cylindrical type up to 6 inches long, bedecked with white wool at the top. The flowers are white, ½ inch long. *M. perbella lanata* is a small flattened globe with pale spines radiating from the tubercles making a pattern of concentric circles. It is ready to bloom with reddish, ½-inch flowers when no more than 1½ inches across. The Fish-hook Pincushion (*M. wildi*) is a clustering type, with cylindrical or globe-like stems and slender tubercles, each tipped with a hooked spine. The ½-inch white flowers are freely produced in a circle around the top of the body.

There are over 200 species of Mammillaria and many varieties all with something to commend them. The above selection, in the main, represents free-flowering kinds.

Notocactus—Ball Cactus: This genus, by some botanists combined with *Malacocarpus,* has several free-flowering species including *Notocactus apricus,* about 2 inches in diameter with yellow flowers larger than the plant. *N. haselbergi* makes an 8-inch globe, with white spines and numerous red flowers 1 inch across. A shining green globular stem with the central spines more than ½ inch long and 1½-inch yellow flowers with contrasting scarlet stigmas, sometimes produced four or more at a time, are the chief characteristics of *M. mammulosus.* It has the reputation of being easy to grow. Silver Ball Cactus (*N. scopa*) may grow up to 1½ feet. Young plants are globular, blooming while still small, clothed with white bristles, each tuft interspersed with longer red spines. The lemon-yellow flowers are 2½ inches across with pale anthers and a scarlet stigma. A striking plant in bloom and out.

Opuntia—Prickly-pear, Cholla, Tuna: The members of this genus are, in general, too large for culture in small pots, but there are two at least which are satisfactory for the purpose. Rabbit Ears (*O. microdasys*) has small "pads" with no spines, but plenty of golden glochids (barbed bristles) in dense tufts arranged in diagonal lines. The variety *albescens* is similar with white, innocuous glochids. Then there is *O. ramossissima,* which, although capable of attaining 6 feet, is very attractive because of its habit of branching when still small. It then reminds one of a miniature edition of Sahuaro.

Rebutia: A group of small South American Cacti with large flowers produced from the side or base of the plants. *Rebutia minuscula* makes a globe about 2 inches in diameter with spiraled tubercles and bright crimson 1½-inch flowers around the base of the plant body. *R. senilis,* also globose, is usually only about 3 inches tall with bristly spines to 1¼ inches long and bright carmine 2-inch flowers. These Rebutias should be shaded from bright sunshine and given more water than the general run of Cacti.

I leave this group of small Cacti with the feeling that I shall be taken to task for leaving out many valuable and favorite kinds. But I have to remember that this is a book of house plants in general and not of Cacti alone.

Large Cacti

We are now to consider those Cacti which are capable of reaching larger dimensions and appeal to those who appreciate bulk and need something more massive than the tiny varieties. While these big brothers can be used as shelf plants when they are young, they are more impressive when they are grown up and most of them do not bloom until they attain a good size.

Aporocactus flagelliformis—**Rat-tail Cactus:** This has long flexible stems about ½ inch in diameter covered with bristly hairs, and

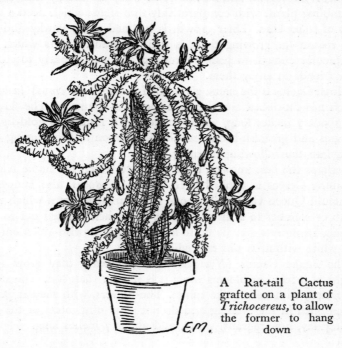

A Rat-tail Cactus grafted on a plant of *Trichocereus,* to allow the former to hang down

crimson flowers 3 inches long. It can be grown as a trailer or trained up on a support; but it is more commonly seen grafted at the top of a straight stem of another Cactus. Its stems are so limp that they can be trained in any way that fancy dictates. It is an easy species to grow and showy in bloom.

Cephalocereus—Old Man Cactus, Woolly Torch Cactus: The name Old Man Cactus is applied to *Cephalocereus senilis,* characterized by the shaggy white hair with which the cylindrical stems are covered. It is a slow grower and, although capable of reaching a height of 40 feet, pot-grown specimens in excess of 2 feet are rare. The flowers (I have never seen one in bloom!) are rose-colored, about 2½ inches long. A similar species, but less common, is known as Woolly Torch Cactus (*C. palmeri*). Crushed limestone or powdered eggshells should be mixed with the soil for these.

Cereus—Night-blooming Cereus: The plants to which the name Night-blooming Cereus is commonly applied have been ejected from the genus *Cereus* and are now to be found under *Harrisia, Hylocereus, Nyctocereus,* and *Selenicereus.* They are mostly climbing or scrambling plants with comparatively thin stems which need a support of some kind. Their growth is inclined to be gawky and the real reason for growing them is their fragrant flowers which are spectacular enough to justify throwing an evening party to enable your friends to enjoy them.

Moon Cactus is the name given to *Harrisia (Eriocereus) jusberti,* which has six-ribbed erect stems 2 inches in diameter. The flowers are about 7 inches long, white petaled with numerous gold-tipped stamens and greenish-brown sepals. They open in the evening and close late the following morning.

Perhaps the best known of the plants to which the name Night-blooming Cereus is applied is *Hylocereus undatus,* also known as Honolulu Queen Cactus. This one has triangular stems which may climb or clamber to a distance of 40 feet when planted out in the tropics. Its flowers may be up to a foot long, yellowish-green outside and white within. It has red, edible fruits.

The Snake Cactus (*Nyctocereus serpentinus*) may grow to a height of 8 feet but blooms when it is smaller than this. The stems are fluted, with needle-like spines. The flowers, with slender petals which open in the evening and do not close until noon of the following day, are fragrant, white, and about 7 inches long.

Queen of the Night (*Selenicereus macdonaldiae*) is a high-growing climber with angled stems about ½ inch thick. The flowers are enormous, up to 14 inches across, with white petals, reddish or yellowish sepals, and conspicuous stamens and pistil.

Some of these plants are extremely tenacious of life. I remember one of them (I think it was *Hylocereus*) which remained alive for many months though deprived of contact with the soil and hanging on a wire attached to the greenhouse roof. It had been inadvertently left behind when the main portion of the plant was removed. They need fairly good soil—in between Cactus and general-purpose mixture—and rather dry conditions at the root during winter, but plenty of water when they are actively growing.

Cleistocactus—Scarlet Bugler, Silver Torch: Scarlet Bugler (*Cleistocactus baumanni*) has 1½-inch cylindrical stems (which may need support) up to 6 feet high. The spines are yellowish brown, but the striking feature is the slender, tubular, orange-scarlet flowers up to 3 inches long. The Silver Torch (*C. straussi*) has conspicuous bristly white spines on erect stems up to 3 feet high, and red to carmine-violet flowers, which may be nearly 4 inches long. This species is reputed to be able to endure a few degrees of frost.

Echinocactus—Barrel Cacti: The Golden Barrel Cactus (*Echinocactus grusoni*) is attractive even as a small plant, but it may reach 4 feet in height and 2½ feet in diameter. There is, or was, a specimen in the Huntington Botanical Gardens, San Marino, California, about thirty years old whose weight is estimated at 400 pounds. It is possible to buy specimens 1½ feet in diameter, but these cost around $50. The beauty of this plant depends mainly on the golden spines, arranged with almost mathematical exactitude, and the contrasting feltlike cushion at the top of the plant in which the red and yellow flowers are imbedded.

Lemaireocereus—Organ-pipe Cactus: The Organ-pipe Cactus botanically is *Lemaireocereus* (*Pachycereus*) *marginatus*. Capable of reaching a height of 25 feet, it is commonly used in Mexico for making living fences. The common name is descriptive of its appearance although its stems, unlike the pipes of an organ, are ribbed. It is one of those kinds which sometimes are embarrassing because of the height to which they grow. I was once in a greenhouse whose owner was compelled to append a "lantern" to accommodate it. If it gets too big for the home, the best plan is to cut off a section of suitable size from the top and root it, discarding the old plant.

Opuntia—Cholla, Prickly-pear, Tuna: One or two Opuntias should be in every collection if only to represent what to many people is the typical Cactus form with flattened oval joints resembling ping-pong bats. Orange Tuna (*Opuntia elata*), which grows to about 3 feet, has almost spineless joints up to 10 inches long. The flowers, 2 inches across, are orange-yellow. *Opuntia monacantha* is perhaps best known in the form of its variety *variegata,* sometimes called Joseph's Coat because of the white, yellow, and pink splotches on the joints. These are oval and may reach the length of a foot. The Grizzly Bear Opuntia (*O. ursina*) grows to about 1½ feet, the plant body being almost completely hidden by shaggy bristle-like spines. The flowers are reddish-yellow, 3 inches across. The Paper-spined Opuntia is *Tephrocactus glomeratus,* which see.

Oreocereus—Mountain Cacti: Coming from the Andes, these Cacti can endure low temperatures. Old Man of the Andes (*Oreocereus celsianus*) grows to 3 feet and has 3-inch branches covered with matted white hairs. Its variety *lanuginosior* has abundant, short woolly hairs. Another species growing unbranched to about 3 feet is *O. trolli.*

Tephrocactus glomeratus—Paper-spined Opuntia: This species, sometimes listed as *Opuntia papyracantha,* has fat oval joints with prominent tubercles and long white flexible spines something like white-pine shavings. A distinctive plant worthy of a place in any collection.

Trichocereus spachianus—White Torch Cactus: An easily grown species with cylindrical, prominently ribbed stems up to 3 feet tall. The flowers are pure white, about 6 inches across. It is frequently used as an understock on which crested or delicate Cacti are grafted. It needs more water than most of its relatives.

This business of making a selection from many hundreds of large-growing kinds has been a difficult one. I have tried to include a variety of types distinctive in appearance and have left out all which are not listed in commercial catalogues.

Culture: The soil must be porous so that stagnant water does not remain about the roots. Most Cacti require an alkaline soil which can be provided by mixing with it mortar rubble, limestone, oyster shells, or eggshells (if you have enough of them!), all of which should be crushed or pounded so that there are no pieces more than ¼ inch across.

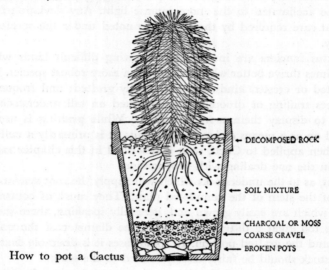

← DECOMPOSED ROCK

← SOIL MIXTURE

← CHARCOAL OR MOSS
← COARSE GRAVEL
← BROKEN POTS

How to pot a Cactus

Watering must be done with care. Although Cacti are adapted to survive dryness (if you want to take a long week end you can go away without worrying about them), during the time they are actively growing and in the summer months they can be watered as freely as you would a Begonia. During the short days of winter they must definitely be kept on the dry side, giving them only enough water to keep the stems from shriveling. Avoid watering when the weather is overcast unless it is made necessary by shriveling stems.

Some types with globular or barrel-like bodies occupy so much of the soil surface that it is difficult to apply enough water from above to moisten the entire mass of soil. The pots of such plants should be partially submerged in a vessel of water until moisture shows on the surface. The way I handle the small specimens is to stand them in small glass saucers, obtained from the 5-and-10, which are filled with water whenever the soil seems to be getting dry. *Any water remaining in the saucer after an hour or two is poured off.*

Most Cacti should be kept in a sunny window during fall, winter, and spring. Watch them especially in summer, and if there is any indication of sunburn shown by yellowing or browning of the body on the exposed side, provide light shade. If they are put outdoors for the summer, don't forget to keep them lightly shaded until they become acclimated to the more intense light. Any deviation from general care required by those listed is noted under the species or variety.

Cactus fanciers are interested in growing difficult kinds which sometimes thrive better when grafted on a more robust species. The fasciated or crested kinds also are usually grafted; and frequently one sees trailing or drooping kinds worked on tall understocks in order to display them more effectively. While grafting is usually looked on as a means of increasing plants, it is primarily a cultural aid when applied to Cacti, so it is described in this chapter rather than in the one dealing with propagation.

First, as to the understocks which will supply the root system and part of the stem of the completed plant. They must, of course, be kinds which are easily grown and, generally speaking, there should not be too great a difference between the diameter of the understock and the grafted portion. In some cases it is desirable that the understock should be fairly closely related to the scion.

The shrublike *Pereskia* is often used as an understock for Christmas Cactus which, however, is very accommodating and can be grafted successfully on other diverse kinds such as *Selenicereus* and *Opuntia*. A plant of striking appearance can be constructed by inserting scions of *Zygocactus* at 3-inch intervals around the upper edge of a large flat joint of an *Opuntia*. This is effective until the scions grow so much that they obscure the understock. An even stranger-looking plant can be created by grafting scions of the Peanut Cactus on each stem tip of a branched *Pereskia*.

Trichocereus spachianus is commonly used as an understock for allied crested varieties; for small globular forms *Selenicereus* is among those favored; *Pereskia* and *Opuntia* are used for Christmas Cactus.

The technique of grafting Cacti is simple and the results relatively certain. If, for example, a high-grafted Christmas Cactus is wanted, you obtain, or grow, a single-stemmed *Pereskia* a few inches taller than the desired height and cut off those extra inches squarely. Then split the stem to a depth of an inch. Take a shoot tip of Christmas

Cactus (some use one joint and some use two) and with a very sharp knife slice a piece off either side of the base to make a wedge which is inserted in the split of the understock and then pinned in place by a couple of slender Cactus thorns thrust through stock

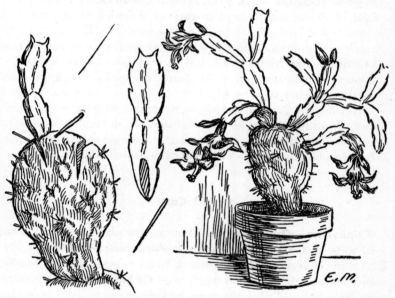

Detail of grafting Cactus (Zygocactus on Opuntia) and plant after a few months' growth

and scion. If *Opuntia* is used as the understock, merely cut slits at 3-inch intervals across the edge of the upper half of the joint and insert the scions prepared as above and pin in place. The grafted plant should be shaded until union has taken place.

Another method which can be used, for example, when grafting the Rat-tailed Cactus on *Selenicereus* is to cut a wedge-shaped piece out of the understock and bevel the scion to fit in it. Pin in place with thorns and tie with soft twine. With some Cacti it may be necessary to trim off some of the thorns to facilitate grafting.

The globular and crested types usually are grafted low, and fleshy-stemmed understocks (rather than the rather woody *Pereskia*) are used. The understock, rooted in a comparatively small pot, not more than 3-inch size, is cut off at the desired height with a single, clean, horizontal cut. The base of the scion is similarly cut, applied to the cut surface of the stock, and held in close contact by two rubber bands which pass below the bottom of the pot and over the top of the graft. The tension should not be too great—merely enough to press the scion gently against the stock. If necessary, a couple of thorns can be used to prevent the scion from slithering around. Two lengths of soft twine can be used instead of the rubber bands if something is used to prevent the twine from cutting into the scion. In this operation three hands, or even four, are desirable.

There is almost no limit to the fantastic creations made possible by grafting bizarre types of Cacti.

When buying Cacti, it is well to remember that those collected directly from the deserts of the Southwest are difficult to establish; and unless the plants are required for a temporary display only, it is better to obtain nursery- or greenhouse-grown plants.

Orchid Cacti

Epiphyllum—**Orchid Cactus:** These are the plants some of which used to be rather generally known as *Phyllocactus*—meaning leafy Cactus in reference to their flattened, leaflike stems, actually a misnomer because they have no true leaves. Of late years the botanists have been busy splitting them up into genera such as *Disocactus, Epiphyllum, Nopalxochia, Schlumbergera* (Easter Cactus), and *Zygocactus* (Christmas Cactus). The horticulturists have also been busy crossing the different sections so that it is difficult to know where we are. Thinking that most home gardeners are less interested in the fine points of botanical differences than they are in growing these gorgeous plants, and because they all need much the same cultural treatment, they are lumped together here under *Epiphyllum* except for the comparatively small-flowered *Zygocactus*.

The plants themselves are awkward and ungainly, their flattened stems with scalloped edges seldom disposing themselves in a sightly manner. But they fully make up for their lack of grace when their colorful blooms, up to 10 inches in diameter in some varieties, are displayed, mostly in spring and early summer, in glowing colors. Even unbranched specimens no more than a foot high will bloom, but some varieties are capable of developing into many-branched plants, 3 or more feet in diameter.

There are dozens of species and garden varieties available including White Orchid Cactus (*Epiphyllum strictum*) which is a night-bloomer and may grow to 6 feet with flowers up to 6 inches long; Red Orchid Cactus (*Nopalxochia akermanni*) up to 3 feet tall with 8-inch flowers, scarlet on the outside, carmine within, and contrasting white stamens; Yellow Orchid Cactus (*Epiphyllum [Phyllocactus] cooperi*) with white and yellow flowers up to 9 inches across; and Easter Cactus, *Schlumbergera gaertneri,* with drooping branches and scarlet flowers 3 inches long. Then there are the hybrids and named garden forms such as Empress, pink; Etoile de Contich, salmon-red with inner petals suffused with violet; Gloria, with 8-inch flame-colored flowers; Latona, orchid-pink; and Scarlet Giant, whose scarlet petals have an orange stripe.

These plants need different treatment from Cacti in general except that, in common with all, the pots in which they are grown must be well drained. To insure this, put at least an inch of flowerpot chips or something similar in the bottom. Use the soil recommended for Begonias and do not pot too firmly. They must have abundant supplies of water at the root during the time they are actively growing, but it must run freely through the soil. They need moist air and should not be exposed to strong sunshine. Even during the winter, when they should be kept on the dry side at the roots, their branches should be sprayed on dry, sunny days. During the summer, keep them outdoors in the shade of a tree or building. In country districts one can often see excellent examples of Orchid Cacti growing in discarded cooking utensils, displayed on a shaded porch or apparently carelessly disposed on the lawn beneath a tree.

The Christmas Cactus (*Zygocactus trunctatus*) needs much the same growing conditions as the preceding kinds. The terminal branchlets are made up of glossy, leaflike, flattened joints measuring about $2'' \times 1''$. The flowers, about $2\frac{1}{2}$ inches long, may be from pink to deep red with gradations between according to variety. They are produced from the tips of the branches any time from October to January, but usually are at their best at Christmas. This is one of those heirloom kinds of plants, lasting for years in the home and increasing in size. There are many varieties and hybrids of this species which doubtless accounts for apparent erratic behavior in the time of blossoming. Although it roots easily from cuttings and grows well on its own roots, its drooping habit of growth has led to the practice of grafting it upon Cacti with stiff, upright stems, or on a *Pereskia* shoot, so that the flowers are displayed well above the pot (see page 209). One of my earliest recollections is of the magnificent display made by Christmas Cactus grafted at intervals along a stem of *Pereskia* that extended from the eaves to the ridge of a greenhouse.

Many are the recipes for growing the Christmas Cactus, and those who are successful with it naturally think their own method is the best; I, for one, would not suggest that they make a change even if it does not coincide with the following suggestions which seem the logical treatment for this species. Put the plants outdoors when the weather has warmed up in the spring. Give them light shade (I have known them to do well, however, when exposed to full sunshine) and water them whenever necessary during dry periods, using a weak liquid manure every two or three weeks. About the middle of September, or before if there is any danger of frost, bring them indoors and place in an east or west window. If you have to use a south window, shade them from bright sunshine to about the end of October. Until flower buds begin to form, keep on the dry side but not so dry that the joints shrivel. During the flowering period, water them moderately, and then keep on the dry side again until new shoots begin to grow when they should be watered freely. There are often complaints of the plants dropping their flower buds. This could be caused by too much or too little water, exposure to cold drafts, the presence of gas in the air, or rough handling.

Other Succulents

The Cacti circumvent their droughty environment by storing moisture in their thickened stems which take over the work ordinarily done by the leaves; and, in some cases, take on some semblance to them. These other succulents for the most part depend on their fleshy leaves, covered with an impervious cuticle, as moisture reservoirs. Unlike the Cacti, which are native to North and South America, succulents are found growing in Europe, Africa, Asia, as well as the Americas.

It has already been mentioned that succulents are found in a number of plant families; but the two which contain the most members suited for our purpose are the Stonecrop Family, represented in our gardens by such familiar plants as Houseleek and Showy Sedum; and the Fig-marigold Family, represented by the Ice Plant grown outdoors as an annual for the effect of the glistening pustules with which the plant is covered.

The member of the Stonecrop group most commonly seen is *Crassula argentea* (*portulacea*), introduced to the public as Japanese Rubber Plant. Native to South Africa and having no connection whatever with rubber, the absurdity of this common name brought about the change to Jade Plant. Under any name it leaves me cold, for it is a dreary plant with fat, uninteresting leaves and a stodgy habit of growth. Its tiny flowers are so seldom produced under house conditions that they cannot be looked on as a redeeming feature. But if you cherish a Jade Plant, don't let anything I say about it take away from your pleasure in growing one. It has, however, many relatives which are distinctive and adaptable to house culture including:

Aeonium tabulaeforme: This close relative of the Houseleeks is a strange-looking plant with overlapping leaves arranged in a rosette, 3 or more inches across, almost as flat as a table top. It is rather rare in cultivation and I have not grown it as a house plant; but it has been recommended by others for the purpose, and it is so distinctive that I suggest giving it a trial if you can obtain it.

Crassula—Jade Plant, Scarlet Paint Brush, et cetera: In addition to the Jade Plant which already has had some mention, this genus contains many plants of diverse form and habit. Among them is Scarlet Paint Brush (*Crassula* [*Rochea*] *falcata*) which in favored regions may attain a height of 8 feet. As a pot plant it is usually a foot or so high with a flat head of bright crimson flowers. The grayish leaves are thick and fleshy, sickle-shaped, crossing at their bases.

Crassula lycopodioides, which has been called by the name Princess-pine, an unfortunate one because of the possibility of a mix-up with Prince's-pine (*Chimaphila*), is an entirely different plant. This Crassula has closely appressed, tiny, bright green leaves on slender branches. The general appearance, as implied by the specific name, is similar to that of some of the Club Mosses (*Lycopodium*).

The name Necklace Vine (*Crassula rupestris*) could be applied to more than one species (though they are not exactly vines) with leaves united at the base so that they appear to be threaded on the stem. In addition to the one above, the ¾-inch leaves of which are glaucous with bright green spots, there is *C. perforata,* with slightly larger leaves, also spotted, which may grow into a shrub 2 feet tall. All these except *C. falcata* make excellent plants in small pots for shelf culture. *C. lycopodioides* does not mind a little shade.

Echeveria (sometimes called Hen-and-chickens) : The Echeverias are rosette-forming plants often with bluish-white glaucous leaves and attractive flowers of coral or orange-red.

Echeveria elegans makes 2-inch, blue-white rosettes with "chickens" around the base and small pinkish flowers with yellow tips rising 8 inches above the rosette.

E. gibbiflora is one of the giants of the genus, reaching a height of 2 feet. The leaves are 7 inches long, glaucous with a pinkish tinge. The flowers are red. The variety *metallica* has purplish leaves with, as the name implies, a metallic sheen.

The best known of all perhaps is *E. glauca,* often used as an edging to formal beds outdoors. The rosettes are 2 to 3 inches across and blue-green. This is a free-blooming species whose flowers are coral-colored without and yellow within.

The pinkish variegation in the leaves of *E. hoveyi* is a distinctive characteristic. This also attains considerable size, but it is attractive as a young plant. The flowers are pinkish.

Mexican Firecracker is the name given to *E. setosa,* a species with fat, 2-inch-long hairy leaves in a globular rosette. The flowers are red tipped with yellow.

The plants of *E. leucotricha* growing on my 2-foot shelves are much admired. The deep green leaves which have carmine tips and, as the leaves become mature, carmine margins are covered with short white hairs, giving a plushlike effect. I am waiting for the flowers which are cinnabar red in color.

Kalanchoe (*Bryophyllum, Kitchingia*) : Some of the plants that we used to know as *Bryophyllum* and *Kitchingia* are now referred to as *Kalanchoe.* The plant variously known as Miracle Leaf, Air Plant, Life Plant, and Floppers is *K. pinnata.* In 5-and-10-cent stores, where the leaves are sometimes sold attached to cards bearing a rigmarole about its wondrous qualities, it is called Good-luck Leaf. Not particularly beautiful, it is interesting because of the plantlets which are formed on the leaf margins—even if a leaf is cut off and pinned on a window curtain. It should be given general-purpose potting mixture, liberal root room, and light shade if you want 6-foot-tall plants. The flowers have "greenery-yallery" or purple-tinted, inflated calyxes and reddish petals. Although not showy, a well-grown inflorescence is rather impressive.

Even more prolific of plantlets is *K. daigremontiana* with curious mottled leaves which remind one of lizards. Although its height is sometimes given as "usually 1½ feet," it may attain 3 feet. Its flowers are not worth much.

The most popular species of all is *K. blossfeldiana*, grown com-

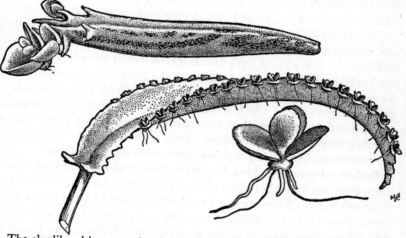

The sluglike object, top, is a leaf (enlarged 2⅔ times) of *Kalanchoe verticillata*, with developing plantlets; just above is *K. daigremontiana* (about life size). Insert is a greatly enlarged plantlet of the latter

mercially in enormous quantities for sale during the winter, when it is covered with small scarlet flowers in clusters. Although a perennial, second-year plants are not nearly so satisfactory as those grown from seeds or cuttings annually. General potting mixture should be used and the plants should be shaded from bright sun during the hottest months. It will take more water than the general run of succulents.

A plant received under the name Panda Plant (it does remind one of a panda, though it is difficult to tell why), *K. pilosa,* a synonym for

K. lanceolata, does not seem to fit the description of the latter. My plant is pictured and listed in a trade catalogue as *K. tomentosa* or Plush Plant, but the name is not included in *Hortus Second.* Whatever its real name may be, it is a first-class shelf plant. The 3-inch fleshy leaves, loosely arranged in a rosette, are blue-green, covered with a lush growth of short white hairs, except on the margins of the upper half, where they are rust-red or sometimes almost black.

A species known as *K. uniflora, Bryophyllum uniflorum,* and *Kitchingia uniflora* is an excellent plant for a hanging container. Its stems, clothed with 1-inch leaves, may trail over the edge to a length of 2 feet. The rose-colored inflated flowers are long-lasting and abundantly produced. It has been in the trade and may appear again—watch for it. It needs moist conditions and a humusy soil.

There are two species which, if planted several together in a small pot, suggest a clump of miniature coconut palms. One, *K. verticillata* (*tubiflora*), has almost cylindrical leaves (with plantlets at the tips) which are arranged in a cluster at the top of the stem with the lowermost ones drooping to give a palmlike effect. Although it is capable of growing to 3 feet, it is most effective when about 8 inches tall. The other, catalogued as *Bryophyllum houghtoni,* I do not remember very well, but its picture shows a growth habit similar to the preceding, but having mottled leaves with serrated edges.

Sedum—Stonecrop, Live-for-ever: Among the subtropical Sedums there are a number of interesting possibilities for house culture. Although many of them grow to a foot or more in height and as much across, it is practicable to use them as small pot plants for the window shelf because of the ease with which individual shoots will root when inserted as cuttings. Mature leaves broken off and left lying on the soil surface often will form roots and ultimately young plants.

The Mexican *Sedum adolphi* has fleshy, inch-long leaves, yellowgreen with bronzy tints. The leaves of *S. allantoides* remind one of a shortened, curved baseball bat. In color they are gray-green as a result of the waxy "bloom" with which they are covered. One which I received as *S. guatemalense,* but which does not fit the botanical description of this species, has red stems and green ¾-inch sausage-shaped leaves, tinged with red at their tips. Erect as a baby, it soon makes long stems which droop over the edge of the pot. Hairlike roots are produced along the stems. The catalogue description of

S. stahli says it has "Chains of red football-shaped leaves in 4 ranks." I'm not sure that this is the true *S. stahli,* but it sounds like an interesting plant to have.

Doubtless the hardy kinds, which have an important place in our rock gardens, could be grown indoors by anyone who has such an affection for them as would suggest this.

Sempervivum—Houseleek: The hardy Sempervivums also can be grown indoors. If this is done, I suggest that it would be a good plan to pot them in the fall and leave them in a coldframe until sometime in January so that they would get a part of the winter's rest to which they are accustomed. Among the interesting species are *Sempervivum arachnoideum* and its varieties (Cobweb Houseleek); *S. calcareum,* whose leaves are tipped with red-brown; and *S. soboliferum,* which has globular rosettes.

Mesembryanthemum—Fig-marigold, Living Stones, Windowed Plants, Pebble Plant, Tiger's Jaw, et cetera: This genus of upward of 1,000 species has been split up into more than 100 genera, known collectively as Mesembryanthema.

The strong-growing kinds, especially the trailers, are widely planted in California to control erosion on banks and, ornamentally, for draping over rocks. It is, however, the smaller species with which we are concerned. They are among the most interesting plants in the vegetable kingdom. Coming from the Karroo and other desert regions in South Africa, they have developed protective mimicry to an amazing extent; and their adaptations to a hot, dry environment and brilliant sunshine are intensely fascinating. Some of them, mimicking the rocks among which they grow, are like chips of granite; and some resemble water-worn stones.

To overcome their droughty environment, they store moisture in their thick fleshy leaves which are covered with an almost impervious cuticle. If you want to demonstrate the effectiveness of this covering, pull off a leaf and split it open. After twelve hours compare it with another leaf pulled off at the same time but not cut open. The split leaf will shrivel to about half size; the other will be scarcely affected. Some species actually grow with their leaves buried beneath the soil, with only the more or less flattened tips visible. These are equipped with translucent "windows" through which light is admitted to the chlorophyll. Some of them never have more than two leaves on a stem at a time; and often they are so closely joined that they look like the solid body of a thornless Cactus. Their flowers are daisy-like (though, botanically, they are far removed from this family), often larger than the plant body, and usually are brilliantly colored—yellow, orange, and magenta are common.

It is impossible here to do more than mention a very few of the genera to give a rough idea of the appearance of some of these plants. If you try a few and are successful with them, you are likely to want to assemble a collection; then you should get the catalogues of specialists and make a selection.

Cigarette Plant is the name given to *Cheiridopsis. C. candidissima* is said to be the best species. It grows in tufts, has white leaves about ½ inch in diameter and 4 inches long, arranged in pairs. The flowers are 2 to 3 inches across, white or pale pink.

In the genus *Conophytum* **(Cone-plants)** the growths consist of two leaves joined together, with a small orifice at the top from which a single flower arises which may be much larger than the growth from which it originates. I have a plant of *C. wiggetae* in which the growths are so closely aggregated in a rounded clump that the normal shape (an inverted cone, average dimensions about 1 $\times$ ¾ inch) of many of them is distorted by pressure. After probing gingerly into the clump, which is 5 inches across and 2 inches high, it seems to me that the leaves are attached to a very short, branching stem system, which is completely invisible unless the growths are pried apart. This timid investigation also disclosed, to my horror, colonies of scale insects, attached out of sight, on the lower part of the growths. It looks as though I shall have to break the clump apart and wipe off the insects by hand, for they are so well hidden between the plant bodies and the remains of the leaves of the preceding year that it is impossible to get at them with an insecticidal spray.

The tips of the leaves of *Faucaria tigrina,* seen in profile, look like the bow of a canoe. The leaves are in pairs and the upper half of each leaf is furnished with recurving teeth, giving a fancied resemblance to the opened jaws of a tiger. There are about 6 pairs of leaves on the almost stemless shoots which grow to form a clump. The flowers, about 1 inch across and bright yellow, are produced in the fall. *F. tigrina superba,* the one commonly offered for sale, has larger flowers.

One occasionally sees plants of **Glottiphyllum** used in made-up dish gardens. Their leaves in general are tongue-shaped, very fleshy, bright green, and cool to touch. *G. longum,* which has leaves 4 inches long, is stemless, with yellow flowers about 3 inches across.

Lapidaria margaritae has thick, stubby leaves, about three pairs of them, 1 inch broad, ¾ inch long, smooth in texture, colored white, yellowish, or brownish, and tinged with rose. A fall-blooming species; the flowers are 2 inches across and bright yellow.

Lithops—Stoneface: The plants in this genus grow somewhat in the same manner as *Conophytum.* In the wild the leaves of most species are partially or completely buried with only the flattened, often windowed top showing; and, when out of bloom, looking like pebbles strewn on the ground. Often the coloration on the growths (pairs of united leaves) forms interesting patterns. This is a large genus and one dealer lists over thirty species. The following were selected on the basis of giving variety in coloring.

Lithops framesi has pinkish-gray growths, 2 inches or so tall, and 1-inch white flowers; *L. lactea,* also with white flowers, has reddish-gray growths with translucent dots and white fragrant flowers; *L. meyeri* is dark, grayish-green with 1½-inch yellow flowers; *L. pseudotruncatella* is one of the best with brownish growths marked with deeper brown lines and flowers of bright yellow which are up to 2 inches across.

Pleiospilos—Living Rocks: These, in general, have larger leaves than most of those previously mentioned. Those of *Pleiospilos bolusi* look like 2-inch chunks of rust-colored stone. Its golden-yellow flowers are 3 inches across. The fat leaves of *P. simulans* are 3 inches long, gray-green with dark green spots and look like chips of granite. The flowers, yellow or white, are 3 inches in diameter.

Titanopsis schwantesi is a plant of unique appearance. The leaves grow in small rosettes and their tips are densely covered with white warty tubercles. The ¾-inch flowers are yellow in spring. Another species, **T. calcarea,** has rust-colored tips and larger yellow flowers.

Trichodiadema densum is very different in appearance from any previously described. It is a tiny shrub about 3 inches tall, its branches thickly clothed with cylindrical leaves ¾ inch long, each one tipped with a diadem of radiating white hairs. Each sepal tip is similarly adorned. The magenta flowers are nearly 2 inches across.

These "living stones," "windowed plants," and "mimicry" plants are reputed to be excellent subjects for house culture. My limited experience with them in my own home leads me to think that they are among the easiest plants to grow provided they can be placed in a sunny window and careful attention is given to watering. My own practice during the winter is to wait until the growths begin to shrivel before giving any water, which is supplied by putting it in the saucer in which the plant is standing. At no time should the soil be kept wet, but when the new leaves are pushing up, it may be kept moist. Use Cactus soil and be sure the pots are well drained.

Practically all these plants are small and slow growers, so they will not crowd you out of house and home unless you grow too many of them.

We turn now to the **Lily Family** and find there a number of xerophytic types and, among the Haworthias, some with windowed leaves.

Many of the **Aloes** (*Aloe* species) are handsome plants and decorative in bloom when grown in regions where the climate permits outdoor cultivation; or when grown in greenhouses where there is plenty of room for their development. Those commonly seen as house plants (with the exception of *A. variegata*) give me the shudders because they are so dreary looking. (I expect the Aloe fanciers will be after my scalp for writing in this strain.) Some of them, maybe all, have a very bitter sap, which when dried becomes the Bitter Aloes of the drugstore, used medicinally and to put on baby's thumb to prevent him, or her, from sucking it. Tiger Aloe (*A. variegata*) is a neat little plant when young, with leaves spotted and banded in white. It is said to grow a stem about 9 inches high, with a foot-long flower stalk and red flowers 1½ inches long, but I have never seen it do this.

Gasteria—Warty Aloe, Ox-tongue: These are the South African plants with thick, fleshy, tongue-like leaves closely arranged in two ranks. They may be smooth or warty, spotted or mottled with white, pale green, or copper. They vary in length from 4 inches to more than a foot. The flowers, while not especially showy, are long-lasting.

Gasteria acinacifolia has white-spotted leaves 14 inches long and a branching flower stalk up to 4 feet tall with reddish flowers about 2 inches long—the largest in the genus.

A much smaller species is *G. brevifolia* with 2″ × 4″ leaves thickly spotted with white. Ox-tongue (*G. hybrida*) is a catalogue name for a plant with white-margined and white-spotted leaves and pink flowers.

The Warty Aloe is *G. verrucosa* with 6-inch grayish leaves decorated with pure white tubercles. The 2-foot inflorescence carries reddish flowers about an inch long.

Haworthia—Cushion Aloe: In this genus the leaves grow in rosettes and the plants are often cespitose—that is, the rosettes develop in dense tufts. The flowers are small, white or greenish, and not especially ornamental. There is a large number of species, but the ones most commonly met with are the following:

Haworthia cymbiformis has pudgy leaves in close rosettes and "windows" in the flattened leaf tips.

My young daughter expresses great admiration for *H. margaritifera,* which she thinks is the best plant in my succulent collection. I don't agree with her. This species makes a rosette of sharply pointed, stiff, fleshy leaves, decorated principally on the underside with white, warty tubercles.

H. setata makes a rosette about 3 inches across. Its distinctive feature is the long slender "teeth" along the margins of the leaves which remind one of a movie star's (female) eyelashes—except that they are the wrong color.

Agave—Century Plant: The most important group of succulents in the **Narcissus Family** is the one which includes the Century Plant. On an occasion when I was visiting a cemetery on the island of St. Thomas in the West Indies, I was amazed to see a metal Century Plant decorating a grave. For a while I could not figure out why anyone should use an artificial plant when wild ones of the same type were growing profusely all around. Then it occurred to me that size was the probable answer—the metal "plant" never got too large for its surroundings. This is the fly in the ointment for those who grow the Century Plant in the house—it invariably gets too big. I have seen Century Plants in the wild 12 feet in diameter; and, while they are not likely to get as large as this when grown as tub plants, they cannot be pruned to keep them in bounds and they grow much too big and awkward to handle long before they reach the flowering stage. Although there are many species, the only ones I would consider as house plants are the striped forms of the

Century Plant (*A. americana marginata*) with yellowish stripes along the leaf margins; *A. americana medio-picta,* yellow striped down the middle, accepted with the strict understanding that they are to be dispossessed as soon as they reach a diameter of 18 inches; and *A. victoriae-reginae,* which never gets more than about a foot in diameter. Its leaves have pale-gray or brownish margins and irregular stripings of gray or white on both upper and lower surfaces. The tips are armed with formidable, needle-sharp spines; but, unlike most Agaves, the margins are free from the curved teeth that make one wary when handling them.

The **Milkweed Family** includes a large number of succulents, most of them contained in the group known as the *Stapeliae.* The number and importance of members of this tribe can be deduced from the fact that there is a large, three-volume work devoted entirely to them. For the most part they have no true leaves. Their fleshy stems have a superficial resemblance to those of Cacti but their flowers are like nothing else on earth. Of intricate construction and unique coloration, often very hairy, they range from the tiny flowers of *Caralluma sinaica,* only ⅛ inch in diameter, to those of *Stapelia gigantea,* which may sometimes reach almost 1½ feet across. The genera likely to be the most easily obtainable are *Caralluma, Hoodia, Huernia,* and *Stapelia.*

Caralluma nebrowni has angled stems up to 7 inches tall and very dark red-brown, starfish-shaped flowers 4 inches across. I should feel a sentimental interest in this species for it is one of many plants named in honor of Dr. N. E. Brown, who was one of my teachers when I was studying at Kew Gardens.

Hoodia gordoni grows to a height of about a foot, its erect, many-ribbed branches, 2 inches in diameter, set with numerous light-brown spines. The flowers are about 3 inches across, nearly flat and almost circular, pale purple with greenish-yellow stripes. Other species are listed in the trade.

Huernia penzigi has angled stems up to 3 inches high and bell-shaped, black-purple flowers; *H. primulina,* the Primrose Huernia, also a low-growing plant, is perhaps the most attractive species with freely produced, creamy-yellow flowers an inch across.

Stapelia is known by the English names **Starfish Flower** and **Carrion Flower,** neither of which is particularly enticing nor as easy to say as its botanical designation. The name Starfish Flower comes from the shape of the blossoms and Carrion Flower from the vile odor emanating from them at times. Because of this last feature, it is fortunate that they are inclined to bloom in summer when it is possible to put them some place out of the house where their perfume is less noticeable.

The **Giant Stapelia,** botanically *Stapelia gigantea,* makes a sprawling plant with erect quadrangular stems up to 8 inches tall. The flowers are enormous, about a foot across under cultivation. They are yellowish in color, barred with numerous fine crimson lines.

S. grandiflora, in spite of its name, is not so large as the preceding. The flowers are up to 6 inches across, dark purplish-brown, rather hairy with purple and whitish hairs.

One of the really hairy species, *S. hirsuta,* known as **Shaggy Stapelia,** in some of its forms has a dense cushion of hairs in the center of the flower which is about 4 inches across. The margins of the corolla lobes of all of them have a thick growth of long whitish or pale purple hairs. The flower color in general is purple-brown, marked transversely with yellowish or purple-brown lines.

The flowers of *S. verrucosa,* about 3 inches across, have yellow ground color with red; in the variety *pulchra* the spots are purplish.

There are scores of additional species of Stapelia, all fascinating to those who enjoy their outlandish flowers. They are not difficult to grow in open sandy soil. They need plenty of sun, normal watering during most of the year, but dryness at the root in winter.

Euphorbia—Medusa's Head: This is a large and varied group belonging to the **Spurge Family** and containing such diverse elements as Poinsettia, Crown-of-thorns, and Snow-on-the-mountain. The succulent members, largely native to Africa, often closely resemble Cacti of the Cereus type. Personally, I do not regard them highly as house plants because of their vicious thorns and their possibly poisonous latex (sap), capable of causing skin irritation. I would make an exception in favor of Medusa's Head (*Euphorbia caput-medusae*), which is sufficiently queer to warrant inclusion in any collection of oddities. It has a globular stem, surmounted by sinuous, slender branches which suggest the snaky hair attributed to the Gorgons of Greek mythology. In mature plants the branches may be up to a foot in length.

The great **Thistle Family** contains a number of succulents of interest to specialists in the group. One which might appeal to growers of house plants is *Kleinia articulata,* Candle Plant, which has jointed fleshy stems covered with bluish-white waxy "bloom" and lobed leaves.

The culture of succulents in general is similar to that of Cacti— porous soil, plenty of sunshine, and very little water during the resting season. When deviations from this regime are in order, they are noted in connection with the species under discussion.

Considerable space has been given to Cacti and succulents because as a group they are well fitted for house culture and because they offer so much in the way of beauty and interest. Even so, there are many others in addition to those here mentioned available for culture by the serious collector.

ORCHIDS

These glamorous subjects have been grown here and there as house plants for many years but they have never achieved wide popularity. This can be attributed to illusions concerning their high cost as a result of reading of the fabulous prices paid for rare kinds; and to the feeling of awe they inspire in the layman who thinks of them as belonging in the completely unattainable class. Actually plants of varieties suited to house culture can be obtained for as little as $5.00, and some of the Cypripediums are listed at $3.00— rather more, perhaps, than most of us want to pay for house plants, but not prohibitive. Many Orchids are tougher than is generally believed, and it is probable that, given good care, there are other kinds, in addition to those usually recommended, amenable to house culture.

My suggestion to those who want to have Orchids in their homes. is to start off with inexpensive kinds such as: *Cattleya bowringiana,* which blooms in October; *C. gaskelliana,* late spring; *C. labiata,* fall; *C. mossiae,* early spring, C. Queen Mary, fall; *C. trianae,* winter; and *C. veriflora,* var. *alba,* winter. These have blooms of the type so often seen in Orchid corsages; and except for the blush-colored Queen Mary, *trianae,* and *veriflora,* they are of that color generally known as "orchid."

Members of an allied genus, *Laelia,* are not quite so showy and their flowers are not so long-lasting, but they are easier to grow. In--

Passion-flower, intricate in design and beautiful in coloring, grows vigorously and requires plenty of room

An ever-popular favorite, the Christmas Cactus, will withstand hard knocks, high temperature, dry atmosphere, and still produce annually its shower of mid-winter blossoms

Billbergia nutans, *a spectacular but neglect-resisting plant for those who like something decidedly out of the ordinary—"pink bracts, green petals edged with blue, and golden anthers"*

expensive ones are *L. anceps,* rose-colored, winter; and *L. crispa,* white, summer.

Another Orchid which, in all probability, would succeed as a house plant in ordinary soil is the one sometimes used outdoors in California in the foundation planting around the house. This is *Epidendrum obrienianum,* a scrambling species with small red flowers in racemes.

The above are epiphytal Orchids—those which in nature grow perched on trees, where there is never any stagnant water about their roots. Under cultivation they may be grown on blocks of wood with Osmunda fiber wired on in the vicinity of the roots; or, more commonly, in flowerpots, a method which is better suited for home culture. To secure free drainage and root aeration, the pots are filled half full of crocks—flowerpots broken into ½-inch pieces. The potting medium is Osmunda fiber—the roots of Osmunda Ferns with the soil shaken out. This is packed *very firmly* around the roots with the aid of a potting stick. Water is applied to the roots only when the fiber becomes quite dry, when a thorough soaking is given. Overwatering the roots is likely to be disastrous; but the foliage should be sprayed twice daily, if the sun is shining, with clear water applied in a fine mist. Plenty of light is essential, but shade from bright sunshine is provided, except in winter. When the weather becomes settled and warm (June), it is a good plan to suspend the Orchids outdoors, in the shade, from the branches of a tree.

Some of the tropical winter-blooming Cypripediums (Lady-slipper) also are adapted to house culture. These are terrestrial Orchids (those which grow in the ground) and include the kinds which the ladies call "green Orchids," often used in corsages. Inexpensive varieties suitable for trial are Actaeus, green and brown, spotted; Hannibal, mahogany and green; Medea, rose; W. W. Luny, green and spotted. The species *Cypripedium insigne* also could be grown.

Cypripediums need moist air and should never be allowed to become dry at the roots. Great care must be taken, however, to avoid overwatering newly potted plants. These should be kept on the dry side until the roots are active in the new compost. Established plants may be watered every two weeks or so in September and October with very weak liquid cow manure. Cypripediums must not be exposed to undiluted sunshine.

Repotting Orchids is something of a problem for the amateur, both in obtaining the Osmunda fiber and in acquiring the knack of packing it to a sufficient degree of firmness. If you live near your dealer, it might be possible to make arrangements with him to repot for you at the right time. Those whose rooms are too dry for Orchids could construct a Wardian case (see Chapter IV) of sufficient size which will permit the provision of adequate humidity.

My own personal experience with Orchids as house plants has been limited but not too disappointing. I had high hopes for *Laelia anceps,* which sent up a strong flowering shoot, but when the flowers opened, they lasted only a day or two and curled up like a "sleepy" Carnation—the condition associated with the presence of artificial gas, of which, as you have already been informed, there is plenty in my home. The leaves, however, seem quite healthy. A plant of *Dendrobium nobile,* when obtained last fall and brought into the house, promptly shed 25 per cent of its leaves, but then seemed to become reconciled to its new environment and finally developed a nice spray of flowers which, while not so gorgeous as those seen at the International Flower Show, were sufficiently thrilling to a house-plant gardener.

SHRUBS AS HOUSE PLANTS

There are a number of plants of a shrubby nature suitable for house culture. Some of them have a tendency to grow too large and must be controlled either by judicious pruning (see Chapter XIII) or by renewing them from time to time by seeds or cuttings. The culture of the most important species and varieties is covered in this chapter. Some, you will find, are dealt with elsewhere—Pelargonium, for example, strictly speaking, is a shrub. When you come across these inconsistencies remember it is convenience, yours as well as mine, and not ignorance, that has inspired the arrangement.

Abutilon—Flowering Maple: More closely related to Hollyhock than to Maple, Abutilons were in greater favor with Grandmother than they are with us—probably because she was able to grow them better as a result of being content (or was she?) to live in a house where the temperature, more often than not, was nearer 50° than 70° during the winter. Abutilons are characterized by Maple-like leaves and hoopskirt, papery flowers very much like those of Hollyhock. Most of those grown as house plants are of hybrid origin and are referred to as *Abutilon hybridum*. Named varieties are Eclipse, with pink flowers and leaves variegated with yellow; Grandiflorum, orange flowers with scarlet veins; Insigne, white flowers veined with red and purple; Savitzi, with yellow flowers and leaves margined with white; Snowstorm, which, as you might guess, has white flowers; and Splendens, with deep red flowers. A package of mixed seeds might be expected to produce some, at least, of these varieties. Abutilons accorded the rank of species by the botanist are:

A. megapotamicum, differentiated from the general run in having rather small unlobed leaves and a very long, bright red calyx. Its petals are yellow and the stamens protrude well beyond the corolla, giving a striking Fuchsia-like effect. Its drooping habit of growth makes it a favorite for culture in hanging containers. *A. pictum* has orange or yellow flowers veined with crimson and leaves which may be variegated or plain green. A Chilean species, *A. vitifolium,* which is hardy outdoors in the mid-South, has blue flowers up to 3½ inches across.

Seeds sown in the spring and grown along in pots outdoors until they are brought indoors in the fall will bloom in winter. Named varieties, and any exceptionally good forms originating from seeds, should be propagated from cuttings in the spring or fall. The tips of the shoots of young plants should be pinched out to promote a bushy habit. Old plants should be pruned in September to encourage new growth for winter blooming. Give them a sunny window and a temperature of about 60°. Use general-purpose potting mixture and when they are in pots as large as you care to handle and these have become crowded with roots, give them liquid fertilizer every four or five weeks.

Camellia japonica, C. sasanqua—Camellia: Camellias are worth growing for their rich, glossy foliage alone; added to this there are the gorgeous flowers, 2 to 6 inches in diameter and beautiful in form. These may be single, semi-double, or fully double in a wide range of color; some are all of one tone, and some are variously mottled and striped with another color. The most popular species is *Camellia japonica* of which there are hundreds of named varieties blooming mostly in winter and early spring. Varieties recommended for house culture are Alba Plena, double white; Donkelaari, semi-double, white petals margined with red; Sarah Frost, double, light red; Pink Perfection, double; Debutante, Peony-type, pink.

Camellia sasanqua is less compact than *C. japonica,* has smaller foliage and blooms in the fall. Listed varieties include Cleopatra, often double, cherry red; Osea, single, brilliant pink; Mine-no-Yuki, semi-double, white with golden stamens.

Camellia thea (more properly nowadays *Thea sinensis*), although not a first-class ornamental because its white flowers are small and poorly displayed, is perhaps worthy of room for its interest as the source of one of the great beverages—tea.

Camellias are very much worth while if you have a cool, well-lighted place in which to grow them in winter. They are not harmed by light frost (actually when planted outdoors they have been known to survive temperatures down to zero), but grown as pot plants it is desirable to give them 45° to 50° during the winter months. Sunshine is supposed to be essential, but I was successful in carrying one (I don't know the variety) to flowering stage in a poorly lighted, unheated basement room. Perhaps they can endure more shade in winter than is generally believed—provided the temperature is kept sufficiently low. Camellias have the exasperating habit of dropping their unopened flower buds on the slightest provocation. Lack of light, too much heat, dryness of the air, and too much or too little water are all supposed to be contributory causes. Spraying the foliage with water every day helps to keep the plants clean and provide the humid atmosphere that is desirable.

The soil should have a reaction of about pH 5.5 to pH 6.5. Use general-purpose mixture, substituting acid peatmoss for leafmold if the base soil approaches alkalinity. When repotting, avoid setting the old ball any deeper in the pot. Put at least a half-inch layer of broken pots or clinkers in the bottom of the pot for drainage, because the plants should be watered freely but resent stagnant moisture at their roots. During the summer set them outdoors with the pots plunged in peatmoss, in dappled shade. Very little pruning is necessary and should be restricted to shortening shoots which spoil the plant's symmetry. This should be done immediately after flowering.

Chrysanthemum anethifolium, C. frutescens—Paris Daisy, Marguerite: There are two species of shrubby Chrysanthemums which are worthy of consideration as house plants. These are *Chrysanthemum anethifolium* or Glaucous Marguerite (glaucous meaning that the leaves are overlaid with "bloom," giving a blue-green effect); and *C. frutescens,* Marguerite, or Paris Daisy, a coarser plant with green leaves. Both species are said to have both white and yellow forms, but I have no recollection of ever having seen a yellow-flowered *anethifolium.* Etoile d'Or is the name of the yellow variety commonly grown; Boston Yellow is another name which may, perhaps, refer to the same variety.

These Marguerites bloom freely around Easter and are commonly seen in florists' shops at that time. Although old plants can be cut back after blooming and grown along to flower another year, it is better to raise new plants annually because Marguerites have extensive root systems and are such voracious feeders that it is necessary to use pots inconveniently large. Old cut-back plants should be set outdoors about the middle of May and cuttings of young shoots inserted in June. These, when rooted, should be potted in general-purpose mixture and shifted into larger pots when roots begin to crowd, until they are in "sixes" or "sevens." Then when these are filled with roots, start feeding with liquid fertilizer. Bring indoors before frost and keep in a sunny window preferably in a temperature between 50° and 60°.

Euphorbia—**Poinsettia, Crown-of-thorns:** The Poinsettia (or Pointsetter as it is often called, as though it were a hybrid between two bird dogs!) is one of those exasperating plants that grow beautifully outdoors during the summer, raise our hopes by retaining their leaves for a while after they are brought in, and then start shedding when it becomes necessary to use artificial heat. Dry air, fluctuations of temperature, gas, and insufficient light seem to be the chief reasons for their failure.

Assuming that you will acquire your Poinsettia at Christmas, you should put it in a sunny window and try to maintain an equable temperature between 60° and 70°. The leaves will begin to fall within two days, two weeks, or two months, depending on the suitability or otherwise of the growing conditions. Water normally until half the leaves have fallen, then gradually reduce the supply until the soil is completely dry. Remove the plant from public view and store it, dry at the roots, in a temperature of about 60°. About the middle of April cut it down to 6 inches; remove from the pot and repot in new soil—general-purpose mixture. Water thoroughly and place in a sunny window, going easy on watering until the new shoots are 6 inches long. When the weather is settled and warm, place outdoors in a sunny location (shade it for a few days) still in its pot, plunged to the rim in sand, soil, or peatmoss; turn the pot every week or two so that the roots do not get into the soil surrounding the pot. Poinsettias make tremendous growth if removed from their pots and planted out; but it is impossible to dig them in the fall without root injury which is fatal to success.

A better method of handling Poinsettia, which involves more work but which you may wish to use if you fancy yourself as a propagator, is to start up the old plant in April (it is not necessary to repot in this case) and take cuttings when the shoots are about 5 inches long. These vigorous youngsters, if potted in larger pots as it becomes necessary, will make better plants than cut-back old stock.

The **Crown-of-thorns** is *Euphorbia splendens,* a shrub with tangled fleshy stems armed with fierce spines which warrant caution in handling it. The leaves are few in number on the tips of the branches and are soon shed if the plant is grown under arid conditions. The flowers are produced in greatest abundance in winter, but a well-grown plant is seldom without a few. It is the scarlet bracts (not petals) accompanying the flowers which make the plant bright and cheerful in spite of its spines and snaky branches. Give it all the sun possible; soil as for Cacti and keep on the dry side during November and December.

Fuchsia hybrida—**Fuchsia, Ladies' Ear-drops:** There are about 2,000 named varieties of Fuchsia, believed to be derived mostly from hybrids of *F. fulgens* and *F. magellanica.* The average grower of house plants will probably be satisfied with the varieties commonly handled by florists such as Carmelita, double white; Gartenmeister Bonstedt, long, slender red blooms, green and bronzy-red foliage; Little Beauty, petals lavender-blue, pink sepals; dwarf and bushy; and Trophie, double flowers, white and violet blue. Those who want to make a hobby of Fuchsias will get in touch with specialists and perhaps join the American Fuchsia Society.

There are a number of Fuchsias of trailing habit suitable for growing in hanging containers, among them *magellanica gracilis,* purple and red, which has been recommended for winter bloom; Muriel, rosy lilac and red; San Francisco, salmon and orange-scarlet.

Fuchsias, in general, are summer-blooming shrubs. They need

cool conditions and shade from hot sun, but plenty of light. The plants are rested by keeping them cool—45° to 50°—during November and December, and giving them only enough water to keep the wood plump. In January they are brought into a day temperature of 60° to 65° (night 50°) and watered. When the buds begin to swell, cut out dead and weak wood and trim to shape. Some growers shake the soil off the roots and repot at this time, using general-purpose mixture. Avoid overwatering until growth is well along, and spray tops with water at least once a day. Young plants can be raised by cuttings of young shoots taken off when they are about 4 inches long. They root very easily in sand in a propagating case. A bushy habit should be promoted by pinching out shoot tips during the early stages of growth.

Fuchsias have so much charm and such beautiful and varied form and coloring that they merit the attention of all who can provide the cool growing conditions of winter and early spring.

Gardenia—Florists' Gardenia, Cape-jasmine: Those who conduct question-and-answer columns for gardeners come to loathe the sight of the name Gardenia because the plant is provocative of more "why does it drop its flower buds" queries than any other house plant. The Florists' Gardenia, commonly known as *G. veitchi,* a winter-flowering form of *G. jasminoides,* is a cantankerous plant even when grown under what are supposed to be ideal conditions of a greenhouse. It is not surprising, therefore, that it is a bad actor when treated as a house plant. The old-fashioned Cape-jasmine, often known as *G. florida* (really a synonym for *G. jasminoides*), is much easier to grow because it flowers during the summer months when it can be kept outdoors and can be induced to take a rest during the winter. This has smaller flowers than *veitchi* varieties.

In spite of its mean disposition, the glossy luxuriant foliage and beautiful waxen flowers of the winter-flowering varieties impel thousands to attempt its culture in the home—and there are some who succeed with it! An acid soil, warmth, sunshine, moist air brought about by spraying the foliage daily, and the use of other humidifying devices are necessary. If the temperature falls much below 60°, the foliage is likely to become yellow; if it goes much above 60° during the hours of darkness, the flower buds are likely to drop. An alkaline soil will also cause the leaves to turn yellow. This is provided against by using acid peatmoss as a source of humus in the potting soil and by mixing a tablespoonful of iron sulphate to each bushel if the base soil is alkaline. (See mixture for acid-soil plants.) Keep the soil moist at all times but avoid waterlogging. Repot just before the plants are placed outdoors for the summer. When pots are filled with roots, water every four or five weeks with liquid fertilizer. Prune and pinch as described in Chapter XIII.

The Cape-jasmine is a much more satisfactory plant to grow if you can forego the pleasure of flowers in winter. It is admirable as a tub plant for porch decoration or when placed at a strategic point in the garden. It can be stored for the winter in a light situation in a temperature of about 50°. Give less water when it is resting.

Hibiscus rosa-sinensis—**Chinese Hibiscus, Rose-of-China:** Although reaching the dimensions of a large shrub (up to 30 feet) or a small tree in the tropics and subtropics, the Chinese Hibiscus can be grown satisfactorily as a pot or tub plant because it does not resent hard pruning and produces its large blooms, reminiscent of Hollyhock to which it is related, on young shoots. It is said that the flowers can be rubbed on the shoes in place of blacking when one needs a shine. There are numerous varieties in the tropics. About a half-dozen commonly available in the North include Brilliant Queen, double, vermilion scarlet; Orange Beauty; Peachblow, double, pink; and Sub-violaceous, with violet-tinted flowers. There is also one with variegated leaves and red flowers, var. *cooperi,* commonly seen in greenhouses, which I have not found listed commercially.

While one may be able to see flowers on greenhouse-grown plants of Hibiscus at almost any season, they are primarily summer and fall bloomers. When grown as house plants, it is desirable to rest them during the winter in a temperature of about 50°, keeping them on the dry side at the roots. At the beginning of March cut them back about one half, bring into a sunny window, repot in general-purpose mixture, and water freely when growth begins. A daily spraying of the tops will help new shoots to "break." They should be kept outdoors during the summer.

Rhododendron—**Azalea:** The Rhododendrons commonly forced by florists and commonly known as Azaleas fall into two groups: varieties of *R. indicum,* the Indian Azalea (a misnomer because the species is native to Japan); and varieties of *R. obtusum* which includes the Kurume Azaleas, some of which (Hinodigiri types) are hardy in the vicinity of New York.

Then there are the Rutherfordiana Azaleas, developed in the main by crossing varieties of the above two groups and the injection of Rhododendron blood. One of the largest commercial growers of Azaleas suggests the following as desirable varieties:

[The letters E, M, and L indicate early forcing, midseason, and late. "Hose-in-hose" means the flowers are produced one within another.]

Indicas

E. Lambertus C. Bobbink. Bright velvety red.

E. Paul Schame. Early; double; salmon-pink.

M. Jean Haerens. Very double; rosy carmine.

M. Albert Elizabeth. Large; semi-double; ivory-white with frilled deep pink edge.

L. Niobe. Large; double white.

Kurume

M. Coral Bells. Pleasing coral-pink shading deeper toward center.

M. Snow. Large; pure white flowers.

E. Jersey Belle. Large; hose-in-hose; vivid coral-salmon.

M. Mauve Beauty. Medium size; dainty flowers.

M. Pink Pearl. Salmon rose shaded lighter.

Rutherfordiana

E. Dorothy Gish. Large; hose-in-hose; deep salmon.

E. Alaska. Early; large double; pure white.

E. Constance. Single; cerise-pink, frilled and ruffled.

E. Pink Ruffles. Hose-in-hose; frilled; deep rose-pink.

M. Salmon Perfection. Beautiful bright salmon; large double flowers.

All plants suitable for early forcing may also be used for late forcing by storing in a cool, well-lighted room until such time as needed for forcing.

These Azaleas can be grown as house plants if they are kept cool —40° to 50°—during November and December. While the florist with humid greenhouse facilities can force the earlier sorts into bloom for Christmas, it usually is fatal to attempt to do this under house conditions. When they are brought indoors in the fall just before frost, keep them in a light position in an unheated but frost-free room, and water the soil whenever it shows signs of becoming dry. Do not attempt to start them into growth before the middle of January; if you can curb your impatience until mid-February, so much the better. About five weeks at 60° will bring them into bloom. Spray the foliage daily during this time. Repot in a larger pot, if necessary, as soon as the flowers have faded, using the acid-soil mixture. If the roots are not unduly crowded, remove loose soil from the surface and replace with a 50-50 mixture of peatmoss and rotted manure and a teaspoonful of cottonseed meal, or dried blood, or tankage. When frost no longer threatens, place them outdoors in full sun or light shade, plunging the pots in peatmoss to keep the roots cool and to lessen the need for watering, which, however, must be attended to during dry spells.

Rosa chinensis minima—vars. **Fairy, or Pygmy Roses:** If properly handled these offer opportunities for late-winter, spring, and summer bloom in the house. These roses are miniature replicas of some of the Hybrid Teas and seldom exceed 6 inches in height, with flowers and foliage in proportion. There are several varieties available, including the one known to gardeners as *Rosa rouletti,* which started all the furor for them. This has an interesting story. It was found growing as a pot plant in the windows of cottages in the village of Mauborget, Switzerland, by a Dr. Roulet, who called it to the attention of his friend the late Henri Correvon, a famous horticulturist of Geneva, who introduced it to general cultivation. According to Correvon, the peasants said it had been grown as a house plant in Mauborget for centuries. Included among other varieties are Baby Gold Star, golden yellow; Midget, very dwarf, red; Oakington Ruby, crimson buds, ruby red when open; Pixie, white; Tom Thumb, deep crimson.

My own experience with these roses has been disappointing, but others report excellent results. They should be obtained in small pots from dealers in January and immediately repotted in 3- or 4-inch pots in general-purpose mixture. Cut them back ½ to ⅔ and keep moist in a temperature between 60° and 70°. Established plants should be rested by keeping them cool (40°) in November and December.

Tibouchina—Princess Flower: The Princess Flower, or Glory-bush, called "Boogiana" by one nurseryman for some obscure reason, has suffered under a plethora of botanical names including *Pleroma* *macranthum, P. grandiflora* (as listed by one dealer), and *Tibouchina semidecandra,* the preferred name today. It has gorgeous royal-purple flowers, 4 to 5 inches across, produced over a long period in summer and fall. The hairy leaves take on a delicate "fall" coloring as they fade. When started from cuttings, the shoots, as they attain a length of 8 inches to a foot, should have their tips pinched out until the required bushiness is obtained. The Princess Flower is best grown outdoors during the summer, and brought into a sunny window in the fall. When active growth ceases the plant should be removed to a cool, well-lighted room and less water given. Cut back about a third in the spring, give a higher temperature (65° to 70°), and keep soil moist. Use general-purpose mixture.

FRUITS

I know a man whose hobby is growing various tropical and subtropical fruits as house plants. This is an interesting project if one's bent lies that way even though the possibility of obtaining edible fruit on such kinds as Avocado, Banana, Date, and Papaya is decidedly remote, unless conditions are exceptionally favorable and one has plenty of room to grow the plants. On the other hand, Fig, Lemon, Christmas Peppers, Pomegranate, Strawberry Guava, and Surinam Cherry can be grown with a reasonable expectation of obtaining some fruit if given good culture. Then there are some which are grown solely for the beauty of their fruits with no utilitarian thoughts whatever. These include Ardisia, Jerusalem-cherry, Otaheite Orange, and Rouge Plant or Rivina.

I have never heard of anyone successfully raising Pineapples (*Ananas*) to the fruiting stage as house plants; but when these lines appear, I expect to be deluged with letters saying it can be done. They are worth growing as foliage plants alone, though if this is the objective it would perhaps be better to use one of the colorful varieties with striped leaves rather than those grown for their fruit. It is easy enough to obtain a Pineapple plant—of a kind. Merely buy a Pineapple fruit when in season and slice off the crown of leaves at the top of the fruit, making the cut at the junction of fruit and leaf bases. Insert this in sand, keep it moist, and it will soon produce roots, when it can be potted in soil. Commercial growers do not use this method of propagation because it is said that such plants take longer to come into bearing—suckers originating at the base of the plant are used instead.

Like all Bromeliads, Pineapples need a well-drained, open rooting medium. Put at least an inch of broken pots or clinkers in the bottom

Top sliced from a Pineapple, with a thin "plate" of the flesh, will root and form an interesting plant

of the pot for drainage, and use a soil mixture of equal parts fibrous loam, peatmoss, thoroughly rotted manure, sand, and granulated charcoal. Pot the plants on into progressively larger pots as they become root-bound if the objective is fruit production. Moist air, 60° minimum temperature, and ample light are necessary.

Coral Berry *Ardisia crispa* (*A. crenulata*) is famous for the lengthy period (two years) that it hangs on to its clusters of Holly-like red berries. It is a first-class, tolerant house plant, and well-grown specimens are beautiful at all times because of their glossy crenulated leaves. Old plants become leggy and bare at the base and may then be air-layered (see Chapter XV). Perhaps a better plan is to raise new plants annually by inserting cuttings of nearly matured young shoots in a warm propagating case. Seeds can also be used, first washing off the pulp before sowing them in the spring. Seedlings, however, show a greater tendency toward legginess than do cuttings. Use general-purpose potting mixture. If possible, keep at 60° during winter. The chief enemy of Ardisia is a brown scale insect which can be controlled by weekly forcible spraying with water. Do not, however, spray during the flowering period.

The **Christmas Pepper** (*Capsicum frutescens* var.) is grown as an annual by starting the seeds, which must be removed from the pods before sowing (in case you are using seed from your own plants), in May or June. The seedlings should be pricked off into small pots and shifted to larger sizes, up to 5 inches, as the pots become filled with roots. Use general-purpose potting mixture. Plunge the pots outdoors in a sunny situation in a bed of sand or peatmoss to keep the soil from drying too frequently. Water during dry spells. Or they may be planted out and dug up with a ball and potted in early September. Keep well watered and shaded for a week or two. Bring indoors before cold weather and keep them in a sunny window. During winter, maintain a temperature of 55° (they will last better if kept cool) if possible, and do not allow the soil to become dry. The tiny, brilliant scarlet fruits are peppery and can be used as a condiment if they seem of greater value for this than for ornament.

The **Papaya** (*Carica papaya*) grows too large for the average home. I have seen it more than 8 feet tall and 5 feet in diameter, growing in a large, enclosed porch heated in winter. It is easy to raise from seeds, but male *and* female plants are needed to obtain fruit, unless you happen to get a specimen in which both sexes are represented. Its foliage, something like that of Castor Bean, is ornamental. General potting mixture, routine care.

Mention has been made elsewhere of the foliage value of Citrus fruits when raised from seeds. If fruits are a desideratum, grafted plants of varieties adapted to pot culture should be purchased. These will come into bearing earlier than seedlings. A Lemon (*Citrus limonia* var.) sold as "Everbearing" is excellent for house culture and produces its fruits freely. Ponderosa, whose fruits are very large—up to 2 pounds—is another variety often grown as a house plant. The Dwarf or Otaheite Orange (*Citrus taitensis*) often sold as fruiting pot plants by florists at Christmas is decidedly ornamental when covered with small oranges which, however, are of little value for eating. Kumquats, *Citrus japonica,* eaten skin and all, are pungent and palatable, though the plants are well worth growing for ornament too. All these Citrus fruits have the added attraction of sweetly scented flowers and glossy foliage. None of them is likely to grow too big to be accommodated in the house with the exception of the Ponderosa Lemon. As to soil, the general-purpose potting mixture will suit them. In winter the temperature should be kept between 55° and 65° if possible. A weekly spraying, except when they are blooming, is desirable to help keep down scale insects. During the summer they should be placed outdoors so that the wood becomes thoroughly ripened.

Surinam Cherry (*Eugenia uniflora*), a Brazilian shrub related to the Clove Tree of commerce, has fragrant half-inch white flowers and small glossy leaves. The ribbed crimson fruits, about the size of Gooseberries, ripen in winter and are quite palatable. Place outdoors during summer, but keep in a sunny window during the cold months. It will not be harmed if the temperature falls to 45°. General potting mixture, routine care.

A **dwarf Fig** (*Ficus carica* var.) is offered by at least one dealer as being particularly adapted to pot or tub culture. Its fruits are produced on the new shoots so it can be pruned back in the spring if this should be necessary to keep the plant from becoming too large. It does produce fruits and, while they are not of first-class quality, growing this variety offers a means of raising one's own fresh Figs, even though living in a climate not suited to Fig culture outdoors. This is one of those shrubs that can be overwintered in a cool cellar and put outdoors when danger of severe frost is past if there is no room for it in the living quarters; or it can be started in the living room six weeks in advance of the time for setting outdoors. Plants which have started to grow should not be exposed to frost and they should be shaded for a week or two to inure them gradually to more intense light. Use general-purpose potting mixture, water freely when growing, keep on dry side when they are resting in winter.

One would scarcely think of **Bananas** as house-plant possibilities, but the Chinese or Dwarf Banana (*Musa cavendishi*) can be fruited when grown in a tub, and I have seen one almost of fruiting size grown in an enclosed porch. Plants should be started as suckers in rather sandy soil in 8-inch pots. When the pot is filled with roots, transplant to a tub 24 to 30 inches in diameter and 24 inches high. As soon as the soil (general-purpose mixture) is filled with roots, give weak liquid manure every two or three weeks. Warmth (60° minimum), moist air, and plenty of sunshine are required. The old trunk (it is not really a trunk, but rather a bundle of leaf stalks) should be discarded after fruiting and a new plant or plants raised from the suckers appearing around the base.

There are some who claim to see great beauty in the foliage of **Avocado** (*Persea americana*). Personally, I think it is stodgy and undistinguished but it is interesting to watch the germination of the large seed. If you have not already done so, the next time you have an Avocado salad, save the seed, soak it in water to remove its outer covering, and then suspend it, large end down, with the base just touching some water in a wide-mouthed, clear glass jar. Three toothpicks stuck into the seed at an equal distance apart will hold the seed at the right level. Sometimes this treatment will cause the seed to decay, but one has to take a few chances in life. If you want to *grow* an Avocado, realizing that you are unlikely to get fruit from it as a house plant, start the seed a half-inch below the surface in a 4-inch pot in sandy soil. It will grow no matter whether it is placed on its side or topside down, but you will save it the trouble of reversing the direction of root and shoot if it is placed with the small end up.

Described as a "luscious tropical fruit" with "a delicious, sweet, and spicy flavor," the **Strawberry Guava** (*Psidium cattleianum*) is to me insipid and seedy. Its foliage is good, however, the 1-inch flowers are white and fragrant, and it has the merit of blooming and fruiting while comparatively small in size. General-purpose potting mixture, routine care.

If you are ambitious to grow **Pomegranate** (*Punica granatum*) in your home, you should get the dwarf (var. *nanum*) single-flowered variety. The double-flowered one is floristically more effective, but not likely to produce fruits. These dwarf varieties make dense, twiggy little bushes clothed with small, narrow, shining leaves; the flowers are large and orange-red. The Pomegranate should be placed outdoors in full sun during the summer months. Bring it in before frost (though light frost will not kill it) and keep in a sunny window in a cool (50°) room to rest with rather less water than normal at the roots. Start into growth by bringing it into living-room temperature in February and water it normally. Repot into larger pot whenever the roots become crowded, using general-purpose potting mixture.

The **Rouge Plant** (*Rivina humilis*) is a relative of the Pokeweed and grows wild in southern United States and tropical America. It is a weedy-looking plant (about 1½ feet tall) until it is redeemed by racemes of small but showy red berries which probably are not wholesome to eat. In the greenhouse it takes care of itself to the extent of developing plenty of self-sown seedlings in the gravel of the benches. I have never grown it at home, but it is reported that it is a good house plant. If seeds can be obtained, it is worthy of a trial, needing no special treatment.

If your rooms are hot and dry and if there is any trace of gas in the air there is not much use in bothering with **Jerusalem-cherry,** *Solanum pseudo-capsicum,* because under these conditions it quickly drops its leaves and berries. If you have small children who are inclined to eat anything of attractive appearance within reach, it might be as well not to allow Jerusalem-cherry in your home, for the fruits are poisonous. These plants, especially a form known as the Cleveland Cherry, are grown commercially in enormous numbers and sold at Christmas. The Patterson variety is compact and preferred for small pots. The **False Jerusalem-cherry** (*Solanum capsicastrum*) is similar but has ovoid pointed fruits. Seeds may be sown indoors in February. Culture same as for Christmas Pepper.

VINES AND TRAILERS

In addition to the pleasure given by their intrinsic beauty, climbing and trailing plants perform the function of adding height to the window garden. They can be grown to frame the window, or can be suspended in a suitable container to furnish the upper parts of the window opening. A few accessories are needed to accommodate the weak-stemmed habit which characterizes this group. The climbers will need supports of some kind or other. These can be elaborate or simple, depending upon taste and pocketbook. The simplest is a plant stake pushed into the soil of the pot, to which the shoots are tied or on which they climb of their own volition. A modification of this is a light wooden trellis attached to a section of board on which the potted plant is stood as described on page 105. One advantage of making a unit of plant and stand is that the whole can be removed from the window to a more convenient place if it should be necessary to spray against insect pests. Another method of supporting climbers is by means of light wire (picture wire is good) attached by hooks or screw eyes to the window frame. If the window is recessed, a simple trellis of wood or wire can be attached

Veltheimia, a dependable winter-flowering bulb with glossy green foliage that makes it an attractive plant even when not in bloom

*Amaryllis (Hippeastrum), one of Grandmother's favorites. The modern
giant hybrids have much larger, but less graceful, flowers*

on blocks to the side framing so that it stands out an inch or two.

Droopers or trailers can be hung from brackets attached to the window casing. A browse around hardware, department, and 5-and-10-cent stores will give you an idea what is available in this line. You will probably find hanging jardinieres and wrought-iron brackets fitted with rings, singly or in twos or threes, in which water-tight pots are placed to hold the potted plants. These, however, are seldom large enough to accommodate a size in excess of 4 inches. I have searched in vain for the type of support that I consider the best for droopers, consisting of a metal saucer to catch drips attached to a bracket which sets flat against the wall or window casing. Of course there is no real reason why one should not fit a glass or pottery saucer into one of the ring-type stands which will permit using a larger flowerpot than does the usual jardiniere.

Whatever you do, don't degrade the appearance of the window by using anything that looks like a makeshift; don't use odd pieces of string knotted together, nor make a trellis from an orange crate, without first planing off the advertisement and applying a coat of paint.

There is considerable variation in size and vigor of trailing and climbing plants, ranging from the fragile grace of the Kenilworth-ivy to the massive solidity of the more robust Philodendrons. Some trailers such as Abutilon, Achimenes, Coleus, Fuchsia, Oxalis, Pelargonium, and Sedum have been disposed of elsewhere, either to avoid divorcing them from their families or removing them from a group to which they more appropriately belong. Sweet-potato, an excellent house vine, will be found in the section "Vegetables as House Plants." Others which we think most definitely belong in this chapter are described below.

Cissus—Kangaroo Vine, Cape Grape, Grape-ivy: These relatives of the Grape provide excellent vines of good constitution for house culture. The best known is Grape-ivy (*Cissus rhombifolia*), whose leaves consist of three glossy toothed and pointed leaflets. It needs a fair amount of light, can endure heat and dryness, and may be used either as a drooper or climber. Of similar habit is *C. adenopodus*, which has tuberous roots and fuzzy leaves which are green above and red beneath. Its leaves also are divided into three leaflets. The Cape Grape (*C. capensis*) is more akin in appearance to the Grape grown for its fruits. The developing leaves are particularly attractive, for they have a dense covering of pinkish-lavender hairs which disappear as the leaf ages. It, like *C. adenopodus,* has tuberous roots and is able to withstand drought and sun. The Kangaroo-vine (*C. antarctica*), native to Australia and a newcomer to the house-plant scene, has comparatively long and narrow leaves, shiny on the upper surface. It is rather awkward in appearance unless trained and pruned to the desired shape. It will grow well in poorly lighted situations.

If ever I can lay my hands on it, I am going to try *C. discolor* in the house, but am not at all sanguine of being able to obtain one or of succeeding in growing it if I do. Under warm greenhouse conditions it is a vigorous grower with exquisite oval or heart-shaped leaves up to 6 inches long, purplish beneath and velvety green above, marked with white, pink, and purple. Sometimes it is known as Climbing Begonia, although in no way related.

All of these are of easy culture (except possibly *C. discolor* in the home) in general-purpose potting soil. They should be kept constantly moist at the roots when they are actively growing. The tuberous-rooted kinds should be rested by keeping the soil fairly dry for a month or two after growth for the season is completed. All of them are subject to attacks by mealybugs, which should be watched for, especially in the angles made by junction of leaves and stems.

Ceropegia woodi—Hearts Entangled, Rosary Vine, String of Hearts: This is a plant which always excites interest with its thick, fleshy, heart-shaped, opposite leaves, about ¾ inch long, which are marbled white on green when grown in shade and white on coppery-bronze in sunshine. The undersides are pinkish overlaid with gray. Under favorable conditions its slender stems may trail to a length of 6 feet. The moisture contained in the leaves makes these stems surprisingly heavy. The small pinkish or light purple flowers add nothing decoratively but they have an interesting structure. The plant produces tubers in the soil and along the stems, which can be used for propagating purposes. It is adaptable to varied conditions. It will grow in sun or shade and can be rested or not, according to its behavior—some plants will keep on growing throughout the year; others indicate their desire for a rest by wilting of the stems. When this happens, water should be withheld for a month or two. The soil recommended for Cacti will suit Ceropegia.

Cyanotis somaliensis—Pussy Ears: This relative of the Wandering Jew has trailing stems and triangular, fleshy, hairy leaves. It has "bright purple and orange hairy flowers," though these I have never seen. Even though it may not be floriferous under house culture, it is worth growing for its unusual-looking leaves. Native to tropical Africa, it can stand plenty of heat and sun. Use general-purpose potting mixture and keep a little on the dry side in winter.

Cymbalaria (Linaria) muralis—Kenilworth-ivy: This dainty little relative of the Snapdragon is rather commonly to be seen growing in chinks between brick and stone walls in England and seems to get along famously on the rather lean diet afforded by crumbling mortar. It has tiny lilac-blue, Snapdragon-like flowers on fragile stems clothed with rounded, lobed leaves. There are color forms with white or pink flowers. It is admirable for use in a hanging or bracket container and plants of good size can be grown in pots as small as 3 inches. It is easily raised from seeds sown in the spring or old plants can be divided then. Its predilection for old walls suggests that it would not be amiss to include a handful of old broken-up mortar in the potting soil or, failing this, a handful of crushed limestone. Sun or part shade.

Ficus pumila (repens)—Creeping Fig: Although the Creeping Fig can be grown as a trailer or drooper, it is more naturally a climber and should be so used whenever the right conditions present themselves. It attaches itself to its support by means of aerial rootlets (I have seen it cling tenaciously even to a painted surface) and in its climbing stage presses its small, heart-shaped leaves flat against the wall, post, or rock on which it is growing. When it has attained sufficient size and has reached the limits of its supports, it puts out an entirely different style of growth with leaves three times the size of those on the climbing shoots. This is known as the arborescent and fruiting stage, but it is seldom seen in the North except in large conservatories. The "Figs" are said to be used in Japan for making preserves.

I once saw this *Ficus* ideally used in a friend's home, planted in a narrow border at the base of a wall (completely clothing it) which formed the inner boundary of an enclosed sun porch. It is an adaptable plant, enduring either warm or freezing conditions in winter with equanimity. If you haven't a wall on which to grow it, allow it to trail over the edge of the pot or insert vertically in the pot a slab of wood with bark attached on which it will climb. It is not particular as to soil; keep it well watered and spray foliage occasionally. It is not much bothered by insects.

Hedera—English Ivy, Canary Ivy, Colchic Ivy: The true Ivies, perhaps because of their low cost, are among the most popular trailing or climbing plants for home use, even though they have a hard time of it and finally succumb, usually to an infestation of spider mites, if kept at 70° and over during the winter. The English Ivy, *Hedera helix,* is an extraordinarily variable species with hundreds of named varieties. The one most commonly sold by florists (ironically enough sometimes as "Old English Ivy") is the Irish Ivy, *H. h. hibernica,* an exceptionally vigorous variety. It was in all probability this variety which "sported" and produced a dwarfish branching form, between 1915 and 1920, which was introduced under the name of Pittsburgh Ivy. This in turn sported freely and gave rise to varieties such as Hahn's Miniature, Long Point, Manda's Crested, Maple Queen, and Sylvanian—all rather compact, freely branching types, good for drooping over the pots but not much for climbing.

Distinctive varieties with long, climbing shoots that can be obtained without too much difficulty are *H. h. cordata,* heart-shaped, unlobed leaves, slow-growing; *H. h. discolor,* which has small leaves variegated with white; *H. h. minor,* Baby Ivy, with five regular lobes and prominent gray veins; *H. h. palmata,* having five rather deeply cut lobes and gray veins; and *H. h. pedata,* also sold as *caenwoodiana* and *donerailensis,* which has a very long central lobe and is a rapid grower. The forms of *H. h. marginata,* which have small three-lobed leaves margined with white, and often tinged with red if grown cool, are very beautiful but not too easy to grow. They are suitable as droopers and also as climbers if not too much is expected of them.

Although they are fairly enduring, keeping these Ivies really happy means giving them moist, cool (45° to 50°) conditions during the winter. If you cannot do this, spray them with water as often as you can and give them a real shower bath once a week by spraying them thoroughly with water from the bathroom hose, taking care to hit both sides of the leaves. This will prevent attacks by spider mites and scale insects, the worst enemies of the Ivy.

Those who have a good planting of Irish Ivy outdoors can cut shoots about 2 feet long in August or September and place the bases in water. They will root readily and remain in good condition for several months. Although Ivies can endure winter sun indoors, they are better off if shaded from its direct beams, and are suitable for growing in a well-lighted north window. General-purpose mixture is satisfactory and they should be kept moist at the roots at all times.

The **Canary Ivy (H. canariensis),** native to the Canary Islands and, in geographical forms, to North Africa (*H. algeriensis*) and Madeira (*H. maderensis*), seems better adapted to survival in hot rooms than *H. helix* varieties—perhaps because acclimated to warmer winters in its native home. The leaves are large, up to 6 inches across, and not so deeply lobed as those of most varieties of English Ivy. There are several variegated forms, including Gloire de Marengo and *H. maderensis variegata*, often seen in "dish gardens," which are not too easy to grow as house plants.

The **Colchic Ivy** (*H. colchica*) may have heart-shaped leaves up to 7 × 10 inches when growing outdoors in a favorable location. I have no information as to its adaptability to house conditions but think it is worthy of a trial.

Hoya carnosa—**Wax-plant:** An old-time favorite as a house plant, Hoya is grown for its clusters of very fragrant, wax-like, white, pink-centered flowers which are produced in summer. The variety *variegata*, which has its thick, fleshy leaves irregularly margined with white, is attractive at all seasons. The Wax-plant climbs naturally with the help of aerial rootlets, and it is desirable to give it something in the nature of a bark-covered slab of suitable length to which it may become attached rather than to tie it to an ordinary plant stake. It should be potted in a humusy mixture such as that recommended for Begonias; during late winter and spring growth should be encouraged by keeping it warm (70°), moist at the roots, and by frequently spraying the top. Throughout late fall and early winter it should be rested by keeping the soil almost dry, watering it only when the leaves show signs of shriveling. During this time a temperature of 50° to 60° is preferred. The "spurs" on which the flowers are produced should not be cut off when the flowers have faded, for they will produce again. Partial shade will be satisfactory.

Ipomoea—**Morning-glory:** Morning-glories, despite the fact that they may climb to 10 feet or more when planted outdoors, are adaptable to pot culture and their cramped quarters have a tendency to force them into bloom earlier than is the case when their roots are unrestricted. Varieties of *Ipomoea nil* have long been favorite pot plants of the Japanese. In this country they are usually sold in mixture under the name Imperial Morning-glories, in various strains such as Fancy Fringed, Double Mixed, and so on. One excellent named variety which is fairly easy to obtain is Rose Marie, which has ruffled double flowers, rose-pink in color. The varieties of *I. nil* are characterized by flowers up to 6 inches across, single or double, variously ruffled, scalloped, and fringed, often mottled, flaked, or bordered with one or more colors. These Morning-glories can be kept within bounds by pinching out the tips of shoots which seem likely to exceed the limits assigned them.

Other Morning-glories that can be used are varieties of *I. purpurea,* the one known as Heavenly Blue being an especial favorite. The Cypress Vine, sometimes sold as *I. quamoclit,* but more correctly known as *Quamoclit pennata,* is worth a trial if only for the beauty of its leaves, which are cut into finely divided segments. It is likely to give an extra dividend of scarlet flowers about 1½ inches long.

It takes these Morning-glories from 8 to 12 weeks to come into bloom from seeds, which may be started by planting three or four ½ inch deep in a 3-inch pot, afterward giving them a shift to a larger size; or by sowing them directly in the 5- or 6-inch pots in which they will bloom. It may accelerate germination if the seeds are soaked in lukewarm water for twenty-four hours prior to sowing them. Nicking or filing a notch in the seed coat serves the same purpose. The soil should not be too rich—use general-purpose mixture diluted by adding two extra parts of sand. They should be given a sunny window to insure free flowering. Morning-glories climb by twining, so it is desirable to stretch three or four vertical wires up the window casing to serve as supports.

Nepeta hederacea—Ground-ivy: This trailer, also known as Gill-over-the-ground, Field-balm, and at least fifteen other vernacular names, is an elegant plant for a hanging container, with its slender stems, clothed with roundish leaves, gracefully hanging 2 feet or more below the pot. The variety *variegata,* whose leaves are variegated with white, and which has the light blue flowers of the type, is preferable. Ground-ivy is a winter-hardy plant and should be rested by keeping it cold for three or four months during the winter. Use general-purpose potting mixture and divide and repot annually after its winter rest.

Philodendron: While all the Philodendrons are climbers, there are some, noted in the chapter on foliage plants, which are too massive to be used for this purpose in the average house. There are two species, however, which may be considered first class for either trailing or climbing. The Heart-leaf Philodendron (*P. cordatum*) is one of the most tolerant house plants and one of the most shade-enduring. I have it growing in a window in a north room in which my wife, for some obscure feminine reason, constantly keeps the shades halfway down. It has not lost a leaf all winter. The leaves of this Philodendron, in the juvenile stage, are about 4 inches long, heart-shaped and long-pointed. Another species, *P. micans,* with leaves of similar size and shape, is much more beautiful because of the velvety appearance of the upper surface. But, unfortunately, it is also much more finicky and difficult to grow, so much so that one of the largest commercial growers of this class of plants has given it up because it does not grow fast enough to meet the demand.

There is nothing much to be said about the culture of *P. cordatum.* Keep the soil moist but not waterlogged and when the trailers get too long, snip off 6 inches from the tip of each one and either insert them in the soil of the pot in which the parent is growing (if it is bare at the base) or put them in the propagating case with a view to starting up a new pot filled with vigorous young plants to take the place of the old one.

Saxifraga sarmentosa—Mother-of-thousands, Strawberry-geranium, Strawberry-begonia: It was difficult to decide whether to include this among the flowering plants, foliage plants, or trailers, for it could equally well be put in any of these categories. It has panicles of white, long-lasting flowers in spring, carried well above the rounded leaves which are reddish below and green above, veined with white. A characteristic feature is the numerous filiform stolons (runners), each carrying one or more plantlets after the manner of the Strawberry. It is particularly effective when a single rosette is planted in a 3-inch pot with the runners trailing over the edge. This method implies starting a new pot annually. Of course it can also be grown with several rosettes in a larger container. While it is capable of surviving zero temperatures outdoors, if planted in a sheltered nook, it can also get along in the living room, though it will be better off in a winter temperature of 50°. Use Begonia soil for potting, keep soil moist, shade from bright sunshine, and start new pots from runners annually.

Scindapsus—Ivy-arum: The Ivy-arum most commonly seen is *Scindapsus (Pothos) aureus,* native to the Solomon Islands, which for some unknown reason has been called the Ceylon Creeper. Built somewhat along the lines of Heart-leaf Philodendron, it gives a coarser effect, and its leaves are irregularly blotched with cream or yellow. There is a variety called *wilcoxi,* in which the variegation is more pronounced, but this is not so good-tempered. A more refined character is *S. pictus argyraeus,* which has small heart-shaped leaves spotted with white. A friend of mine had this growing for two years in the house in a 5-inch bulb pan. During this time it made shoots 15 feet long which were trained back and forth on a little trellis about 2 feet high. It is best when used as a climber; *S. aureus* can be used either to climb or droop.

Both of these Ivy-arums are sure bets in the house provided they are given reasonable care. They do not demand sunshine, but the variegation of the leaves will be more evident if they get three or four hours of sun daily. Use general-purpose mixture for *S. aureus;* Begonia mixture for *S. argyraeus;* keep moist and propagate from shoot tips when necessary.

Sedum morganianum—Donkey's Tail: Really this plant should be included among the succulents, but a well-grown specimen is so striking as a trailer that it is discussed here. The name given above is not listed in *Hortus Second,* but it is so known in the trade. It makes trailing shoots 2 to 3 feet long, clothed from tip to base with closely crowded, gray-green, ¾-inch long, cylindrical leaves with pointed tips. The flowers are red, produced at the ends of the shoots, but they are a minor matter compared with the decorative effect of the long, drooping shoots. Grow it in Cactus soil; water less frequently during the winter, but often enough to prevent the leaves from shriveling.

Senecio mikanioides—German-ivy: This is an old-time house plant with thin, bright green leaves shaped like those of English Ivy, and small, yellow composite flowers. It is seldom offered for sale nowadays, but at least one firm offers it under the name "Water or Parlor Ivy" and says that it "grows in either soil or water." It climbs by twining, but can also be used as a trailer. Like so many of our house plants, it prefers to be cool (50°) during winter. Use

Easily cared-for and fast-growing vines for sunny windows: Kangaroo Vine (*Cissus antarctica*)

eart-leaf Philodendron (*P. corda-m*) supported in this case by a piece of tree bark

Excellent small-leaved decorative vines
the Creeping-figs, *Ficus pumila* (*repen*
The usual form is at the left

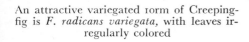

An attractive variegated form of Creeping-
fig is *F. radicans variegata,* with leaves irregularly colored

H.h. cordata

H.h. marginata

*H.h. Green
Feather*

H.h. caenwoodiana

H.h. minor

H.h. marmorata

A few of the many types of Ivy adapted to house culture.
The Ivies top the list of vines for permanent decorative effects in window gardening

For a long season of bloom: Lily-of-the-valley can be started from cold-storage pips at any season and will give almost continuous bloom from monthly plantings

Fuchsia, too, will blossom all summer. It is one of the few good plants that will do well in fairly deep shade. Shrublike growth

general-purpose mixture for potting; keep in a light situation but shade from bright sun except in winter; normal watering. If you have any difficulty in purchasing it, you can probably get some slips from a neighbor (if you live in a country district) which will readily root if placed in water or in moist sand.

***Thunbergia alata*—Black-eyed Susan Vine:** Although of perennial duration, the Black-eyed Susan Vine is usually grown as an annual. In spite of its name the flowers do not always have blackened eyes. In one variety the flower is pure white, in another it is orange with a white center; but mostly the flowers are white, cream, buff, yellow, or orange with dark purple or blackish centers. It is not so rampant as some climbers and the shoots seldom exceed 4 feet in length. It may be trained up or allowed to hang down over the pot. It takes about three months from seed sowing to blooming, so if they are desired for winter flowering, the seeds should be started in September or October. Sow about five seeds to a 5-inch pot, and after seedlings are well along, pull out all but the three strongest ones. Use general-purpose soil mixture; give the plants the benefit of a sunny window and water normally. If they become infested with spider mites, as they sometimes do, discard them and start afresh from seeds.

***Tradescantia* and *Zebrina*—Wandering Jew:** Plants known as Wandering Jew have wandered into three botanically distinct genera: Commelina, Tradescantia, and Zebrina. The first-named, so far as I know, is seldom if ever used as a house plant; the other two are among the commonest and also the toughest in spite of their seeming fragility. Differing in rather obscure botanical characters, *Tradescantia fluminensis* and *Zebrina pendula* seem to the gardener to have much in common—similar habit of growth, great variation within each species, and ease of culture. The flowers are white in *T. fluminensis* and the leaves are plain green, or striped with white or yellow, according to variety. In *Z. pendula* the flowers are purple; the undersides of the leaves are red-purple, the upper has a metallic appearance—in general, silvery with green or purplish markings on the center and margins. There are innumerable variations on this theme. I have one growing in a 4½-inch pot with a dozen shoots, most of them more than 2 feet long, clothed with leaves which are light red-purple beneath and bronze on the upper surface. It has been producing its purple flowers for several months. The variety *quadricolor* is striped with green, white, and red on green of a different shade. While the plants are likely to grow better when shaded, the color of the leaves is more intense when they are exposed to plenty of sunshine. They are not climbers but are among the best for trailing or drooping.

Wandering Jew is not particular as to soil and will grow for lengthy periods in plain water. When the plants are approaching the limit of attractive growth (2 to 3 feet, according to variety, quality of soil, and size of pot), a few tips 4 inches long should be cut off, rooted in water or sand, and ultimately put in soil to start a new pot. I am glad to be able to finish this section with a group of plants about which I do not have to say "should be kept cool in winter!"

GIFT PLANTS

The florist trade makes a practice of raising enormous quantities of showy flowering plants for the holidays—Christmas, Easter, Thanksgiving, et cetera. These often fall into the category of "gift plants"—not that the florist gives them away, but because they are often chosen for presentation to relatives and friends. Some of them are suitable for year-round house culture, but many are not, and the best we can hope for from them is that they will not collapse before blossoming has come to an orderly termination. I am not going to insult you, gentle reader, by telling you that plants (except artificial ones) received as gifts must have the soil about their roots kept moist, but evidently there are some who need this information, for it is said that there are those who complain to the florist that their plant died after a couple of days in the house—something which they couldn't understand, for they had done nothing to it!

It is well to bear in mind constantly that these florists' plants were grown in well-lighted greenhouses, with temperature and humidity carefully controlled according to the varied needs of the plants. When they are received we should try as nearly as possible to give them the same conditions: non-fluctuating temperature and moist air for Poinsettias, coolness for Primulas. As I have pointed out elsewhere, the plants experience a less abrupt change of conditions between greenhouse and home if they are obtained during the spring, summer, and early fall, when little or no artificial heat is needed, rather than in the depth of winter. An Easter Azalea has a much better chance of survival as a house plant than one obtained at Christmas. For one thing, it has not been debilitated by severe forcing.

Let us take a look at some of these "gift plants" and see what can be done with them. Except where otherwise indicated, living-room temperature is satisfactory.

Acacia—Mimosa: If you had asked me a year ago regarding the possibilities of Acacia as a house plant, I would have said "nothing doing"; but having successfully brought *A. armata (paradoxa),* the Kangaroo Thorn, through the winter to the flowering stage in March, I am inclined to hedge. This stupendous accomplishment (to me) was brought about by keeping the plant in an unheated room (45° to 50°) from September until toward the end of January, when it was brought to the plant room where the temperature of the window area is around 60° except on warm, sunny days.

Acacias are those plants that you see in late winter with tiny yellow or pale to deep orange flowers arranged in decorative little pompons or spikes. The genus is a large one with about 450 species, but only a very few of them are grown commercially as pot plants, although there are many which are favorite flowering shrubs or trees for outdoor planting in frostless regions. If you are fortunate enough to receive an Acacia, place it in a sunny window in a cool room. When the flowers have faded, cut back the leading shoots and shift to a larger pot if the roots are crowded. Spray daily to encourage growth of new shoots and put outdoors when danger of frost is past. Bring indoors in the fall and keep in a well-lighted room between 40° and 50°.

Astilbe—Florists' "Spirea." *Astilbe japonica* is a winter-hardy plant often forced into early bloom. One of the few plants which do not resent overwatering, it should be stood in a dish kept constantly filled with water. When the flowers have faded, it should be regarded as having fulfilled its function as a house plant, and be planted outdoors in a moist situation (see page 185).

Christmas Begonia. *Begonia socotrana* hybrids—Gloire de Lorraine, Cincinnati, et cetera—are those kinds so smothered with panicles of pink flowers that the foliage is barely visible. They are not to be considered as permanent house plants for most people.

The flowers will last longer in the house if the plant is kept cool (50°) in a well-lighted window.

Christmas Pepper (*Capsicum frutescens*) : These plants should be given a sunny window, 60° temperature, soil kept constantly moist. For culture, see page 236.

Cineraria (*Senecio cruentus*) : The gorgeous blooms of Cineraria fill almost everyone who receives one at Easter with the desire to keep it for another year. This is a vain hope, for although the plant is a perennial, it is almost impossible to carry it over under house conditions. In any case, better plants are obtained when raised from seeds annually. When plants are received from the florist, keep them as cool as possible (45° to 50°) if you want the flowers to last. Although it is said they are adapted to window-garden culture, I believe them to be among the most difficult plants to raise successfully under the limitations of a home. Those who wish to make the attempt will find their culture described on page 177.

Cyclamen indicum—Florists' Cyclamen: Another difficult subject. Cyclamens require the same cool conditions as the preceding and plenty of water at the roots which should be supplied by sub-irrigation. Stand the pot in a bowl of water until moisture shows on the surface to avoid getting water in the crown of the plant. There are some who are able to grow this as a house plant; therefore, the "how to do it" is described on pages 173–75.

Cytisus canariensis—Florists' Genista: Many have been disappointed because of their inability to keep alive the Genista with sweetly fragrant, pealike yellow flowers. It is *not* a good house plant, and about all one can do is to keep it cool and watered until the flowers fade.

Easter Lily, White-trumpet Lily (*Lilium longiflorum*) : I suppose that the Easter Lily in its many varieties, all much alike to the untrained eye but exhibiting differences which are important to the florists, heads the list of gift plants in point of numbers. As received from florists, the golden stamens usually are removed from the open flowers to avoid having the pollen shed and mar the purity of the waxen trumpets. It is a pity that this has to be, because they add so much to the beauty of the flower. Plants of this Lily which have been made to bloom at Easter are useless for forcing another year but they may be kept watered until danger of frost is past and then turned out of their pots and planted in the garden, where, if all goes well, they may produce another crop of blooms in the fall. In favored regions they may live indefinitely outdoors. This Lily is not among the easily grown house plants, but those who wish to give it a trial will find suggestions for handling it on page 189.

French Hydrangea (*Hydrangea macrophylla*): This is a very popular plant with florists for Easter and an extraordinarily thirsty one—it may need soaking *twice* a day. The colors may be white, pink, lavender, or blue. Pink varieties become lavender or blue when grown in acid soil which gives them access to the aluminum responsible for the change in color. Although recommended as a house plant, those who live in regions where it is hardy outdoors (New York City and southward along the coast) will probably prefer to plant it out when the flowers have faded. If you want to keep it as a house plant, cut the flowering shoots back to two "joints" when the flowers have faded and repot, using general-purpose mixture, bringing it up to pH 7 by the addition of ground limestone (try ½ pound per bushel to start with) if blue coloring in the flowers is not desired. Place outdoors, plunge pot in sand or ashes, and feed with liquid manure when the pots are filled with roots.

After the first frost, store them in a cold cellar and keep the roots on the dry side. Some time in January bring them upstairs in a temperature of 50° for two or three weeks, then place in a sunny window and raise to 60° to 65°, and don't neglect the watering. If smaller plants are desired, start them annually from cuttings made in February. These should be potted into progressively larger pots until the fall, when treatment should be the same as that accorded older plants.

Heather (*Erica*): The plants often sold as "Heather," or even "Scotch Heather," are not Heather (which is *Calluna vulgaris*) at all. They are Heaths and most of them are native to South Africa. The growing of Heaths as pot plants is a ticklish proposition even when a greenhouse is available, and their culture is usually left to specialists. I would say they are impossible as permanent house plants. All one can do is to keep them cool, water them normally, and hope that not all of the leaves will fall off before the flowers fade.

Jerusalem-cherry—(*Solanum pseudo-capsicum*): This is likely to be one of the most disappointing house plants when received from the florist at Christmas because when placed in a hot, dry room it sheds its berries and leaves in embarrassing profusion. The only way to prevent this is to *keep it cool*—50°; and moisten the air as much as possible. Culture same as Christmas Pepper.

Primrose (*Primula*): All types of Primroses should be kept as cool as possible and watered freely. The culture of those commonly grown is given on page 176.

Rose—(*Rosa*): Plants of Hybrid Tea, Hybrid Perpetual, and Rambler Roses are commonly forced into bloom for the Easter trade. None of these is adapted for permanent culture in the home—in point of fact, their size puts them in the white-elephant class in small homes. They are winter-hardy in all but the most severe climates, and the best thing to do with them after the flowers have faded is to plant them outdoors.

Then there are the dish gardens. When made up commercially, they are likely to be overcrowded with roots squashed and mutilated in the endeavor to get more plants into the container than it can properly hold. More important, perhaps, is the probability that the arrangement will contain plants which are culturally incompatible. The best way to handle the situation is to keep the garden as is until you have had an opportunity to admire it and properly express your appreciation in the presence of the donor; and then take out and repot separately the plants which do not belong and rearrange the remainder.

The plants mentioned in this section do not, of course, exhaust the list of those which you may receive as gifts. There are the hardy spring-flowering bulbs, useless for indoor growth another year, but which can be planted in the garden (if the soil in the pots is kept watered until it is safe from the weather standpoint to put them outdoors); and there are Marguerites (see *Chrysanthemum frutescens,* page 228) and a host of others which you will be able to locate by referring to the Index.

FLOWERING HOUSE PLANTS THROUGHOUT THE YEAR

It is possible to have house plants in bloom all through the year, provided one has sufficient room to accommodate the rather large selection of kinds desirable to make a real show, and provided the right treatment is given them.

There are some plants which are practically everblooming, such as African-violet, Wax Begonia, and Patience Plant; and these, of course, appear high up in the lists of those who crave free-flowering. Some plants may be made to bloom at almost any time by giving the proper cultural treatment. Calla-lilies, for example, will start growing any time after their tubers have been rested by drying and still start to bloom in about eight weeks if given sunshine and a temperature of 70°.

By making use of retarded Lily bulbs and Lily-of-the-valley pips held in cold storage until needed for forcing, flowers can be had at will by giving the necessary cultural conditions and sufficient time for growth—about four months and three to four weeks respectively.

By changing the time of seed sowing, the normal blooming season for a given kind can be greatly varied. For example, Cineraria seeds may be sown in May, August, and September, giving a blooming season from fall to spring. Far be it from me, however, to recommend Cinerarias as house plants; their culture presents too many pitfalls for the amateur. Many of the plants we ordinarily grow as summer-blooming annuals outdoors can be made to bloom in winter by starting the seeds during the summer or fall.

Some plants have their regular season for blooming regardless of how much they are pushed around by the gardener; the Poinsettia, for example, comes into bloom in December, if at all, regardless of whether the cuttings were started in May or in August. Others are inclined to be erratic, so that it is difficult to predict with accuracy when flowers will make their appearance. Amaryllis bulbs, as purchased from a dealer, may bloom any time from January to March —probably because of differences in the ripening of the bulbs.

The most important flowering house plants are listed in the following table. Not all of them can be considered good house plants. Some, marked by an asterisk, are best regarded as one would cut flowers—although ordinarily they last much longer. Perhaps it should be emphasized that the time of bloom as given is not necessarily natural for the species (e.g., Sweet Alyssum), and that many of the plants listed can be flowered at a time other than that selected as most likely to be preferred by the grower.

The time allowed for bringing hardy bulbs into bloom is necessarily approximate. Much depends upon uncontrollable temperature variations which may be experienced under house conditions, sunshine, and geographical location. Also it should be remembered that, as the natural blooming season approaches, less time is needed to produce flowers.

Timetable for Flowering House Plants

KEY

*	Not recommended for permanent culture as house plants
H	Winter hardy plants
HB	Winter-hardy bulbs
TB	Tender bulbs
A	Annual

	When in bloom	*Treatment*
Abutilon, Flowering Maple	Almost ever blooming	Seeds or cuttings for new plants in May. Prune old plants in September for winter bloom.
Acacia spp., Mimosa, Wattle (*)	Spring	Usually transitory as house plants. Keep at 50°–60° when received in bloom from florist.
Achimenes spp. and vars.	Late spring—summer	Start tubers January–March.
African-violet. *See Saintpaulia*		
Allium neapolitanum, Flowering Onion (TB)	Winter	Pot bulbs in October; keep cold in plunge pit 6–8 weeks; 6–8 weeks at 60°.
Alyssum maritimum, Sweet Alyssum. *See Lobularia*		
Amaryllis. *See Hippeastrum*		
Antirrhinum majus, Snapdragon (A)	Winter	Start winter-flowering strains from seeds or cuttings in June or July. Winter temperature 50°–55°.
Aporocactus (C e r e u s) flagelliformis, Rat-tail Cactus	Mid-December to mid-January	From cuttings or grafts after flowering. Retain old plants.
Apostle-plant. *See Marica*		

	When in bloom	*Treatment*
Astilbe japonica, Spirea (H)	Winter	Pot up in October; 6 weeks cold; allow 10–14 weeks at 60° for bloom.
Azalea. *See Rhododendron*		
Begonia coccinea (rubra), Angel Wing Begonia	Spring	No special treatment needed to bring these into bloom at the time indicated. Many other Begonias of long-blooming habit available as house plants.
Begonia dregei	Winter	
Begonia feasti	Winter	
Begonia feasti bunchi	Winter	
Begonia heracleifolia	February–April	
Begonia manicata	Spring	
Begonia metallica	Spring	
Begonia ricinifolia	Winter, early spring	
Begonia scharffi (haageana)	Summer, but almost everblooming	
Begonia semperflorens vars., Wax Begonia, especially Christmas Cheer, Darling, Gloire de Chatelaine, Masterpiece	Everblooming	Sow seeds in May or dig up seedlings from self-sown seeds in the border in September for best winter blooms.
Begonia templini	January–April	
Begonia tuber-hybrida, Tuberous Begonia	Summer	Start tubers March-April.
Beloperone guttata, Shrimp Plant	Winter, long-blooming	Cuttings in May.
Black-eyed Susan Vine. *See Thunbergia*		
Bloodroot. *See Sanguinaria*		
Brodiaea (Triteleia) uniflora, Spring Star Flower (Nearly HB)	Spring, long-blooming	Pot in September–October; keep as near 50° as possible during winter.
Browallia speciosa (A)	Winter, early spring	Sow seeds in June–August.
Calla-lily. *See Zantedeschia*		
Campanula isophylla	August–November	Cuttings in spring.

	When in bloom	Treatment
Camellia japonica	Winter–spring	Cuttings in summer; 18 months to flowering size. Keep 45°–50° in winter.
Camellia sasanqua	Fall	Cuttings in spring.
Christmas Cactus. *See* Zygocactus		
Chrysanthemum frutescens, Marguerite	Winter, spring	Cuttings June–July.
Chrysanthemum hortorum vars.	September–January, according to variety	Cuttings in March; or plants may be dug from open ground when buds have formed.
Cineraria. *See Senecio*		
Claytonia virginica, Spring Beauty (H)	March, April	Pot up in fall; keep in coldframe, mulched, until end of February. Allow 4–5 weeks at 50°.
Clivia (*Imantophyllum*) miniata (TB)	Spring	Keep rather dry at 55° November and December; raise to 65° in January, and water freely.
Colchicum autumnale, Meadow Saffron (HB)	September, October	Pot bulbs September; plant outdoors when flowers fade.
Colchicum speciosum		
Convallaria majalis, Lily-of-the-valley (H)	Winter	Use retarded pips; allow 3–4 weeks at 70°.
Crocus, spring-flowering species and varieties (HB)	February, March	Pot corms in fall; keep in plunge pit until February 1; then grow in 50° temperature.
Crocus, fall-flowering species and varieties (HB):		
Crocus longiflorus	November, December	
Crocus sativus	September, October	Pot corms in August; plant outdoors when flowers fade.
Crocus speciosus	September, October	
Crocus zonatus	September, October	

	When in bloom	*Treatment*
Crown-of-thorns. *See Euphorbia splendens*		
Cyclamen persicum, Florists' Cyclamen (*)	December–April	Seeds August to November; allow 15–18 months from seed to flowers.
Cytisus canariensis, Florists' Genista (*)	Spring	Keep it cool when received in bloom from florist.
Dicentra cucullaria, Dutchman's Breeches (H)	March, April	Treat as for *Claytonia.*
Epiphyllum makoyana. See Schlumbergera gaertneri		
Eranthis hyemalis, Winter Aconite (HB)	January, February	Keep cold until end of December; allow 4 weeks at 50° to bloom.
Erica melanthera, Heath (*)	Late winter	Keep at 50°–60° when received in bloom from florist.
Euphorbia pulcherrima, Poinsettia	December–February	Keep dry February to April.
Euphorbia splendens, Crown-of-thorns	Winter, but almost never out of bloom	Rest by reducing water in November and December.
Foam Flower. *See Tiarella*		
Freesia hybrida (TB) *Freesia refracta* (TB)	Winter and spring	Pot bulbs August–February; allow 12–14 weeks to bloom at 50°.
Fuchsia magellanica gracilis	Winter	Cuttings in spring.
Fuchsia speciosa vars.	April–October	Cuttings in summer. Rest old plants by keeping on dry side November, December; start growth at 50° in January.
Gardenia (jasminoides) florida	Summer	Keep cool (50°) November–March.
Gardenia veitchi, Florists' Gardenia	Winter, early spring	Pinch out tips of 6-inch shoots May–August.
Genista. *See Cytisus*		
Geranium. *See Pelargonium*		

	When in bloom	Treatment
Gloxinia. *See Sinningia*		
Grape-hyacinth. *See Muscari*		
Heliotropium arborescens, Heliotrope	September–December	Seeds May; cuttings July; keep flowers pinched off until September.
Hepatica triloba (H)	March	Treat as for *Claytonia,* but will bloom if brought indoors in November. Allow 3 weeks at 50°–60° for bloom.
Hibiscus rosa-sinensis, Chinese Hibiscus	Summer, fall	Keep at 50° in winter; prune in March; give 70°; water freely.
Hippeastrum hybridum, Amaryllis (TB)	Winter, early spring	Usually about 10 weeks at 65° from time of planting bulbs; 2–3 years from seed sown in spring.
Hyacinthus orientalis, Hyacinth (HB)	Winter, early spring	Pot bulbs September–October, in plunge pit 8 weeks; 3 weeks at 50°; 4–5 weeks at 65°.
Hyacinthus praecox, Roman Hyacinth	Winter, early spring	Pot bulbs August–October, 6 weeks in plunge pit; 2–3 weeks at 50°; 4–5 weeks at 65°.
Hydrangea macrophylla, French Hydrangea	March, April	Keep dry and cold (30°) October–January; then 60°; plenty of water.
Impatiens holsti *Impatiens sultani,* Zanzibar Balsam	Almost everblooming	For winter bloom start seeds May, June; cuttings June–July.
Ipomoea purpurea, Morning-glory (A)	Winter	Ten to twelve weeks from seeds to first bloom.
Jacobinia obtusior (often goes under name of *J. carnea*), Brazilian Plume	Fall, winter	Cuttings in March.
Kalanchoe blossfeldiana (*K. globulifera coccinea*)	December–May	Cuttings or seeds in March.
Kalanchoe (*Kitchingia*) *uniflora*	March, April	Cuttings in May.

Wild flowers, too, can contribute to the garden indoors. Plants potted in the fall, kept in a frame over winter, and brought indoors in early February or a bit later, will delight you with their pre-season bloom. Above are Foamflower (*Tiarella cordifolia*), and at right Bloodroot (*Sanguinaria canadensis*)

Preview of spring in the indoor garden!
Easily forced plants of hardy bulbs can provide an
almost continuous display from Christmas to Easter

	When in bloom	*Treatment*
Lachenalia, South African Cowslip (TB)		
Lachenalia aurea	January, February	Pot bulbs August, September; keep cool (50°).
Lachenalia pendula vars.	December, January	
Lantana camara	Winter	Cuttings or seeds in May; keep flowers picked off until October.
Lilium longiflorum, Easter Lily (TB)	March–April	Pot in October; keep cool (60°) until rooted; allow 13–14 weeks at 60° after rooting.
Lobularia benthami, Sweet Alyssum (A)	Winter	Seeds August–September.
Marguerite. *See Chrysanthemum frutescens*		
Marica gracilis	March	Keep at 65°–70°; divide after flowering.
Marica northiana, Apostle-plant	March	
Marigold. *See Tagetes*		
Mt. Etna-lily. *See Sternbergia*		
Muscari botryoides, Grape-hyacinth (HB)	Winter	Pot bulbs October–November; 6 weeks cold for rooting; 6–8 weeks at 60°.
Myosotis scorpiodes, Forget-me-not (H)	Winter	Seeds May–June; keep flowers picked off until fall.
Myosotis sylvatica, Ball Early (A)	Winter	Seeds August.
Myosotis sylvatica, Blue Bird	Spring	Seeds August.
Narcissus, hardy sp. and vars. (HB)	Winter	Pot bulbs early in fall; 6–8 weeks in plunge pit; 5–6 weeks at 60°.
Narcissus, tender vars., Paper-white, Chinese Sacred Lily, Soleil d'Or (TB)	Winter	Pot October–January; allow 6–8 weeks at 60°–70°.
Nasturtium. *See Tropaeolum*		
Nicotiana alata, Flowering Tobacco, Jasmine Tobacco (A)	Winter	Dig up seedlings in fall from self-sown seeds, or sow seeds in July.

	When in bloom	*Treatment*
Nopalxochia (*Epiphyllum*) *akermanni,* Orchid Cactus.	February–June	Start normal watering in February.
Ornithogalum arabicum (TB) *Ornithogalum thyrsoides* (TB) *Ornithogalum thyrsoides aureum*	Winter	Pot bulbs October–November; allow 8 weeks at 60°–70° to bloom.
Oxalis cernua, Bermuda Buttercup (TB)	Winter	Pot bulbs September, allow 8–10 weeks to bloom.
Patience Plant. *See Impatiens*		
Pelargonium domesticum, Lady Washington Geranium	March–April	Cuttings April–May; keep on dry side after flowering; prune and repot August–September; keep at 50°–60°.
Pelargonium hortorum, Geranium	All year	For winter bloom, cuttings May–July; keep flower buds pinched off until October.
Pelargonium peltatum, Ivy-leaf Geranium	February–September	Cuttings April–May.
Primula obconica, Poison Primrose	Winter, spring	Sow seeds January–March, winter temperature 50°–55°.
Primula sinensis vars. Chinese Primrose	Winter, spring	Sow seeds January–March, winter temperature 50°–55°.
Rhododendron indicum vars., Greenhouse Azalea	Winter, early spring	Keep at 40°–50° until January; allow 4–6 weeks at 60° for flowering.
Rhododendron obtusum vars., Kurume Azalea		
Rosa chinensis minima vars. Fairy Rose (Pigmy, Pixie, *Rouletti,* Tom Thumb, et cetera)	Winter, spring	Pot in fall; keep in coldframe until January, then give temperature of 60°.

	When in bloom	*Treatment*
Saintpaulia ionantha, African-violet	Almost everblooming	For winter bloom start seeds or cuttings in January; rest old plants in summer by giving less water.
Sanguinaria canadensis, Bloodroot (H)	March	Treat as for *Claytonia;* allow 2–3 weeks to bloom.
Saxifraga sarmentosa, Mother-of-thousands (H)	Spring	Start new pots in May; allow room for rosettes to develop.
Schlumbergera (Epiphyllum) gaertneri, Easter Cactus	April	Water freely when growth begins.
Senecio cruentus, Cineraria (*)	Fall to spring	Sow seeds May, August, September.
Shortia galacifolia, Oconee Bells (H)	March, April	Treat as for *Claytonia.*
Shrimp Plant. *See Beloperone*		
Sinningia speciosa, Gloxinia	June–August	Start tubers February–March, 70°; about 4 months to bloom. Seeds sown in February bloom in 7 months.
Snapdragon. *See Antirrhinum*		
South African Cowslip. *See Lachenalia*		
Spirea. *See Astilbe*		
Sternbergia lutea, Mt. Etna Lily (HB)	September	Pot bulbs August, early September; plant outdoors after blooming.
Tagetes patula, French Marigold (use winter-blooming varieties) (A)	Winter	Sow seeds August–September.
Thunbergia alata, Black-eyed Susan Vine (A)	Winter, long-blooming	Starts blooming 10–12 weeks from seed sowing.
Tiarella cordifolia, Foam Flower (HB)	March, April	Treat as for *Claytonia.*
Trillium nivale, Snow Trillium (H)	March–April	Treat as for *Claytonia.* Allow 3 weeks at 50° for bloom.
Triteleia. *See Brodiaea*		

	When in bloom	Treatment
Tropaeolum majus, Nasturtium (A)	Winter, early spring	Start seeds or cuttings in August for winter bloom.
Tulipa, Tulip (HB) early vars., late vars.	Winter, early spring	Pot bulbs in fall; 6–8 weeks in plunge pit; 2 weeks at 50°; 4–6 weeks at 60° for early vars., 6–8 weeks for late vars.
Veltheimia viridifolia (TB)	Winter	Keep dry during summer. Start watering in September.
Zantedeschia aethiopica, Calla-lily (TB) *Zantedeschia elliottiana,* Golden Calla *Zantedeschia rehmanni,* Pink Calla	Almost any time	Start well-ripened tubers 8 weeks before blooms are required. *Z. elliottiana* tubers should be exposed in a warm, dry room for 3–4 weeks after receipt from dealer.
Zygocactus truncatus, Christmas Cactus	Early Winter	Avoid overwatering in November and early December, but give enough water to prevent stems from shriveling.

CHAPTER XVIII

Foliage Plants

THE so-called "foliage" plants are in general more tolerant than those grown primarily for their flowers. While they are not so gay-looking as a pot of well-flowered Tulips, Primroses, or Poinsettias, many of them do exhibit striking coloration—not so brilliant, perhaps, as that of some flowers, but effective nonetheless. In some, the normal green of the leaves is striped, spotted, or mottled with white or yellow; in others, it is wholly or partly masked by other pigments, as in Crotons and some of the Begonias, which may also exhibit an iridescent sheen or have a metallic appearance. Often the colors are arranged in striking patterns, and sometimes the lower leaves are typically green while the newer ones are marked with carmine or other colors. Frequently it is the graceful form of the leaves as in palms and ferns which warrants the designation foliage plants.

There is certainly no lack of variety in form, size, and color of plants grown for their foliage, and it can be said of them that while on the whole they may not be so spectacular as some of the flowering plants, for the most part they function throughout the year. Exceptions are those such as the Fancy-leaved Caladiums which die to the ground and go completely dormant during the winter, but even these make a show over a much longer period than the general run of flowering plants.

Some of the Bromeliads and Begonias considered under flowering plants also have attractive foliage and are worthy of culture for their leaves alone.

For convenience in dealing with their cultural requirements and to avoid as far as possible that "catalogue appearance," foliage plants are here grouped as far as possible according to their botanical affinities, starting with the Aroids.

AROIDS

These are plants belonging to the same family as the Jack-in-the-pulpit and Calla-lilies—an enormous group which contains a large number of the toughest of our house plants.

The most familiar is Chinese Evergreen which hails from Borneo and the Celebes. For a while we were told to call it *Aglaonema marantifolium,* then its alias was *A. modestum,* and now it has to pass as *A. simplex.* It is not specially beautiful or exciting—not even when it produces its greenish-white Calla-like inflorescence; but it grows almost equally as well in water as in soil and can thrive in dim light and dry air. Better "lookers" are the dwarf (8-inch) *A. costatum,* whose broad, bright green leaves are spotted with white, and *A. commutatum,* which reaches 2 feet with pale gray-green markings along the veins of its lance-shaped leaves. Mature plants may produce tight clusters of scarlet berries. These two are not quite so tolerant as the Chinese Evergreen.

The fancy-leaved Caladiums (see page 194) have a completely dormant period and are primarily suited for summer display, but by starting the tubers very early (January) or very late (June) it is possible to have them in good leaf in early spring and early fall respectively.

The various species of *Dieffenbachia,* Dumb Cane, or Mother-in-law Plant (so-called because a piece of the stem placed on the tongue renders one speechless for three days) are characterized by thick, fleshy stems and large, handsome, broad leaves (up to 2 feet long and half as much wide, though usually less than this in the house) variously mottled, spotted, or striped with white, yellow, or greenish brown. Several species and varieties are available from time to time in the florists' stores. Good ones are: *bowmanni; picta,* in several varieties; *seguine* and its varieties; and *splendens.* As house plants they are at their best when 1½ to 2½ feet high; but, whether grown in home or greenhouse, Dieffenbachias have the habit of becoming leggy and topheavy. When this occurs, they should be air-layered as described in the Propagation chapter.

There is a group of Aroids which in nature climb on trees by means of aerial roots. Some of these are sufficiently stout to be grown as pot plants for a time without any support. One of the most striking is the Mexican Bread Fruit, sometimes called Swiss Cheese Plant, because of the holes naturally formed in the much-divided leaves—a development which, presumably, enables the large leaves, roundish in outline (up to 3 feet wide when planted out and given room), to withstand hurricanes without tearing. This is capable of standing much neglect and dim light. As a potted plant it is usually about 2 feet high. Its botanical name is *Monstera deliciosa* but is generally known to florists as *Philodendron pertusum*.

The best-known Philodendron, all species of which are native to tropical America, is *P. cordatum*, the Heart-leaf Philodendron, a very enduring trailer which is not adapted for upstanding culture without a support. But there are others such as: *corsonianum*, with leaves up to 2 feet long and 1 foot broad with purplish undersides; *gloriosum*, leaves 10 inches long with reddish margins and pale green veins; *mamei*, about the same size, with pinkish stalks, blade spotted with silver; *verrucosum*, 8-inch shiny leaves with paler lines, lined with salmon-violet beneath and red stalks covered with fleshy bristles. There is a vast difference between the juvenile and adult appearance of these Philodendrons, especially in leaf size. *P. cordatum*, usually seen with 3-inch leaves as a trailer growing in a 4-inch pot, may have leaves up to 16 inches when planted out in rich soil in a greenhouse and allowed to climb.

There is almost no limit to the size of these climbers when given suitable growing conditions; most of them easily reach 20 feet or more, but in the home they range from 1½ to 2 feet unless given something on which to climb.

The botanists seem to have had no dearth of jawbreaking names when they came to naming members of this family, as witness *Homalomena*, *Scindapsus*, and *Zantedeschia*—all good house plants. This is a sort of introduction before springing on you *Schismatoglottis roebelini*, whose name may have to be changed, when the botanists get around to it, to *Aglaonema roebelini*. So far as I know it has no common name to give us an "out," which is possibly the reason it is not more commonly grown. It reaches a height of about 18 inches, usually with several stems clothed with leaves, the blades of which are 10 × 4 inches, gray-green with featherings of deep green extending from the midrib. Easy to grow but hard to get.

Nephthytis: One frequently sees *Nephthytis afzeli* decoratively used in New York City restaurants and other places of business, though the owners probably don't know it under this name and, so far as I know, it has no English cognomen. The fact that it grows in the situations mentioned is an indication of its adaptability. It has arrowhead leaves on slender climbing stems and is usually given a bark support.

Another mouthful is provided by *Syngonium podophyllum albo-lineatum,* whose leaves are deeply lobed and marked with white. Small plants of this are often a component of the dish gardens made up by florists. Well-grown plants may attain a height of about 18 inches. Another species of similar size but different appearance is *S. auritum,* whose leaves consist of a large central lobe with two small lobes at its base. Its decorative value consists of the bright green, highly varnished character of the leaves.

This listing of worth-while Aroids could extend from A to Z were it not that Zantedeschia is included in the bulb chapter, so we will conclude with "X" for *Xanthosoma lindeni,* Indian Kale, which is native to Colombia. You may not be able to obtain this because it is slow to propagate and hence does not interest the commercial men, but it is an excellent house plant and you should keep your eyes open and, if you see one listed, grab it.

The cultural requirements of all these Aroids are simple: fairly rich soil (general potting mixture); well-drained pots, so that they may be watered freely without danger of waterlogging; and a moderate amount of light. They succeed well in a north window— Monstera and some of the Philodendrons can get along in even less light. If the foliage can be sprayed with water daily, so much the better; if this is not done, wash the leaves at weekly intervals, using a sponge wet with lukewarm soapy water. The climbing types should be brought down to earth by air-layering if they get too tall for their location.

LILY FAMILY

When we think of the Lily Family it brings to mind the gorgeous flowers of Tulip and Lily; or perhaps, if we are gastronomically in-

Screw-pine (*Pandanus veitchi*) for subdued light and high temperature; and the graceful *Phoenix roebelini*, equally accommodating

Two favorite old-timers, the Asparagus "Ferns." The Lace-fern (*Asparagus plumosus*) above; and Emerald-feather (*A. sprengeri*) below

clined, the succulent delights of Asparagus and Onion. But there are some well-known foliage plants in the groups, though they are not spectacularly beautiful.

The Asparagus-fern, which the florist adds gratis to the package when you buy a half-dozen Roses, can be grown as a house plant. *Asparagus plumosus* is a tall-growing vine, but the variety *compactus* can be grown without support, as can *nanus*. If these show any tendency to climb, the tips of the developing shoots should be cut off. Emerald-feather (*Asparagus sprengeri*) is really a vine, growing to a height of 10 feet or more if planted in rich soil and trained up on wires; but when grown as a pot plant, its shoots arch over and hide the pot—exceptionally good specimens such as the one I once saw grown in a farmhouse and exhibited at a county fair may have shoots 3 or 4 feet long hanging well below the pot. This species is the best Asparagus for house culture, but its branches do not have the fernlike character of the preceding. Its tiny white flowers are attractive but not showy; they are followed by red berries if conditions are favorable. Both kinds need rich soil and plenty of water when growing; in winter it is desirable but not essential to provide a temperature near 50°. Emerald-feather is a voracious feeder and should be given liquid manure every two or three weeks when it is actively growing. Old mangy shoots should be cut away to make room for new growth.

One of the most famous house plants, though not so popular as it was in Victorian days, is *Aspidistra*, the Cast-iron Plant, so-called because of its ability to thrive almost anywhere. Its long, glossy leaves arising from the rootstock are heavy but decorative. The purplish-brown flowers are borne at the soil line and often pass unseen. There is a variety, *A. elatior punctata* with leaves spotted with yellow; and *A. elatior variegata* is striped green and white. Neither is as good-looking as the green-leaf type. Many homes have venerable specimens in 12- or 14-inch pots, but it is easier to handle if divided before it gets so large, and grown in 6-inch pots. Rich soil, ample watering, and a little light are all it needs, plus washing the leaves occasionally to shine them up and remove scale insects.

Cordyline and *Dracaena* are closely related, and many of the species have at one time or another been included in both genera. *Cordyline australis*, the Fountain Dracaena (often sold as *C. indivisa*) has long, narrow leaves gracefully arching from a central stem. It is commonly used as the central plant in large plant vases during summer. It is easily grown as a house plant and can be raised from seeds. A New Zealand species, it can endure light frosts and is better off if kept cool in winter. An East Indian species, *C. terminalis*, which has stalked, lance-shaped leaves, is not so easy to grow, but if you have a warm room in which the air is moist, one or more of the dozens of its varieties are worthy of a trial. The leaves often exhibit remarkable coloration: in *imperialis* they are metallic green rayed with crimson or pink; *amabilis* is suffused with rose and white; *baptisti* is irregularly striped with yellow and pink. And so it goes; some have deep purple leaves; some are white when young, changing to green margined with rose when mature; and some are red all over. Strong light is needed to bring out the colors of the leaves.

The soil should be the general potting mixture; a moist atmosphere and daily spraying of the foliage are desirable; and abundant watering at the roots, but no waterlogging. When the stem becomes too long in proportion to the tuft of the foliage, the top can be air-layered; and after the layer has been removed, the stem remaining can be cut into 3-inch lengths, buried ½ inch deep in sand in a propagating case (70° to 80°) if more young stock is desired.

There are several species of *Dracaena* which make first-class house plants and which vary greatly in size and general appearance. *D. fragrans* is the one which often grows up so that it hits the ceiling and has to be discarded, or given to an institution, unless the owner has the foresight to air-layer it before it gets to the ceiling-touching stage. The arching, Corn-like leaves may be 2 feet or more long and 3 inches wide. Occasionally this species and its varieties take it into their heads to throw up a panicle of flowers, which is just too bad, for the flowers—though fragrant—are not ornamental and their production destroys the symmetry of the plant. The varieties of this species offered commercially usually are faintly striped with yellowish green. The variety *lindeni* has creamy-white stripes.

The Gold-dust Dracaena, *D. godseffiana,* has a branching habit and small, oval, deep green leaves irregularly spotted with yellow or white. It seldom reaches more than a foot or two in height. *D. sanderiana* has leaves about 6 inches long and an inch broad striped with white. Its stems rarely branch and, as they may reach a height of several feet, give an effect of slenderness. Years ago, when

I worked for a Fifth Avenue florist and tended house plants in the homes of the wealthy, I noticed that in neglected window boxes *D. sanderiana* was the plant that survived after all the others had gone to their last rest. No special treatment beyond ordinary routine care is needed by these Dracaenas.

There are two kinds of Lily-turf, hardy outdoors, which can be grown as pot plants in the house and are well adapted for rooms cool in winter or in an enclosed unheated porch. *Ophiopogon jaburan* has grasslike leaves up to 2 feet long which are striped with yellow in the variety *aureus* and white in *variegatus.* The small drooping flowers in racemes are white or lilac. *Liriope muscari,* related to and sometimes sold as *O. jaburan,* has erect, purple flowers; it, too, has varieties with striped leaves. Both kinds form close tufts completely filling the pot in which they grow, necessitating division and repotting in the spring. Use general potting mixture and keep soil constantly moist.

The common Snake-plant (one might say very common!) *Sansevieria trifasciata laurenti,* is one of the most inelegant of all plants, with its stiff, 30-inch, upright leaves and the entire lack of form of the plant as a whole. Its yellow stripes, however, do provide a color note; but its chief claim to consideration is its toughness and ability to survive in darkish corners under conditions of neglect. It is erratic in its blooming habit, occasionally sending up its spike of fragrant flowers at unpredictable times. They are yellowish and not particularly ornamental. *S. zeylanica* is similar in habit, but the leaves have transverse bands of light green. *S. hahni,* which is occasionally seen as young plants in dish gardens, has its comparatively short leaves arranged in rosettes. The chief thing to avoid in growing Snakeplants is overwatering, especially in winter. The general potting mixture suits them; propagation is effected by division of the rootstock, and, except for *laurenti,* leaves cut into pieces 3 inches long and inserted in sand.

MISCELLANEOUS PLANTS

We now come to a miscellaneous lot which cannot conveniently be grouped here by botanical affinities, so they are arranged alphabetically.

Coleus—Painted Nettle: In the days when summer bedding was the thing, dozens of Painted Nettles, chiefly varieties of *Coleus blumei,* were available from florists. It is still possible to get named forms, but unless you happen to live near a florist who has them, probably the best way to get a stock of these colorful plants is to buy a package of seeds, set the seedlings out in the garden in the spring, and rigorously select the best forms for propagation by cuttings. This last is easy, for tip cuttings make roots with rapidity if inserted in moist, sandy soil and covered with a glass and kept shaded for a couple of weeks. A barber near me raises them for sale in olive-oil cans in the window of his store, which faces east. I hope it is a profitable side line for him.

If it were not for the brilliant coloring of the sometimes velvety-looking leaves, Coleus would give the impression of weediness. In some, the leaves are clear yellow; in others, the green is veined or blotched with red, brown, yellow, or pink. In size they range from the 1½-inch leaves of a rather common trailing variety (*C. pumilus*) to the 8-inch leaves produced on specimen plants partly by culture (limiting the plant to one or a few shoots) and partly by selecting a naturally large-leaved variety.

The chief drawback to Coleus culture is the mealybugs' fondness for them. If a plant becomes badly infested, it is better to junk it, reserving a few cuttings, from which the bugs can be removed manually, to carry on the line. The foliage of Coleus is sensitive to insecticides of sufficient strength to kill mealybugs. Use general potting mixture; keep soil moist; give enough light to bring out the leaf colors; and raise new plants annually from cuttings (they will root any time) to replace mangy old one.

Ficus—Rubber Plant: The Fig Family gives us three outstanding species for house culture: the India Rubber Plant (*Ficus elastica*)—the plant for which Brooklyn is famous; the Fiddle-leaf Fig (*Ficus lyrata*); and the Climbing Fig (*Ficus pumila*). The last named may be used as a climber or trailer (see Vines), but the variety *minima* is very attractive as an upright potted plant if given a short log, 3 inches in diameter, on which to climb. The two first named, particularly *F. lyrata,* are handsomer when grown as single-stem plants. They can be air-layered if they become too leggy. The fiddle-shaped leaves of *F. lyrata,* which may be up to 18 inches long, have much more character than those of the ordinary Rubber Plant. General

(*Above*) Coleus, one of the most colorful and easily grown foliage plants.
Watch out for mealybugs!

(*Right*) Giant Hybrid Amaryllis (*Hippeastrum*). For something quick, sure,
and dramatic, try it

The Birdsnest Fern
(*Asplenium nidus*) is
popular and not too
difficult to manage

Maidenhair Fe
(*Adiantum cune*
tum) is another fai
easy kind that is n
tably attractive

potting mixture; routine culture, plus occasional washing of the leaves.

Hedera—**English Ivy:** We usually think of English Ivy as a trailing or climbing vine, but there are some forms of definitely upright habit and some which are sufficiently compact to be grown without support. In the first group we have *Hedera helix conglomerata*, with several forms sold under such names as *minima* (not to be confused with a climbing variety of that name), *erecta*, and *russelliana*. These have stiff stems and crowded, leathery, often ruffled leaves. Then there is the Pittsburgh Ivy, introduced about twenty-five years ago, which "sported" so freely that at least a dozen forms have been selected and named. Among these are: Albany, with curious distorted leaves; Green Feather, somewhat laciniated; Hahn's Miniature, Manda's Crested, Maple Queen, and Merion Beauty. A collection of these forms, varied in leaf characters and habit, makes an interesting hobby for those who have none but north windows in which to grow their plants, more especially if it is a room which can be kept at about 50° in winter. The chief enemies to be watched for are spider mites, which flourish in heat and dry air, and scale insects. These can be prevented by thorough spraying of the leaves, both sides, at least once a week, using water from the hose applied with considerable force. Otherwise, care is routine.

Helxine soleiroli—**Baby's Tears, Japanese Moss, Irish Moss:** There have been several attempts to manufacture a common name for this little creeper from Corsica and Sardinia, none of which have been appropriate except for "Corsican Carpet Plant," which is dull and pompous. It is related to the Stinging Nettles (although it does not sting) and, as we have seen, it comes from the Mediterranean; therefore, the names Japanese Moss and Irish Moss are obvious misnomers. Baby's Tears, the name now generally accepted, does not seem particularly apt, but it is the best that anyone has been able to pull out of his hat so far. The tiny leaves are produced on slender, crowded stems to give the plant a Mosslike appearance. Its shoots do not trail very far when deprived of contact with the soil, so in spite of its creeping habit, it is not very successful when it is desired to have the shoots trail below the level of the bottom of the pot. One of the best methods of displaying it is to build up a pyramid of soil-filled pots of diminishing size, sinking each pot an inch or two in the soil of the pot below. Small, rooted divisions dibbled in the exposed soil of each tier will quickly grow so that the whole becomes merged in a green, fountainlike effect.

Helxine is sensitive to artificial gas, but otherwise is easy to grow in ordinary soil in partial shade.

Maranta—Arrowroot: At one time considered capable of cultivation only in a warm, moist greenhouse; two species of *Maranta* have recently won their spurs as house plants. One is a variegated form (*M. arundinacea variegata*) of the Arrowroot of commerce; usually about a foot high as a pot plant with oblong leaves variegated with yellow. The other is *M. leuconeura,* dwarf, with elliptical leaves about 6 inches long, of velvety appearance, with large, decorative spots. These should be potted in Begonia mixture, kept moist, but not sopping wet, and given partial shade. Spraying the foliage daily with clear water is helpful.

Pandanus—Screw-pine: Screw-pines are beautiful as young plants but one often sees heirlooms which are just the reverse, with browned leaf tips and a forest of suckers cluttering the base. Plants of this nature should have been discarded years before, and would have been were it not for a sentimental attachment to them, plus ignorance of the fact that they can easily be rejuvenated and perpetuated by sucker cuttings taken when the old plant is approaching unwieldy size. There are two species commonly grown as house plants—*Pandanus utilis,* whose leaves are decorated with reddish spines; and *P. veitchi,* striped white and green, also armed with vicious spines along the margins. Both species have gracefully recurving sword-shaped leaves arranged spirally which causes everyone to wave his hand in circles when describing them. *P. baptisti* has no spines, which makes it ideal from the standpoint of no scratched hands, but unfortunately the leaves are not really strong enough to support their own weight, and some are certain to collapse in the middle, giving the plant a bedraggled appearance.

The Screw-pines commonly produce "prop" roots from the stem which enables one to observe very easily the root cap, which is prominent in Pandanus and characteristic of all roots though not often so visible. It is part of house-plant tradition that overhead watering by allowing water to settle in the rosette of leaves causes rotting of the center. I'm not convinced that this is so. Screw-pines can endure confined quarters for their roots, but when they become potbound they should be watered occasionally with liquid manure; and, when the potbound condition is so extreme that they begin to heave themselves out of their pots, they should be shifted to a larger size. Use general potting mixture, keep them well watered, and give them a moderate amount of light.

Peperomia—Watermelon Begonia: Probably the commonest Peperomia under cultivation is the one sometimes called Watermelon Begonia (it has no connection whatever with Watermelon or Begonia!) which may be either *Peperomia sandersi* or its variety *argyreia,* which has more pronounced silver stripes between the veins of the heart-shaped, fleshy leaves on red stalks. Its flowers are worthless decoratively. Another species which has become rather common in recent years is *P. obtusifolia,* a rather stodgy plant with fat green leaves on erect or semi-trailing stems. There is a variety variegated with cream-colored markings on the leaves; it is a popular component of florists' dish gardens and terrariums.

These plants require moist air and shade from bright sunshine. They are often used in terrariums but will grow in the open air of the living room. Use general-purpose potting mixture and keep it moist. Young plants can easily be raised from leaf cuttings inserted in sand in a propagating case or under a tumbler.

Tolmiea menziesi—Picka-back Plant: During recent years the Picka-back Plant has come very much to the fore as a house plant. It is native to the Pacific coast from Alaska to California and is hardy outdoors, or nearly so, as well as in the house. Its flowers are green and not ornamental, so it is grown for its interesting foliage which, while not especially beautiful, has a fresh greenness which is attractive. Its noteworthy feature, however, is the little plants which develop at the tip of the leafstalk and these in turn may also produce plantlets of still smaller size, reminding one of Swift's jingle:

> So, naturalists observe, a flea
> Has smaller fleas that on him prey;
> And these have smaller still to bite 'em
> · And so proceed ad infinitum.

The culture of Picka-back does not present any special problems— merely give it reasonably good soil, water freely, and shade from bright sunshine, especially in summer. When the plants begin to look moth-eaten, as they will when aged, start new ones by potting up leaves with plantlets attached in sandy, humusy soil. It is well adapted to water culture, and leaves placed in a jar so that the water barely touches the leaf blade will soon grow.

FERNS

Many of the plants in the foliage classification are, technically, flowering plants although their flowers may have little ornamental value. Aspidistra, a foliage plant if ever there was one, belongs to the Lily Family and has purple-maroon flowers an inch across. But many amateurs grow it for years, never seeing the flowers even though it blooms annually, so modestly are they displayed. But there is no doubt whatever about the Ferns; they definitely are flowerless plants and make up for it from our standpoint by the beauty and elegance of their fronds.

While many of the most desirable Ferns are difficult (or impossible) for culture in the house unless they are contained in a Wardian case to give them the atmospheric moisture they need (Maiden-hair Ferns in general, for example), there are enough amenable kinds to provide sufficient variety in size and form. Many Ferns in nature inhabit shaded places, and their ability to thrive in a subdued light makes them particularly valuable in dimly lighted locations. It must not be inferred, however, that their use in sunny windows is prohibited. Most of them can be thus placed provided they are protected from direct sunshine by thin curtains.

Ferns are attractive from babyhood to maturity, and those which ultimately attain considerable size may be grown as youngsters even in small apartments, but gardeners whose hearts are wrenched when they have to discard a plant when it starts to crowd them out of house and home will want to know which species to avoid.

One of these big sisters is the **Mexican Tree-fern** (*Cibotium schiedei*) which may make a trunk 15 feet high with fronds 5 feet long. While it is not likely to grow so large under house conditions, I have seen specimens 6 feet in diameter and 3 or 4 feet high. A well-grown specimen, about 3 feet in diameter, with its gracefully curving, much-divided, light green fronds, is exquisite, and I can recommend it highly if you can bear to part with it when it gets too big for you.

The **Sword Fern** (*Nephrolepis exaltata*) and some of the varieties of the **Boston Fern** (*N. exaltata bostoniensis*), more graceful than the first named, are capable of assuming huge proportions. The Sword Fern has fronds up to 5 feet long; and the same is true of Boston Fern varieties such as *roosevelti*. As a matter of fact, the decline of Boston Ferns in popularity is attributed to the passing of old-style roomy houses and the modern craze for apartment living. But there are dwarf forms available for those who are cramped for space, such as Mill's Boston, which grows to only a third of the size of the type and has very tough, long-lasting leaves. More than a hundred forms of Boston Fern have had names attached to them at one time or another, ranging from once-pinnate types to those whose fronds are so much divided that they resemble Moss. This would seem to offer plenty of scope for the "collector," but I doubt if a tithe of them could be purchased nowadays, and probably many varieties are lost to cultivation, which is a pity because they *are* good house plants, almost infinite in variety. The drooping fronds of many of them hide the pots which may be considered an advantage.

The **Hare's-foot Fern** (*Polypodium aureum*) is distinctive with its massive glaucous (blue-green) fronds decorated on the undersides with clusters of golden spore cases. The variety *mandaianum* with ruffled pinnae (leaflets) is particularly attractive and in the greenhouse may make leaves 6 feet in length. Although not likely to be so vigorous as this in a home, it is on the large side as Ferns go.

There are plenty of Ferns to choose from in the middle-size bracket. One of the most striking, because it does not have the divided fronds characteristic of so many other kinds, is *Asplenium nidus,* the **Birds-nest Fern.** This has machete-shaped leaves, often with wavy margins, arranged in circles around a central core of stem. Although these leaves may attain a length of 4 feet under very favorable conditions, they seldom exceed 2 feet when grown in the home. Young specimens a foot or less high are particularly attractive.

I believe the toughest of all Ferns is *Polystichum adiantiforme* (*P. capense, P. coriaceum*), the **Leather-leaf Fern.** I once had this thriving beautifully in a pot on the floor beneath a plant stand in a north window shaded by the porch roof. Under cultivation the

fronds, triangular in outline, are about 1½ feet long and nearly
as much broad, shiny and leathery in texture.

The **Staghorn Ferns** are unusual in having fronds of two kinds.
These plants are epiphytes (not parasites), attaching themselves to
trees by means of sterile clasping fronds which, succulent and greenish when developing, ultimately become cinnamon-colored and
parchment-like. They flare outward at the top, leaving a space between them and the tree trunk which serves as a catchall for leaves
and debris falling from the tree above. This debris decays and forms
"soil" in which the roots ramify. The fertile fronds are grayish
green, reminiscent in shape of the horns of the European reindeer.

The decorative and long-lived
Staghorn Fern

The common Staghorn Fern (*Platycerium bifurcatum*) is a tolerant
house plant and does not mind temperatures as low as 40°. Usually
these Ferns are grown on a hunk of Osmunda fiber wired to a board
or a piece of tree trunk and their watering presents a problem in a
room where drips on the floor are anathema. I have solved it in my
own home by a contraption which looks something like a Rube
Goldberg cartoon. On a shelf I have a marmalade jar filled with
water which is conducted to the surface of the fiber in which the
Fern is growing by means of a length of glass wick. The unabsorbed
water drips into another jar and this, from time to time, is returned to the upper receptacle. Once a week the plant should be
taken to the bathroom and thoroughly sprayed with water. This
will keep it free from scale insects and moisten any part of the
rooting medium missed by the drips. If you have an enclosed porch
with a brick or stone floor which the daily watering will not harm,
in which the temperature never falls below 40°, with a north-facing
wall on which Platycerium can be hung, you have an ideal spot in

which to grow these Ferns (at least those which are not strictly tropical); and you will have something in the plant line that is distinctly out of the ordinary.

The **Mother Spleenwort** (*Asplenium bulbiferum*), beautiful enough with finely divided fronds, has an additional claim to consideration in the interest afforded by bulbils or plantlets which develop on the fronds. In nature these fall off and take root, thus serving as a means of propagation. It occurs in the wild from Malaya to New Zealand and is adapted to a wide range of temperature—it can be grown either in the living room, or in an enclosed porch provided the temperature does not go below 40°. Its dimensions under cultivation usually are about 2 × 2 feet.

Two species which are very much alike in general appearance when young but which can easily be distinguished by the color of the leafstalks are **Holly Fern** (*Cyrtomium falcatum*), green stalks, and **Green Cliff-brake** (*Pellaea viridis*) with dark brown stalks. Both are handsome, with height and spread of about 1½ feet. The first named has Holly-like pinnae (leaflets) and is more tolerant of house conditions than the Cliff-brake which, however, has a little more distinction. They are adaptable to a wide range of winter temperatures—35° to 70°.

There are three species of **Brake Fern** suitable as house plants, all of which are represented by several varieties. The Cretan Brake (*Pteris cretica*—the "P" is silent), which has fronds about a foot long, has varieties such as Ribbon Brake with a white line through each leaf division; Riverton Brake whose pinnae are ruffled and lobed; and several varieties with tassled tips to the leaf divisions— May's Brake, Wilson Brake (a compact variety), and Wimsett Brake.

The Sword Brake (*Pteris ensiformis*) may get a little taller than the preceding. Its outstanding varieties are Victoria Brake, banded with white; and Siebold's Brake, a ruffled variety with two kinds of fronds—the fertile ones, tall, upright, and narrow; the others, dwarf, spreading, and broad.

Spider Brake (*Pteris serrulata* or *multifida*) has leaf divisions narrower than those of *P. cretica*, but otherwise similar. There are many crested and variegated varieties such as *cristata, variegata,* and *nana,* a dwarf form.

Probably the smallest of the Ferns commonly grown in the house is *Polystichum tsus-simense* (no, it's not a misprint!), the **Tsusima**

Holly-fern, which seldom attains a foot in height. It is tufted in habit with dark green upright fronds.

The **Squirrel's-foot Fern** or **Ball Fern** (*Davallia bullata*) also is on the small side, with fronds up to 10 inches long. This is the species formerly imported from Japan in immense quantities in the guise of "Fern balls" consisting of dormant rhizomes bound up with Moss, which started into growth when kept moist. Even though it is deciduous (shedding its leaves annually) it is worth growing if obtainable.

It is generally conceded that the **Maidenhair Ferns** are among the most graceful and attractive. Unfortunately they have a sinister reputation as house plants and most people fail with them unless they have a Wardian case in which they can be grown. One species, however, the Trailing Maidenhair (*Adiantum caudatum*), is quite conformable. It does not look much like a Maidenhair, having drooping fronds which root and produce plantlets at their tips. It is attractive when displayed in a hanging pot or basket.

A typical Maidenhair and the one most likely to succeed is *A. cuneatum*, which may have fronds 15 inches long, but usually they are shorter. In locations not too urban in character, in a room where the air is humid and not contaminated with artificial gas and kept from undiluted sunshine, this species and its many varieties are worth a trial.

While they are not true Ferns, **Selaginellas** may be considered here, for they are close allies. The ones most commonly grown as house plants are *Selaginella emmiliana*, which looks like a Fern, with closely branching stems, usually 6 inches long, clothed with very tiny leaves; and *S. kraussiana browni*, which, when well grown, looks for all the world like a cushion of bright green Moss. This variety grows exceptionally well even under adverse conditions, and I am favorably impressed with it even though my enthusiasm was somewhat dashed when my youngest scornfully asked, on seeing what I considered a beautiful mound of greenery completely filling a 6-inch pan, "Is that all it does?"

The **Resurrection Plant,** *Selaginella lepidota,* might be made to thrive if it were possible to obtain freshly gathered specimens. This is the plant, commonly sold in novelty stores, which looks like a dried-up ball of Moss. When placed in water the fronds unroll, revealing their green upper surfaces.

Doubtless other Selaginellas, some upright, some trailing, some exhibiting unique metallic coloring, could be successfully grown—I have not tried them.

About twenty years ago millions of Ferns (*Cyrtomium, Polystichum, Pteris*) were raised annually to provide material for filling "Fern dishes" to be put in elaborate filigreed silver holders and placed in the center of the dining table. Fern dishes are no longer the vogue which, perhaps, is just as well, since a Fern's expectancy of life in the cramped and crowded dish and dim surroundings was not a good insurance risk. These little Ferns are very attractive, and the process of raising them from spores and watching their development is of absorbing interest, so you may want to try it. The process is described in Chapter XV, page 131.

General culture: As previously mentioned, Ferns in general are good bets when light conditions are not too bright. If the leaves turn yellowish green when grown in a south window and you are sure it is not due to lack of nutrients, give them more shade or remove to a window with a north or west aspect.

Except for species such as the Ball Fern, which can endure drought when it is dormant, Ferns must be kept constantly moist at the root. All Ferns need ample watering when in active growth; however, avoid waterlogging the soil, though this is not likely to happen if the pots are well drained.

If the fronds become yellowish and you are sure it is not due to too intense light, it is usually a sign that nutrients are lacking. Feeding with liquid manure (page 55), nitrate of soda, or sulphate of ammonia (page 56) will correct this condition provided other environmental factors are favorable.

Repotting, if necessary, is done at the beginning of the growing season. Some kinds—as Adiantum and Pteris—may have to be divided at this time to prevent them from attaining unwieldy size. Boston Fern varieties do not respond well to division—raise young plants from runners to replace specimens which have grown too large. See Chapters IX and XV.

Keep a close watch for insect pests—particularly the Fern scale, the males of which are slender and white, the females rotund and brownish. Learn, if you do not already know, how to distinguish between them and the spore cases which develop on the back of the fronds. You may feel insulted by this advice, but the receipt of many letters from frantic amateurs asking for expeditious measures against scale insects when none were present leads me to think the suggestion may deter some from laboriously removing spore cases by hand under the impression they are destroying scale insects!

Ferns appeal more to some gardeners than to others. Their beauty of form compensates for lack of flowers; and there are varieties not devoid of coloring other than the normal green. In this chapter a baker's dozen or so of genera suited to house culture has been listed. Anyone who feels impelled to make a hobby of a collection of Ferns could, I am sure, easily find dozens more equally tolerant.

PALMS

There was a time when Palms as house plants were as much in evidence as the ubiquitous Rubber Plant, but they are out of favor nowadays and the only one that is really widely used is *Howea fosteriana,* the **Kentia Palm.** Native to Lord Howe Island, that Utopia where every prospect pleases and not even man is vile, the collection of its seeds for sale to florists in America and Europe is the only industry. Kentias are in great demand as "rented" Palms for use at balls, parties, weddings, and funerals; and to some extent as house plants.

The toughness of Kentia was impressed on me many years ago when working in the decorative department of a Fifth Avenue florist. Dozens of these Palms ranging up to 10 feet in height were used on any job of considerable size. Every time they left the store their leaves were bundled together with newspapers, the number of thicknesses depending upon the severity of the weather. Then, looking like wrapped mummies, they were stuffed in a horse-drawn wagon and taken to their destination, which might be a hotel, a drafty concert stage, or a private home. There they were unwrapped and the kinks shaken out of their leaves. The following day they were tied and wrapped again, packed in the cold, cold wagon, hustled into the dismal back room of the store, unwrapped, and crowded together, pot touching pot, on the bench. Even with this program of rough handling, alternations of heat and cold, and crowding, they survived for many weeks, but ultimately had to be discarded or sent to a greenhouse to recuperate.

Plants of Kentia purchased from a florist usually are "made up"— that is, a large plant is set in the center of the pot with three smaller, younger ones around it to avoid the naked appearance of the base. They are admirable for porch decoration in summer if room can be found for them indoors in winter.

One of the most beautiful and useful Palms (because of its small growth) is *Syagrus (Cocos) weddelliana,* the **Weddell** or **Cocos Palm,** which used to be fairly common; but since one of the chief producers has gone out of the business of raising it it has become very scarce. This is regrettable, because its graceful leaves made up of narrow, bright green, shiny pinnae are decidedly ornamental.

Its place has been taken to some extent by a relative of the Date Palm, *Phoenix roebeleni.* This perhaps is of even more elegant habit but its leaves do not have the shiny brightness of the Weddell Palm.

Less than ten years ago a dwarf palm from Guatemala, *Neanthe bella,* was given considerable publicity but apparently has not been widely propagated so that it is difficult to obtain. In its natural habitat it grows in shade, in thin soil subject to rapid drying, so that it is tolerant of the dim light and dry air of our homes. A pinnate-leaved Palm, it has the interesting feature of flowering when two or three years old; so if you are lucky enough to have both a male and a female (the sexes are produced on separate plants) it may be possible to enjoy the sight of its dark green, ultimately black fruits displayed on the orange-yellow branches of the inflorescence. So dwarf is this Palm that it is possible for it to reach its full development when growing in a 6- or 8-inch pot.

Fan-leaved Palms are not so well suited to house culture as the more graceful feathery types because their lateral spread is so great that they take up too much room in a home of average size. The Chinese Fan Palm (*Livistona chinensis*), however, takes up little room as a young plant and is worth getting if the opportunity presents itself. *L. chinensis,* when mature, has a trunk 30 feet tall with leaf blades up to 6 feet in diameter on stalks 6 feet long, and *L. rotundifolia* is capable of attaining a height of 80 feet, so don't expect them to grow to maturity in your home.

Palm seeds are occasionally offered in the catalogues of firms dealing with unusual seeds and of those featuring house plants, and there is no difficulty in obtaining seeds of the Date Palm during the winter months when the fruit is on the markets. The seeds are not difficult to raise if sown ½ inch deep in sandy, humusy soil, kept moist, in a temperature of about 70°. Don't be too disappointed in the appearance of the seedlings. With the exceptions of species like *Neanthe bella* and *Cocos weddelliana,* whose leaves early in life acquire the graceful character of adult specimens, most Palms are very unattractive in the young state with some leaves undivided and some just beginning to hint at what they will be like when they are grown up.

Palms, in general, should be potted in a fairly heavy, rich soil (general-purpose potting mixture), and when they become potbound (a condition they do not resent so long as it is not extreme), they should be watered with liquid manure every few weeks during the active growing season.

They will endure reduced light and may indeed be injured if transferred from the home to undiluted sunshine outdoors.

If you find it possible to make yourself wash the leaves every week with a sponge wet with lukewarm soapy water (myself, I hate the job, having been compelled to spend hundreds of weary hours sponging Palms when I was a journeyman gardener), it will keep them free from scales and mealybugs and spruce them up generally.

This does not exhaust the list of plants grown for their foliage; others will be found in the General List of House Plants. The Bromeliads, members of the Pineapple Family, many of which have spectacular foliage, are discussed under Flowering Plants because their unique flowers seemed to justify their inclusion there.

CHAPTER XIX

General List of House Plants

(Where no details are given after a plant's name, see Index for reference to discussions in previous chapters.)

Abrus precatorius, Rosary Pea, Crab's Eyes. A small vine, not particularly attractive, which has been recommended. Sow seeds in general-purpose mixture; keep moderately moist in sunny window.

Abutilon hybridum and others; Flowering Maple.

Acacia, Mimosa. *A. armata,* Kangaroo Thorn.

Acalypha hispida, Chenille Plant. Although this has been recommended, it is a difficult house plant in my experience. Raised from cuttings; general-purpose potting mixture; moderately moist; sunny window.

Achimenes spp., tuberous, summer-flowering plants.

Acorus gramineus variegatus. A grasslike plant, 10 inches tall, related to Sweet Flag. This and the variety *pusillus,* usually no more than 3 inches high, are often used in dish gardens and terrariums. Division; general-purpose potting mixture; plenty of water; sun or shade.

Adiantum spp., Maidenhair Fern.

Aechmea spp., Pineapple relatives.

Aeonium tabulaeforme, succulent.

Agapanthus umbellatus, African Lily. A blue-flowered, summer-blooming, bulbous plant, 3 feet tall. Grown in tubs for porch and garden decoration; stored nearly dry in cool cellar over winter. Division; general-purpose mixture; moist when growing; sun or light shade.

Agathaea coelestis. See Felicia amelloides.

Agave spp., Century Plant and others.

Ageratum houstonianum. Bedding plant with small blue flowers in heads. Often recommended. Small plants may be dug up from garden in fall and potted. Subject to attack by white flies.

Aglaonema spp., Chinese Evergreen and others.

Allium neapolitanum, Flowering Onion. Small white flowers in umbels. Treat as hardy spring-flowering bulb, but don't expose to severe freezing.

Aloe spp., Aloes.

Alternanthera amoena. Dwarf plants, with varicolored leaves suitable for terrariums, which see.

Alyssum maritimum. See Lobularia.

Amaryllis. See Hippeastrum.

Amorphophallus, Devil's Tongue. *See Hydrosme.*

Anacharis canadensis, Ditch Moss (aquatic).

Ananas sativus, Pineapple.

Anthericum. See Chlorophytum.

Anthurium spp., Flamingo Flower and others.

Antigonum leptopus, Coral Vine, Rosa de Montana. A vine with racemes of bright pink flowers; has been recommended. Seeds or cuttings; general-purpose mixture, without manure; moderately moist; full sun.

Antirrhinum, Snapdragon.

Aporocactus flagelliformis, Rat-tail Cactus.

Araucaria excelsa, Norfolk Island Pine. A handsome pyramidal evergreen, formerly popular, now rarely seen. General-purpose mixture; constantly moist; light shade. Must be kept cool, 45°–50°, in winter.

Ardisia crenulata, Coral Berry.

Areca. See Chrysalidocarpus lutescens.

Aregelia marmorata, Pineapple relative.

Aristolochia elegans, Calico Flower. A vine with 3-inch flowers, which has been recommended. Probably difficult. Seeds in spring; general-purpose mixture; moist; sun or partial shade.

Asparagus spp., Emerald-feather—Asparagus Fern.

Aspidistra elatior, Cast-iron Plant.

Asplenium spp., Birds-nest Fern and others.

Astilbe japonica, Florists' Spirea.

Astrophytum spp., Bishop's Cap Cactus—Sand Dollar, et cetera.

Aucuba japonica, Gold-dust Plant. An almost hardy shrub, 2–3 feet tall as a tubbed plant, with gold-spotted leaves, suitable for an unheated enclosed porch. Cuttings; general-purpose mixture; moist; partial shade.

Azalea. See Rhododendron.

Azolla caroliniana, Mosquito Plant (aquatic).

Begonia spp.

Beloperone guttata, Shrimp Plant.

Bertolonia maculata. A dwarf herb with handsome velvety green leaves and purple-bordered veins. Suitable for terrariums, which see.

Beta vulgaris, Beet.

Billbergia spp., Pineapple relatives.

Brassica rapa, Turnip.

Brodiaea uniflora, Spring Star-flower.

Bromeliads, a family which contains the Pineapple and Spanish Moss and plants variously known as Bromels, Air-pines, et cetera.

Bryophyllum. The plants mentioned in this book, known under this name, have been referred to *Kalanchoe.*

Buxus sempervirens suffruticosa, Dwarf Box. Young plants used in terrariums. Cuttings; general-purpose mixture; sun.

Cabomba caroliniana (aquatic).

Cacti.

Caladium bicolor, Fancy-leaved Caladiums.

Calceolaria crenatiflora, Calceolaria. Has been suggested as house plant, but I am ready to take off my hat three times to anyone able to grow it as such. Culture as for *Senecio cruentus.*

Calathea. Tropical plants grown for their beautiful foliage. Although some might possibly thrive in the open air of the living room (a relative, *Maranta leuconeura* does), they are more likely to be successful in a terrarium. For this purpose dwarf kinds should be chosen, such as: *Calathea illustris, C. roseo-picta,* and *C. undulata.* However, they are not commonly offered commercially, and difficulty is likely to be experienced in obtaining them. Division; Begonia soil; moist conditions; partial shade.

Caltha palustris, Marsh-marigold.

Camellia spp., Tea-plant—Camellia.

Campanula isophylla, Ligurian Harebell, sometimes erroneously called Star of Bethlehem. A plant with gray-green leaves and somewhat trailing stems; abundant pale blue flowers produced over a long period in fall. Cuttings; general-purpose mixture with handful of crushed limestone to a 6-inch pot; moderately moist; shade from bright sun; cool (50°) in winter.

Capsicum annuum, Christmas Pepper.

Caralluma nebrowni, a succulent.

Carica papaya, Pawpaw.

Cattleya spp., Orchid.

Centaurea cyanus, Cornflower. An annual with variously colored flowers, primarily blue.

Cephalocereus senilis, Old Man Cactus.

Ceratopteris (aquatic).

Cereus peruvianus, one of the Cacti.

Ceropegia woodi, Rosary Plant, Hearts Entangled.

Chamaecereus sylvestri, Peanut Cactus.

Chamaerops humilis, a dwarf Fan Palm from the Mediterranean region, which can endure light frost. Try in enclosed unheated porch. See Palms for culture.

Cheiridopsis candidissima (succulent), Cigarette Plant.

Chimaphila spp., Pipsissewa. For terrariums.

Chiogenes hispidula, Teaberry, Creeping Snowberry. Native plant for winter terrariums.

Chionodoxa luciliae, Glory of the Snow. *See Hardy Bulbs.*

Chlorophytum elatum, Spider-plant. A very common plant of easy culture, the striped-leaf form being in greatest favor. Division; general-purpose mixture; moist; sun or partial shade.

Chrysalidocarpus lutescens, Golden Feather Palm. Graceful, pinnate leaves with yellow stalks. See section on Palms for culture.

Chrysanthemum frutescens, Paris Daisy, Marguerite.

Chrysanthemum hortorum, Garden Chrysanthemum.

Cibotium schiedei, Mexican Tree Fern.

Cineraria. See Senecio cruentus.

Cissus, Grape-ivy, Cape Grape, Kangaroo Vine.

Citrus spp., Grapefruit, Otaheite Orange, Lemon, et cetera.

Claytonia virginica, Spring Beauty.

Cleistocactus spp., Scarlet Bugler, Silver Torch.

(*Above*) Interesting and easily cared for plants for hot, dry rooms are to be found among the Cacti, with their widely varied forms and exotic blossoms in many colors

(*Above*) Blooms of the yellow-flowered *Echinocereus luteus*

(*Right*) Flats of Cacti grown from seed—a slow, but not too difficult an undertaking

Two plants for a room decorated in the modern manner: the Watermelon-begonia (*Peperomia sandersi*), left;

and variegated *P. obtusifolia*. Both of these add a nice decorative touch

Clerodendron thomsoniae. A twining vine having showy crimson flowers with creamy-white calyxes, which has been recommended. Cuttings; general-purpose mixture; moist, except in fall when it should be rested by reducing the supply of water; sunny window.

Clivia miniata, Kafir Lily.

Cobaea scandens, Cup-and-saucer Vine. A strong-growing vine with large greenish or purplish flowers. Needs at least a 6-inch pot for good results. Raise annually from seeds sown in late winter; general-purpose mixture; moist; sun or light shade.

Cocos weddelliana, Cocos Palm, *Syagrus.*

Codiaeum spp., Croton.

Colchicum spp., Meadow Saffron.

Coleus spp., and varieties, Painted Leaf.

Conophytum wiggetae (succulent), Cone Plant.

Convallaria majalis, Lily-of-the-valley.

Coprosma baueri. A New Zealand shrub (or small tree when planted out) with shining leaves blotched with yellow in the variety *variegata,* the one most commonly cultivated. Rooted cuttings useful in cool-room terrariums; as a tubbed shrub for frost-free, unheated, enclosed porches. Cuttings; general-purpose mixture; moist; cool in winter; sun or light shade.

Cordyline spp., Dracaena (which also see).

Cotyledon spp. Succulents suitable for sunny windows. Many plants formerly known as *Cotyledon* are now referred to as *Echeveria.* Cuttings; Cactus soil; on dry side in winter, moist when growing; sun or very light shade.

Crassula spp. (succulents), Jade Plant, Necklace Vine, et cetera.

Crinum longifolium. A summer-flowering bulb with large pink or white flowers which requires too much room for the average grower. Propagated by offsets from the bulbs; bulb soil; moist when growing; dry and cool in winter; sun.

Crocus spp.

Cryptanthus spp., Pineapple relatives.

Cyanotis somaliensis, Pussy Ears.

Cycas revoluta, Sago "Palm." The processed leaves are perhaps more familiar as a backing for funeral pieces than as part of a house plant. Too spiky and spreading for the average home. Seeds (when obtainable); general-purpose mixture; moist, somewhat dry and cool in winter; sun or light shade.

Cyclamen indicum, Florists' Cyclamen.

Cymbalaria muralis, Kenilworth Ivy.

Cyperus alternifolius, Umbrella Plant. A semi-aquatic with umbels of grasslike leaves on stems up to 4 feet. The varieties *gracilis* and *nanus,* which are dwarfer, are preferred for house culture. There is a variety (*variegata*) with stems and leaves striped white. Cuttings of umbels in water; general-purpose mixture; wet; sun or light shade.

Cypripedium spp., Lady Slipper Orchid.

Cyrtomium falcatum, Holly Fern.

Cytisus canariensis, Florists' Genista, Broom.

Daphne odora, Fragrant Daphne. A small evergreen shrub with intensely fragrant white to purple flowers in late winter. Variety *marginata* has leaves bordered with yellow. Cuttings; equal parts loam, leafmold, peatmoss, sand; moist; 50° in winter; sun or light shade.

Daucus carota sativa, Carrot.

Davallia bullata, Squirrel's Foot Fern.

Dendrobium nobile (Orchid).

Dicentra spp., Bleeding Heart, Dutchman's Breeches.

Dieffenbachia spp., Dumb Cane, Mother-in-law Plant.

Dizygotheca elegantissima, False Aralia. This plant with the dizzy name is a shrub or small tree, but when grown in a pot is usually seen with a single stem about a foot tall, clothed with elegant compound leaves with slender, gracefully drooping leaflets. A similar plant (*D. [Aralia] veitchi*) has wavy-margined leaves and its variety *gracillima* has white midribs. All of these are rare and difficult to obtain, but very much worth while. Cuttings; general-purpose mixture; moist soil and air; warmth; partial shade.

Dolichos lablab, Hyacinth Bean. Has been recommended. A climber with purple or white flowers and purple seed pods; often grown as a porch vine outdoors. Seeds in late winter; general-purpose mixture; moist; sun.

Dracaena spp., Corn Plant, et cetera.

Dyckia spp., Pineapple relatives.

Echeveria spp. (succulents).

Echinocactus spp., Barrel Cactus.

Echinocereus spp., Hedgehog Cactus, Rainbow Cactus.

Echinopsis spp., Sea Urchin Cactus, Easter Lily Cactus.

Epidendrum obrienianum (Orchid).

Epigaea repens, Trailing Arbutus. Treat as other hardy native plants.

Epipactis spp., Rattlesnake-plantain, is *Goodyera.* Hardy native plant. See above.

Epiphyllum ackermanni, Orchid Cactus, is *Nopalxochia ackermanni.*

Eranthis hiemalis, Winter Aconite.

Erica spp., Heath.

Espostoa lanata, Snowball Cactus.

Eucharis grandiflora, Amazon Lily. A tropical bulb with beautiful fragrant white flowers. Has been recommended, but requires warmth and moist air. Division; general-purpose mixture; moist when growing, on dry side when resting; partial shade.

Eugenia uniflora, Surinam Cherry.

Euonymus fortunei, Winter Creeper. Winter-hardy shrubs or vines used in terrariums. Cuttings; general-purpose mixture; moist; partial shade.

Euphorbia spp., Crown-of-thorns, Poinsettia, et cetera.

Farfugium grande, Leopard-plant. *See Ligularia.*

Faucaria tigrina (succulent),Tiger's Jaw.

Ficus spp., Fig, Rubber Plant, et cetera.

Fittonia verschaffelti and its variety *argyroneura* are suitable for terrariums. The former has oval leaves with red veins, the latter has white veins. Cuttings; general-purpose mixture. Has been grown without the aid of a terrarium.

Freesia spp., Freesia.

Fritillaria spp., Fritillary.

Fuchsia spp., Fuchsia.

Gardenia spp., Cape Jasmine, Gardenia.

Galanthus nivalis, Snowdrop.

Gasteria spp. (succulent), Warty Aloe, Ox-tongue.

Gaultheria procumbens, Wintergreen.

Gloriosa superba, Glory Lily.

Glottiphyllum longum (succulent), Tongue-leaf.

Gloxinia speciosa, Gloxinia, is *Sinningia speciosa.*

Goodyera spp., Rattlesnake-plantain. Hardy native plants.

Grevillea robusta, Australian Silk-oak. A tree with fernlike leaves which makes a handsome pot plant when young. Seeds in spring; general-purpose mixture; moist; sun or light shade.

Guzmannia zahni, Pineapple relative.

Gymnocalycium spp., Chin Cacti.

Gynura aurantiaca, Velvet Plant. Its most striking feature is the egg-shaped leaves, densely covered with velvety violet or purple hairs. Cuttings; general-purpose mixture; moist; sun.

Hamatocactus setispinus, Strawberry Cactus.

Harrisia jusberti, Moon Cactus.

Haworthia spp. (succulents), Cushion Aloe, Windowed Plant.

Hechtia argentea, Pineapple relative.

Hedera spp., English Ivy, Canary Ivy.

Heliotropium arborescens, Heliotrope.

Helxine soleiroli, Baby's Tears, etc.

Hepatica americana, Hepatica.

Hibiscus sinensis, Chinese Hibiscus.

Hippeastrum hybridum, Amaryllis.

Homalomena rubescens. An aroid with broad, arrowhead leaves, with reddish stalks; seldom offered in the trade. See Index for culture reference.

Hoodia gordoni (succulent).

Houstonia coerulea, Bluets, Quaker Ladies.

Howea forsteriana, Kentia Palm.

Hoya carnosa, Wax-plant.

Huernia spp. (succulents).

Hyacinthus spp., Dutch Hyacinth, Roman Hyacinth

Hydrangea macrophylla, French Hydrangea.

Hydrocleis nymphoides (aquatic).

Hydrosme rivieri, Devil's Tongue.

Hylocereus spp., Night-blooming Cereus.

Iberis amara, Candytuft. Annual.

Impatiens spp., Patience Plant, Zanzibar Balsam.

Ipomoea spp., Morning-glory, Sweet-potato.

Iresine lindeni, Blood-leaf. A plant with reddish leaves commonly used for outdoor bedding. Has been recommended, but the plant I tried looked very unhappy in the house. Cuttings; general-purpose mixture; moist; sun.

Iris spp., English, Dutch, and Spanish Irises—Netted Iris. Those experienced in growing hardy bulbs in the house might like to try these. The Netted Iris (*I. reticulata*) is dwarf with deep violet flowers marked with orange. See Index for culture reference.

Ixora coccinea, a tropical evergreen shrub with clusters of small red flowers, has been recommended but failed to grow for me. Cuttings; general-purpose mixture; moist air and soil; sun.

Jacobinia obtusior, Plume Flower. Showy pink or crimson flowers in dense terminal clusters; unattractive leaves. A plant I tried bloomed and got along very well until the heat was turned on, when it began to fail. Cuttings; general-purpose mixture; moist; sun or part shade.

Kalanchoe spp., Life Plant, Panda Plant, et cetera.
Kleinia articulata (succulent), Candle Plant.

Lachenalia spp., Cape Cowslip.
Laelia spp., Orchids.
Lantana camara, Lantana.
Lapidaria margaretiae (succulent).
Laurus nobilis, Sweet Bay Tree. This shrub, or tree, with fragrant leaves used in cooking and perfumery, was formerly much used, when trimmed to pyramidal or standard form, for outdoor use in summer and hallway embellishment of large establishments in winter. Cuttings; general-purpose mixture; moist; cool in winter; sun.
Lemaireocereus marginatus, Organ Cactus.
Leucojum vernum, Spring Snowflake. Hardy bulb.
Ligularia kaempferi aureo-maculata, Leopard-plant. This has large rounded leaves blotched with yellow or white; usually 8 to 12 inches tall as a pot plant. Division; general-purpose mixture; moist; cool in winter (45°); sun or partial shade.
Lilium longiflorum, Easter Lily.
Lippia citriodora, Lemon Verbena. A shrub of mediocre appearance grown for its fragrant leaves. Cuttings; general-purpose mixture; moist when growing, on dry side and cool in winter; sun.
Lithops spp. (succulents), Flowering Stones, Stoneface.
Livistona spp., Fan Palms.

Lobelia erinus vars., Bedding Lobelias. Young plants can be dug up from the flower border, potted, and brought indoors in the fall, but usually with not much success.

Lobivia spp., Cob Cactus.

Lobularia benthami, Sweet Alyssum.

Lophophora williamsi (Cactus), Peyote, Sacred Mushroom.

Ludwigia sp. (aquatic).

Lycopodium spp., Club Mosses.

Lycoris radiata. A bulbous plant with bright red flowers in umbels in the fall. Usually stored in cellar during winter and used for porch decoration in summer. Offsets; bulb soil; moist when growing; dry in winter; sun.

Mammillaria spp., Pincushion Cactus, Lace Cactus, et cetera.

Maranta spp., Arrow-root (in part).

Marica northiana, Apostle Plant.

Mesembryanthemum, Ice Plant. Most of the plants formerly known under this name have been transferred to other genera, collectively known as the Mesembryanthema. Those most likely to be of interest are described and discussed in the Succulent section.

Mimosa pudica, Sensitive Plant. A roadside weed in the tropics. The sensitivity of its leaves is always intriguing. It has been suggested as a house plant, but although I have had no difficulty in growing it as an annual outdoors, where its little pompons of pink blossoms are attractive, it has resolutely failed to thrive for me in the house. Treat as an annual.

Mitchella repens, Partridge Berry.

Monstera deliciosa, Mexican Bread-fruit.

Musa nana (cavendishi), Dwarf Banana.

Muscari spp., Grape Hyacinth.

Myosotis spp., Forget-me-not.

Myriophyllum sp., Milfoil.

Narcissus spp., Daffodil, Paper-white Narcissus, et cetera.

Neanthe bella (Palm).

Neoregelia spp., Pineapple relatives.

Nepeta hederacea, Ground-ivy.

Nephthytis afzeli.

Nerine spp., including Guernsey Lily. Has been recommended, but it is doubtful if many would want to give it a cool, sunny window throughout the winter (when the leaves are active) for the sake of its admittedly showy blooms in late fall. The bulbs should be dried off in their pots from May to August. Bulb soil; sun.

Nerium oleander, Oleander. A shrub with showy pink flowers which can be stored in a cool, well-lighted cellar during the winter. *See Shrubs.*

Nicotiana alata, Flowering Tobacco.

Nidularium spp., Pineapple relatives.

Nierembergia caerulea, Blue Cup Flower. Has been recommended. Can be dug up from flower border in the fall.

Nopalxochia akermanni, Cactus.

Notocactus spp., Ball Cactus.

Nyctocereus serpentinus, Snake Cactus.

Nymphoides spp. (aquatics).

Ophiopogon spp., Lily-turf, Snakebeard.

Opuntia spp., Cacti.

Oreocereus spp., Mountain Cacti.

Ornithogalum arabicum, O. thyrsoides. Tender bulbs.

Osmanthus fragrans, Fragrant Olive. A shrub with tiny fragrant flowers in winter. Has been recommended for house culture. Needs to be kept cool during winter. Cuttings; general-purpose mixture; moist; sun or partial shade.

Othonna crassifolia, Little Pickles. A succulent trailer, with cylindrical fleshy leaves and small yellow Daisies. Cuttings; Cactus soil; rather dry in winter; sun.

Oxalis spp., Bermuda Buttercup, et cetera.

Oxalis rubra, a summer-flowering species; can be dried off in winter (keep cool). Division; general-purpose mixture; moist in summer; sun.

Pandanus spp., Screw-pines.

Passiflora spp., Passion Flower. These vines have been used successfully as house plants. Seeds and cuttings; general-purpose mixture; moist; sun or partial shade.

Pedilanthus tithymaloides, Redbird-cactus (not a Cactus, really), Slipper Flower. Succulent stems; 2 feet tall when grown in pots; oval, pointed leaves bordered with white in *variegata*. Has been grown successfully in the house but probably difficult to purchase. Culture as for Cacti.

Pelargonium spp., Geraniums of varied types.

Pellaea viridis, Cliff Brake-fern.

Peperomia spp., Watermelon "Begonia" and others.

Pereskia spp., Cactus.

Persea americana, Avocado.

Philodendron spp.

Phoenix roebelini (Palm).

Phyllocactus spp., Orchid Cacti.

Pilea involucrata, Panamiga, and *P. microphylla,* Artillery Plant. Cuttings; general-purpose mixture; moist; partial shade. Useful in terrariums.

Pittosporum tobira variegata. A shrub with white markings on leaves. Young plants can be used in terrariums. Cuttings; general-purpose mixture; moist.

Platycerium bifurcatum, Staghorn Fern.

Pleiospilos spp., Living Rocks.

Podocarpus neriifolia. A tree related to conifers, with narrow leaves. Used in seedling stage in dish gardens and terrariums.

Polypodium spp. (Ferns).

Polyscias balfouriana and *P. guilfoylei* are shrubs with ornamental foliage, suitable when young for house and terrarium culture. Easy to grow but probably difficult to obtain.

Polystichum spp., Leather-leaf Fern and others.

Portulacaria afra. A succulent shrub of undistinguished appearance sometimes used in dish gardens.

Pothos aureus is *Scindapsus aureus.*

Primula spp., Primroses of various kinds.

Psidium cattleianum, Strawberry Guava.

Pteris spp., Brake Ferns.

Punica granatum, Pomegranate.

Quamoclit pennata, Cypress Vine.

Rebutia spp., Cacti.

Rhipsalis spp., Mistletoe Cacti. Epiphytic, with small white or creamy flowers. Culture same as Orchid Cacti.

Rhododendron spp., Azaleas.

Rhoeo discolor, Three-men-in-a-boat, Moses-on-a-raft, Purple-leaved Spiderwort. A rather ungainly plant whose leaves are purple beneath. Small white flowers in boatlike bracts. Culture of *Zebrina.*

Rivina humilis, Rouge Plant.

Rosa chinensis minima, Fairy Rose, Pygmy Rose.

Sagittaria spp. (aquatics), Arrowhead.

Saintpaulia ionantha, African-violet.

Salvinia auriculata (aquatic).

Sanguinaria canadensis, Bloodroot.

Sansevieria spp., Snake-plant, Bowstring Hemp.

Sauromatum guttatum, Monarch-of-the-East.

Saxifraga sarmentosa, Mother-of-thousands, Strawberry Geranium.

Schismatogolittis roebelini.

Schizobasopsis (*Bowiea*) *volubilis,* Climbing Onion. This has been suggested as a house plant and might appeal to those who like oddities. Twining, much-branched, bright green stems are produced from aboveground bulbs 3 to 5 inches across. Division; Cactus soil; dry in winter; sun.

Scilla sibirica, Siberian Squill. Hardy bulbs.

Scindapsus spp., Pothos.

Sedum spp., Stonecrop, Live-for-ever.

Selaginella spp.

Selenicereus macdonaldiae (Cactus), Queen-of-the-night.

Sempervivum spp., Houseleek.

Senecio cruentus, Florists' Cineraria.

Senecio mikanioides, German Ivy.

Sequoia sempervirens, Redwood.

Serissa foetida variegata. A little shrub with ½-inch oval leaves bordered with yellow; sometimes used in dish gardens. Cuttings; general-purpose mixture; moist; sun or partial shade.

Shortia uniflora. Oconee Bells.

Sinningia speciosa, Gloxinia.

Skimmia japonica. Has been recommended. A small evergreen shrub with fragrant white flowers and red berries. Culture same as Camellia.

Solanum pseudo-capsicum, Jerusalem-cherry.

Sparaxis spp., tender bulbs.

Spathiphyllum floribundum. An aroid with small white spathes. Has been recommended, but in my experience is not happy under house conditions. See section on Aroids.

Spironema fragrans, sometimes sold as *Tradescantia dracaenoides.* A strong-growing relative of Wandering Jew, with hanging stems terminated with rosettes of broad, oblong-lance-shaped leaves. Small white fragrant flowers in clusters on tall branching stems. A tolerant house plant, but difficult to obtain. Culture as *Zebrina.*

Stapelia spp. (succulents), Carrion Flower.

Sternbergia lutea, Mt. Etna Lily.

Strelitzia reginae, Bird-of-paradise Flower. Has been recommended. Stemless; leaves rising to 3 feet, 1½ feet long, ½ foot wide. Inflorescence purple, yellow, and blue. Culture of *Clivia.*

Swainsona galegifolia, Swan Flower. A shrub with long, flexible stems and racemes of Pea-shaped flowers—white, pink, red, or rose-violet according to variety. Seeds; general-purpose mixture; moist; sun.

Syagrus weddelliana, Cocos or Weddell Palm.

Syngonium spp.

Tagetes patula, French Marigold.

Talinum patens, Flame Flower. Related to, but nothing like, Portulaca. The variety *variegatum* is marked with white or pink. Small red flowers on branched stalks. Seeds; general-purpose mixture; not too moist; sun.

Tephrocactus glomeratus, Paper-spined Opuntia.

Thuja plicata, Giant Arborvitae.

Thunbergia alata, Clock Vine.

Tiarella cordifolia, Foam Flower.

Tibouchina (Pleroma) semidecandra, Princess Flower.

Tillandsia spp., Pineapple relative.

Titanopsis schwantesi, succulent belonging to the Mesembryanthema.

Tolmiaea menziesi, Picka-back Plant.

Torenia fournieri, Wishbone Plant, Blue Wings.

Tradescantia fluminensis, Wandering Jew.

Trichocereus spachianus, White Torch Cactus.

Trichodiadema densum, one of the Mesembryanthema.

Trillium nivale, Snow Trillium.

Tropaeolum majus, Nasturtium.

Tulipa, Tulip.

Utricularia spp. (aquatics), Bladderwort.

Vallisneria spiralis (aquatic), Eel Grass.

Veltheimia viridifolia is a South African bulb with a handsome rosette of leaves which are about 12 × 3 inches. The flowers, yellowish or tinged with red, clustered on a central stalk, are reminiscent of those of *Kniphofia.*

Vinca major, Periwinkle. A trailing evergreen with plain or variegated foliage. Often used in the foreground of outdoor window boxes in summer, it can be brought into an unheated enclosed porch where it will survive and perform a decorative function if the temperature does not fall too much below freezing. Division; cuttings; general-purpose mixture; moist; sun or shade.

Vriesia spp., Pineapple relatives.

Xanthosoma lindeni, Indian Kale, Spoon Flower.

Yucca aloifolia, Spanish Bayonet. There are several varieties of this plant with variously striped leaves which are good-looking but need careful handling because of their very spiky leaves. Culture as for succulents in general.

Zantedeschia spp., Calla-lily, Golden Calla, Pink Calla.

Zebrina pendula, Wandering Jew.

Zygocactus truncatus, Christmas Cactus.

CHAPTER XX

Plants for Special Conditions

HERE is a selection from the main list of plants for various locations and purposes. There is no hard-and-fast dividing line between plants suitable for north, south, east, and west windows, which explains why the same plant may appear in more than one list. This versatility is also an indication of the plant's adaptability to varied conditions. Climatic factors, too, have a bearing on a plant's ability to thrive in any given location. A species which demands all the sun available in a cloudy region could be expected to get along in an east, west, or even a north window in those favored sections where the sun is always shining, or nearly so, during the hours of daylight. I should mention that flowering plants in general, if grown in a north window, may bloom sparsely or not at all during the winter. Most house plants are benefited by all the sun available during the winter months, but some of them will need some shade as the days begin to lengthen and the sun gains power.

These lists are intended to be nothing more than a rough guide. Before making a final selection the cultural requirements for each species should be consulted.

Easily grown plants: None but the toughest kinds are represented here. Beginners would do well to start with a selection from this list.

Agave spp.
Aglaonema commutatum
Aglaonema simplex
Aspidistra elatior
Chlorophytum elatum
Coleus blumei varieties

Dieffenbachia spp.
Dracaena fragrans varieties
Dracaena sanderiana
Ficus elastica
Ficus lyrata
Helxine soleiroli

Howea forsteriana
Impatiens sultani
Marica northiana
Monstera deliciosa
Nephthytis afzeli
Pandanus veitchi
Philodendron cordatum
Polystichum adiantiforme

Sansevieria spp.
Schismatoglottis roebelini
Scindapsus aureus
Scindapsus pictus argyraeus
Tolmiaea menziesi
Tradescantia fluminensis
Zebrina pendula

Plants for north windows: Locations away from the source of light in sunny rooms. Most of them will grow better in east or west windows.

Aglaonema spp.
Araucaria excelsa
Aspidistra elatior
Begonia spp.
Bromeliads
Chlorophytum elatum
Dieffenbachia spp.
Ferns in variety
Hedera spp. and varieties
Helxine soleiroli
Impatiens sultani
Monstera deliciosa
Nephthytis afzeli

Peperomia obtusifolia
Peperomia sandersi
Philodendron cordatum
Saintpaulia ionantha
Sansevieria spp.
Saxifraga sarmentosa
Scindapsus aureus
Scindapsus pictus argyraeus
Selaginella spp.
Syagrus (Cocos) weddelliana
Tolmiaea menziesi
Tradescantia fluminensis
Zebrina pendula

Plants for south windows: Most of these will grow almost as well in east or west windows.

Abutilon hybridum
Ageratum houstonianum
Begonias (in winter)
Beloperone guttata
Bromeliads
Cacti in general. (Orchid and Christmas Cacti should not be exposed to strong, undiluted sunshine.)

Ceropegia woodi
Chrysanthemum frutescens
Citrus spp.
Coleus varieties
Cyanotis somaliensis
Euphorbia pulcherrima
Euphorbia splendens
Freesia varieties
Gardenia veitchi

Gynura aurantiaca
Heliotropium arborescens
Hippeastrum hybridum
Hyacinthus spp.
Ipomoea spp.
Iresine lindeni
Iris spp.
Lantana camara
Lilium longiflorum
Lobularia benthami
Marica northiana
Myosotis spp.

Narcissus varieties
Nicotiana alata
Oxalis spp.
Pelargonium spp.
Rosa varieties
Tagetes patula
Thunbergia alata
Tibouchina semidecandra
Tropaeolum majus
Tulipa varieties
Veltheimia viridifolia
Zantedeschia spp.

Plants for east and west windows: Can be grown in south windows if shaded by thin curtains when necessary.

Achimenes spp.
Acorus gramineus pusillus
Acorus gramineus variegatus
Anthurium scherzerianum
Araucaria excelsa
Astilbe japonica
Begonia spp.
Beloperone guttata
Bromeliads
Caladium bicolor
Campanula isophylla
Cattleya spp.
Cissus spp.
Citrus spp.
Cymbalaria muralis
Dendrobium spp.
Dicentra spectabilis
Dieffenbachia spp.
Dracaena spp.
Epiphyllum spp.
Eucharis grandiflora
Ferns in variety

Ficus spp.
Fuchsia varieties
Grevillea robusta
Hedera spp.
Hoya carnosa
Hydrangea macrophylla
Impatiens sultani
Ligularia kaempferi aureo-mac-ulata
Marica northiana
Ophiopogon spp.
Palms in variety
Pandanus spp.
Phyllocactus spp.
Rhododendron spp.
Senecio mikanioides
Sinningia speciosa
Torenia fournieri
Tradescantia fluminensis
Zantedeschia spp.
Zebrina pendula
Zygocactus truncatus

For cool (45°–55°) temperatures:

Acorus gramineus pusillus
Acorus gramineus variegatus
Araucaria excelsa
Aspidistra elatior
Aucuba japonica
Camellia japonica
Camellia sasanqua
Campanula isophylla
Chrysanthemum hortorum varieties
Coprosma baueri
Crocus
Cyclamen indicum
Cymbalaria muralis
Cyrtomium falcatum
Daphne odora
Eranthis
Euonymus fortunei
Freesia spp.

Hedera spp.
Helxine soleiroli
Laurus nobilis
Ligularia kaempferi aureo-maculata
Myosotis spp.
Ophiopogon spp.
Osmanthus fragrans
Pelargonium spp.
Pittosporum tobira variegata
Primula spp.
Pteris spp.
Rhododendron spp.
Saxifraga sarmentosa
Senecio cruentus
Skimmia japonica
Tolmiaea menziesi
Vinca major

For dish gardens: Some of these are useful only when they are small, and some—such as *Dieffenbachia, Hedera,* and *Tradescantia* —may quickly grow too large.

Acorus gramineus pusillus
Acorus gramineus variegatus
Aglaonema spp.
Asparagus sprengeri (seedlings)
Bromeliads
Buxus sempervirens suffruticosa
Cacti in variety
Coleus varieties
Dieffenbachia spp.
Dracaena godseffiana
Dracaena sanderiana
Euonymus fortunei
Ferns, young plants in variety
Gaultheria procumbens

Hedera, small varieties
Helxine soleiroli
Maranta leuconeura
Pandanus veitchi, young plants
Peperomia obtusifolia
Peperomia sandersi
Philodendron, young plants
Phoenix roebeleni, young plants
Pilea involucrata
Pilea microphylla
Podocarpus neriifolia
Portulacaria afra
Saintpaulia ionantha
Sansevieria, small plants

Saxifraga sarmentosa
Schismatoglottis roebelini
Scindapsus aureus
Scindapsus pictus argyraeus
Serissa foetida variegata
Succulents in variety

Syagrus weddelliana
Syngonium podophyllum alboli-
   neatum
Tradescantia fluminensis
Zebrina pendula

"Permanent" evergreen plants of massive character for background and framing:

Aspidistra elatior
Chrysalidocarpus lutescens
Cibotium schiedei
Cissus adenopodus
Cissus antarctica
Cissus capensis
Cissus rhombifolia
Dieffenbachia spp.
Dracaena fragrans varieties
Ficus elastica
Ficus lyrata
Hedera helix hibernica
Howea forsteriana

Hoya carnosa
Livistona chinensis
Marica northiana
Monstera deliciosa
Nephthytis afzeli
Pandanus utilis
Pandanus veitchi
Philodendron spp.
Phoenix roebelini
Sansevieria trifasciata laurenti
Scindapsus aureus
Senecio mikanioides

Index

(NUMERALS IN BOLDFACE INDICATE ILLUSTRATIONS)